I0010457

Flux Architecture

Learn to build powerful and scalable applications with Flux, the architecture that serves billions of Facebook users every day

Adam Boduch

PUBLISHING

BIRMINGHAM - MUMBAI

Flux Architecture

Copyright © 2016 Packt Publishing

All rights reserved. No part of this book may be reproduced, stored in a retrieval system, or transmitted in any form or by any means, without the prior written permission of the publisher, except in the case of brief quotations embedded in critical articles or reviews.

Every effort has been made in the preparation of this book to ensure the accuracy of the information presented. However, the information contained in this book is sold without warranty, either express or implied. Neither the author, nor Packt Publishing, and its dealers and distributors will be held liable for any damages caused or alleged to be caused directly or indirectly by this book.

Packt Publishing has endeavored to provide trademark information about all of the companies and products mentioned in this book by the appropriate use of capitals. However, Packt Publishing cannot guarantee the accuracy of this information.

First published: May 2016

Production reference: 1180516

Published by Packt Publishing Ltd.
Livery Place
35 Livery Street
Birmingham B3 2PB, UK.

ISBN 978-1-78646-581-8

www.packtpub.com

Credits

Author
Adam Boduch

Reviewer
August Marcello III

Commissioning Editor
Edward Gordon

Acquisition Editor
Smeet Thakkar

Content Development Editor
Divij Kotian

Technical Editor
Gebin George

Copy Editor
Charlotte Carneiro

Project Coordinator
Nikhil Nair

Proofreader
Safis Editing

Indexer
Rekha Nair

Graphics
Jason Monteiro

Production Coordinator
Manu Joseph

Cover Work
Manu Joseph

About the Author

Adam Boduch has been involved with large-scale JavaScript development for nearly 10 years. Before moving to the front end, he worked on several large-scale cloud computing products using Python and Linux. No stranger to complexity, Adam has practical experience with real-world software systems and the scaling challenges they pose.

He is the author of several JavaScript books, including *JavaScript Concurrency*, and is passionate about innovative user experiences and high performance.

About the Reviewer

August Marcello III is a highly passionate software engineer with nearly two decades of experience in the design, implementation, and deployment of modern client-side web application architectures in the enterprise. An exclusive focus on delivering compelling SaaS-based user experiences throughout the Web ecosystem has proven both personally and professionally rewarding. His passion for emerging technologies in general, combined with a particular focus on forward-thinking JavaScript platforms, have been a primary driver in his pursuit of technical excellence. When he's not coding, he could be found trail running, mountain biking, and spending time with family and friends.

Many thanks to Chuck, Mark, Eric, and Adam, who I have had the privilege to work with and learn from. I'm grateful to my family, friends, and the experiences I have been blessed to be a part of.

www.PacktPub.com

eBooks, discount offers, and more

Did you know that Packt offers eBook versions of every book published, with PDF and ePub files available? You can upgrade to the eBook version at www.PacktPub.com and as a print book customer, you are entitled to a discount on the eBook copy. Get in touch with us at customercare@packtpub.com for more details.

At www.PacktPub.com, you can also read a collection of free technical articles, sign up for a range of free newsletters and receive exclusive discounts and offers on Packt books and eBooks.

https://www2.packtpub.com/books/subscription/packtlib

Do you need instant solutions to your IT questions? PacktLib is Packt's online digital book library. Here, you can search, access, and read Packt's entire library of books.

Why subscribe?

- Fully searchable across every book published by Packt
- Copy and paste, print, and bookmark content
- On demand and accessible via a web browser

For Melissa, thanks for all the love and support.

For Jason, Simon, and Kevin, thanks for brightening my day, everyday.

Table of Contents

Preface

I love Backbone.js. It's an amazing little library that does so much with so little. It's also unopinionated—there are endless ways to do the same thing. This last point gives many Backbone.js programmers a headache. The freedom to implement things the way we see fit is great, until we start making those unavoidable consistency errors.

When I first started with Flux, I couldn't really see how such an architecture could help out a mere Backbone.js programmer. Eventually, I figured out two things. First, Flux is unopinionated where it matters—the implementation specifics. Two, Flux is very much like Backbone in the spirit of minimal moving parts that do one thing well.

As I started experimenting with Flux, I realized that Flux provides the missing architectural perspective that enables scalability. Where Backbone.js and other related technologies fall apart is when something goes wrong. In fact, these bugs can be so difficult that they're never actually fixed—the whole system is scarred with workarounds.

I decided to write this book in the hope that other programmers, from all walks of JavaScript, can experience the same level of enlightenment as I have working with this wonderful technology from Facebook.

What this book covers

Chapter 1, What is Flux?, gives an overview of what Flux is and why it was created.

Chapter 2, Principles of Flux, talks about the core concepts of Flux and the essential knowledge for building a Flux architecture.

Chapter 3, Building a Skeleton Architecture, walks through the steps involved in building a skeleton architecture before implementing application features.

Chapter 4, Creating Actions, shows how action creator functions are used to feed new data into the system while describing something that just happened.

Chapter 5, Asynchronous Actions, goes through examples of asynchronous action creator functions and how they fit within a Flux architecture.

Chapter 6, Changing Flux Store State, gives many detailed explanations and examples that illustrate how Flux stores work.

Chapter 7, Viewing Information, gives many detailed explanations and examples that illustrate how Flux views work.

Chapter 8, Information Lifecycle, talks about how information in a Flux architecture enters the system and how it ultimately exits the system.

Chapter 9, Immutable Stores, shows how immutability is a key architectural property of software architectures, such as Flux, where data flows in one direction.

Chapter 10, Implementing a Dispatcher, walks through the implementation of a dispatcher component, instead of using the Facebook reference implementation.

Chapter 11, Alternative View Components, shows how view technologies other than React can be used within a Flux architecture.

Chapter 12, Leveraging Flux Libraries, gives an overview of two popular Flux libraries — Alt.js and Redux.

Chapter 13, Testing and Performance, talks about testing components from within the context of a Flux architecture and discusses performance testing your architecture.

Chapter 14, Flux and the Software Development Life Cycle, discusses the impact Flux has on the rest of the software stack and how to package Flux features.

What you need for this book

- Any web browser
- NodeJS >= 4.0
- A code editor

Who this book is for

Are you trying to use React, but are struggling to get your head around Flux? Maybe, you're tired of MV* spaghetti code at scale? Do you find yourself asking what the Flux?!

Flux Architecture will guide you through everything you need to understand the Flux pattern and design, and build powerful web applications that rely on Flux architecture.

You don't need to know what Flux is or how it works to read the book. No knowledge of Flux's partner technology, ReactJS, is necessary to follow along, but it is recommended that you have a good working knowledge of JavaScript.

Conventions

In this book, you will find a number of text styles that distinguish between different kinds of information. Here are some examples of these styles and an explanation of their meaning.

Code words in text, database table names, folder names, filenames, file extensions, pathnames, dummy URLs, user input, and Twitter handles are shown as follows: "When the HOME_LOAD action is dispatched, we change the state of the store."

A block of code is set as follows:

```
// This object is used by several action
// creator functions as part of the action
// payload.
export constPAYLOAD_SORT = {
  direction: 'asc'
};
```

 Warnings or important notes appear in a box like this.

 Tips and tricks appear like this.

Reader feedback

Feedback from our readers is always welcome. Let us know what you think about this book—what you liked or disliked. Reader feedback is important for us as it helps us develop titles that you will really get the most out of.

To send us general feedback, simply e-mail feedback@packtpub.com, and mention the book's title in the subject of your message.

If there is a topic that you have expertise in and you are interested in either writing or contributing to a book, see our author guide at www.packtpub.com/authors.

Customer support

Now that you are the proud owner of a Packt book, we have a number of things to help you to get the most from your purchase.

Downloading the example code

You can download the example code files for this book from your account at http://www.packtpub.com. If you purchased this book elsewhere, you can visit http://www.packtpub.com/support and register to have the files e-mailed directly to you.

You can download the code files by following these steps:

1. Log in or register to our website using your e-mail address and password.
2. Hover the mouse pointer on the **SUPPORT** tab at the top.
3. Click on **Code Downloads & Errata**.
4. Enter the name of the book in the **Search** box.
5. Select the book for which you're looking to download the code files.
6. Choose from the drop-down menu where you purchased this book from.
7. Click on **Code Download**.

You can also download the code files by clicking on the **Code Files** button on the book's webpage at the Packt Publishing website. This page can be accessed by entering the book's name in the **Search** box. Please note that you need to be logged in to your Packt account.

Once the file is downloaded, please make sure that you unzip or extract the folder using the latest version of:

- WinRAR / 7-Zip for Windows
- Zipeg / iZip / UnRarX for Mac
- 7-Zip / PeaZip for Linux

Errata

Although we have taken every care to ensure the accuracy of our content, mistakes do happen. If you find a mistake in one of our books — maybe a mistake in the text or the code — we would be grateful if you could report this to us. By doing so, you can save other readers from frustration and help us improve subsequent versions of this book. If you find any errata, please report them by visiting http://www.packtpub.com/submit-errata, selecting your book, clicking on the **Errata Submission Form** link, and entering the details of your errata. Once your errata are verified, your submission will be accepted and the errata will be uploaded to our website or added to any list of existing errata under the Errata section of that title.

To view the previously submitted errata, go to https://www.packtpub.com/books/content/support and enter the name of the book in the search field. The required information will appear under the **Errata** section.

Piracy

Piracy of copyrighted material on the Internet is an ongoing problem across all media. At Packt, we take the protection of our copyright and licenses very seriously. If you come across any illegal copies of our works in any form on the Internet, please provide us with the location address or website name immediately so that we can pursue a remedy.

Please contact us at copyright@packtpub.com with a link to the suspected pirated material.

We appreciate your help in protecting our authors and our ability to bring you valuable content.

Questions

If you have a problem with any aspect of this book, you can contact us at questions@packtpub.com, and we will do our best to address the problem.

1
What is Flux?

Flux is supposed to be this great new way of building complex user interfaces that scale well. At least that's the general messaging around Flux, if you're only skimming the Internet literature. But, how do we define *this great new way of building user interfaces*? What makes it superior to other more established frontend architectures?

The aim of this chapter is to cut through the sales bullet points and explicitly spell out what Flux is, and what it isn't, by looking at the patterns that Flux provides. And since Flux isn't a software package in the traditional sense, we'll go over the conceptual problems that we're trying to solve with Flux.

Finally, we'll close the chapter by walking through the core components found in any Flux architecture, and we'll install the Flux npm package and write a hello world Flux application right away. Let's get started.

Flux is a set of patterns

We should probably get the harsh reality out of the way first—Flux is not a software package. It's a set of architectural patterns for us to follow. While this might sound disappointing to some, don't despair—there's good reasons for not implementing yet another framework. Throughout the course of this book, we'll see the value of Flux existing as a set of patterns instead of a de facto implementation. For now, we'll go over some of the high-level architectural patterns put in place by Flux.

Data entry points

With traditional approaches to building frontend architectures, we don't put much thought into how data enters the system. We might entertain the idea of data entry points, but not in any detail. For example, with **MVC** (**Model View Controller**) architectures, the controller is supposed control the flow of data. And for the most part, it does exactly that. On the other hand, the controller is really just about controlling what happens after it already has the data. How does the controller get data in the first place? Consider the following illustration:

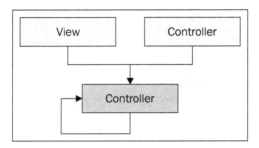

At first glance, there's nothing wrong with this picture. The data-flow, represented by the arrows, is easy to follow. But where does the data originate? For example, the view can create new data and pass it to the controller, in response to a user event. A controller can create new data and pass it to another controller, depending on the composition of our controller hierarchy. What about the controller in question—can it create data itself and then use it?

In a diagram such as this one, these questions don't have much virtue. But, if we're trying to scale an architecture to have hundreds of these components, the points at which data enters the system become very important. Since Flux is used to build architectures that scale, it considers data entry points an important architectural pattern.

Managing state

State is one of those realities we need to cope with in frontend development. Unfortunately, we can't compose our entire application of pure functions with no side-effects for two reasons. First, our code needs to interact with the DOM interface, in one way or another. This is how the user sees changes in the UI. Second, we don't store all our application data in the DOM (at least we shouldn't do this). As time passes and the user interacts with the application, this data will change.

There's no cut-and-dry approach to managing state in a web application, but there are several ways to limit the amount of state changes that can happen, and enforce how they happen. For example, pure functions don't change the state of anything, they can only create new data. Here's an example of what this looks like:

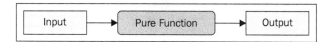

As you can see, there's no side-effects with pure functions because no data changes state as a result of calling them. So why is this a desirable trait, if state changes are inevitable? The idea is to enforce *where* state changes happen. For example, perhaps we only allow certain types of components to change the state of our application data. This way, we can rule out several sources as the cause of a state change.

Flux is big on controlling where state changes happen. Later on in the chapter, we'll see how Flux stores manage state changes. What's important about how Flux manages state is that it's handled at an architectural layer. Contrast this with an approach that lays out a set of rules that say which component types are allowed to mutate application data—things get confusing. With Flux, there's less room for guessing where state changes take place.

Keeping updates synchronous

Complimentary to data entry points is the notion of update synchronicity. That is, in addition to managing where the state changes originate from, we have to manage the ordering of these changes relative to other things. If the data entry points are the *what* of our data, then synchronously applying state changes across all the data in our system is the *when*.

Let's think about why this matters for a moment. In a system where data is updated asynchronously, we have to account for race conditions. Race conditions can be problematic because one piece of data can depend on another, and if they're updated in the wrong order, we see cascading problems, from one component to another. Take a look at this diagram, which illustrates this problem:

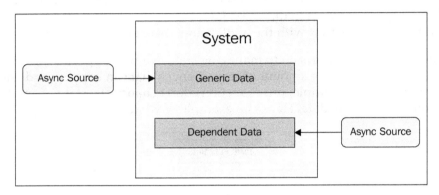

When something is asynchronous, we have no control over when that something changes state. So, all we can do is wait for the asynchronous updates to happen, and then go through our data and make sure all of our data dependencies are satisfied. Without tools that automatically handle these dependencies for us, we end up writing a lot of state-checking code.

Flux addresses this problem by ensuring that the updates that take place across our data stores are synchronous. This means that the scenario illustrated in the preceding diagram isn't possible. Here's a better visualization of how Flux handles the data synchronization issues that are typical of JavaScript applications today:

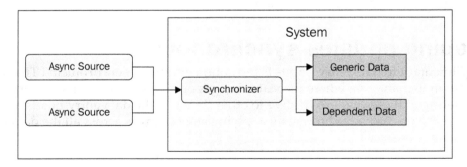

Information architecture

It's easy to forget that we work in information technology and that we should be building technology around information. In recent times, however, we seem to have moved in the other direction, where we're forced to think about implementation before we think about information. More often than not, the data exposed by the sources used by our application doesn't have what the user needs. It's up to our JavaScript to turn this raw data into something consumable by the user. This is our information architecture.

Does this mean that Flux is used to design information architectures as opposed to a software architecture? This isn't the case at all. In fact, Flux components are realized as true software components that perform actual computations. The trick is that Flux patterns enable us to think about information architecture as a first-class design consideration. Rather than having to sift through all sorts of components and their implementation concerns, we can make sure that we're getting the right information to the user.

Once our information architecture takes shape, the larger architecture of our application follows, as a natural extension to the information we're trying to communicate to our users. Producing information from data is the difficult part. We have to distill many sources of data into not only information, but information that's also of value to the user. Getting this wrong is a huge risk for any project. When we get it right, we can then move on to the specific application components, like the state of a button widget, and so on.

Flux architectures keep data transformations confined to their stores. A store is an information factory — raw data goes in and new information comes out. Stores control how data enters the system, the synchronicity of state changes, and they define *how* the state changes. When we go into more depth on stores as we progress through the book, we'll see how they're the pillars of our information architecture.

Flux isn't another framework

Now that we've explored some of the high-level patterns of Flux, it's time to revisit the question: what is Flux again? Well, it is just a set of architectural patterns we can apply to our frontend JavaScript applications. Flux scales well because it puts information first. Information is the most difficult aspect of software to scale; Flux tackles information architecture head on.

So, why aren't Flux patterns implemented as a framework? This way, Flux would have a canonical implementation for everyone to use; and like any other large scale open source project, the code would improve over time as the project matures.

The main problem is that Flux operates at an architectural level. It's used to address information problems that prevent a given application from scaling to meet user demand. If Facebook decided to release Flux as yet another JavaScript framework, it would likely have the same types of implementation issues that plague other frameworks out there. For example, if some component in a framework isn't implemented in a way that best suits the project we're working on, then it's not so easy to implement a better alternative, without hacking the framework to bits.

What's nice about Flux is that Facebook decided to leave the implementation options on the table. They do provide a few Flux component implementations, but these are reference implementations. They're functional, but the idea is that they're a starting point for us to understand the mechanics of how things such as dispatchers are expected to work. We're free to implement the same Flux architectural pattern as we see it.

Flux isn't a framework. Does this mean we have to implement everything ourselves? No, we do not. In fact, developers are implementing Flux libraries and releasing them as open source projects. Some Flux libraries stick more closely to the Flux patterns than others. These implementations are opinionated, and there's nothing wrong with using them if they're a good fit for what we're building. The Flux patterns aim to solve generic conceptual problems with JavaScript development, so you'll learn what they are before diving into Flux implementation discussions.

Flux solves conceptual problems

If Flux is simply a collection of architectural patterns instead of a software framework, what sort of problems does it solve? In this section, we'll look at some of the conceptual problems that Flux addresses from an architectural perspective. These include unidirectional data-flow, traceability, consistency, component layering, and loosely coupled components. Each of these conceptual problems pose a degree of risk to our software, in particular the ability to scale it. Flux helps us get out in front of these issues as we're building the software.

Data flow direction

We're creating an information architecture to support the feature-rich application that will ultimately sit on top of this architecture. Data flows into the system and will eventually reach an endpoint, terminating the flow. It's what happens in between the entry point and the termination point that determines the data-flow within a Flux architecture. This is illustrated here:

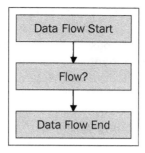

Data flow is a useful abstraction, because it's easy to visualize data as it enters the system and moves from one point to another. Eventually, the flow stops. But before it does, several side-effects happen along the way. It's that middle block in the preceding diagram that's concerning, because we don't know exactly how the data-flow reached the end.

Let's say that our architecture doesn't pose any restrictions on data flow. Any component is allowed to pass data to any other component, regardless of where that component lives. Let's try to visualize this setup:

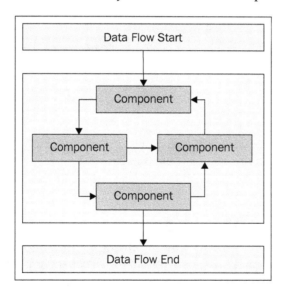

As you can see, our system has clearly defined entry and exit points for our data. This is good because it means that we can confidently say that the data-flows through our system. The problem with this picture is with how the data-flows between the components of the system. There's no direction, or rather, it's *multidirectional*. This isn't a good thing.

Flux is a *unidirectional* data flow architecture. This means that the preceding component layout isn't possible. The question is — why does this matter? At times, it might seem convenient to be able to pass data around in any direction, that is, from any component to any other component. This in and of itself isn't the issue — passing data alone doesn't break our architecture. However, when data moves around our system in more than one direction, there's more opportunity for components to fall out of sync with one another. This simply means that if data doesn't always move in the same direction, there's always the possibility of ordering bugs.

Flux enforces the direction of data-flows, and thus eliminates the possibility of components updating themselves in an order that breaks the system. No matter what data has just entered the system, it'll always flow through the system in the same order as any other data, as illustrated here:

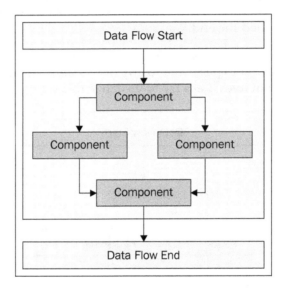

Predictable root cause

With data entering our system and flowing through our components in one direction, we can more easily trace any effect to it's cause. In contrast, when a component sends data to any other component residing in any architectural layer, it's a lot more difficult to figure how the data reached its destination. Why does this matter? Debuggers are sophisticated enough that we can easily traverse any level of complexity during runtime. The problem with this notion is that it presumes we only need to trace what's happening in our code for the purposes of debugging.

Flux architectures have inherently predictable data-flows. This is important for a number of design activities and not just debugging. Programmers working on Flux applications will begin to intuitively sense what's going to happen. Anticipation is key, because it let's us avoid design dead-ends before we hit them. When the cause and effect are easy to tease out, we can spend more time focusing on building application features — the things the customers care about.

Consistent notifications

The direction in which we pass data from component to component in Flux architectures should be consistent. In terms of consistency, we also need to think about the mechanism used to move data around our system.

For example, publish/subscribe (pub/sub) is a popular mechanism used for inter-component communication. What's neat about this approach is that our components can communicate with one another, and yet we're able to maintain a level of decoupling. In fact, this is fairly common in frontend development because component communication is largely driven by user events. These events can be thought of as fire-and-forget. Any other components that want to respond to these events in some way, need to take it upon themselves to subscribe to the particular event.

While pub/sub does have some nice properties, it also poses architectural challenges, in particular scaling complexities. For example, let's say that we've just added several new components for a new feature. Well, in which order do these components receive update messages relative to pre-existing components? Do they get notified after all the pre-existing components? Should they come first? This presents a data dependency scaling issue.

The other challenge with pub-sub is that the events that get published are often fine-grained to the point where we'll want to subscribe and later unsubscribe from the notifications. This leads to consistency challenges because trying to code lifecycle changes when there's a large number of components in the system is difficult and presents opportunities for missed events.

The idea with Flux is to sidestep the issue by maintaining a static inter-component messaging infrastructure that issues notifications to every component. In other words, programmers don't get to pick and choose the events their components will subscribe to. Instead, they have to figure out which of the events that are dispatched to them are relevant, ignoring the rest. Here's a visualization of how Flux dispatches events to components:

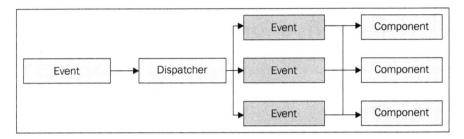

The Flux dispatcher sends the event to every component; there's no getting around this. Instead of trying to fiddle with the messaging infrastructure, which is difficult to scale, we implement logic within the component to determine whether or not the message is of interest. It's also within the component that we can declare dependencies on other components, which helps influence the ordering of messages. We'll cover this in much more detail in later chapters.

Simple architectural layers

Layers can be a great way to organize an architecture of components. For one thing, it's an obvious way to categorize the various components that make up our application. For another thing, layers serve as a means to put constraints around communication paths. This latter point is especially relevant to Flux architectures since it's important that data flow in one direction. It's much easier to apply constraints to layers than it is to individual components. Here is an illustration of Flux layers:

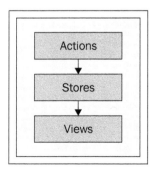

This diagram isn't intended to capture the entire data flow of a Flux architecture, just how data-flows between the main three layers. It also doesn't give any detail about what's in the layers. Don't worry, the next section gives introductory explanations of the types of Flux components, and the communication that happens between the layers is the focus of this book.

As you can see, the data-flows from one layer to the next, in one direction. Flux only has a few layers, and as our applications scale in terms of component counts, the layer counts remains fixed. This puts a cap on the complexity involved with adding new features to an already large application. In addition to constraining the layer count and the data-flow direction, Flux architectures are strict about which layers are actually allowed to communicate with one another.

For example, the action layer could communicate with the view layer, and we would still be moving in one direction. We would still have the layers that Flux expects. However, skipping a layer like this is prohibited. By ensuring that layers only communicate with the layer directly beneath it, we can rule out bugs introduced by doing something out-of-order.

Loosely coupled rendering

One decision made by the Flux designers that stands out is that Flux architectures don't care how UI elements are rendered. That is to say, the view layer is loosely coupled to the rest of the architecture. There are good reasons for this.

Flux is an information architecture first, and a software architecture second. We start with the former and graduate toward the latter. The challenge with view technology is that it can exert a negative influence on the rest of the architecture. For example, one view has a particular way of interacting with the DOM. Then, if we've already decided on this technology, we'll end up letting it influence the way our information architecture is structured. This isn't necessarily a bad thing, but it can lead to us making concessions about the information we ultimately display to our users.

What we should really be thinking about is the information itself and how this information changes over time. What actions are involved that bring about these changes? How is one piece of data dependent on another piece of data? Flux naturally removes itself from the browser technology constraints of the day so that we can focus on the information first. It's easy to plug views into our information architecture as it evolves into a software product.

Flux components

In this section, we'll begin our journey into the concepts of Flux. These concepts are the essential ingredients used in formulating a Flux architecture. While there's no detailed specifications for how these components should be implemented, they nevertheless lay the foundation of our implementation. This is a high-level introduction to the components we'll be implementing throughout this book.

Action

Actions are the *verbs* of the system. In fact, it's helpful if we derive the name of an action directly from a sentence. These sentences are typically statements of functionality – something we want the application to do. Here are some examples:

- Fetch the session
- Navigate to the settings page
- Filter the user list
- Toggle the visibility of the details section

These are simple capabilities of the application, and when we implement them as part of a Flux architecture, actions are the starting point. These human-readable action statements often require other new components elsewhere in the system, but the first step is always an action.

So, what exactly is a Flux action? At it's simplest, an action is nothing more than a string—a name that helps identify the purpose of the action. More typically, actions consist of a *name* and a *payload*. Don't worry about the payload specifics just yet—as far as actions are concerned, they're just opaque pieces of data being delivered into the system. Put differently, actions are like mail parcels. The entry point into our Flux system doesn't care about the internals of the parcel, only that they get to where they need to go. Here's an illustration of actions entering a Flux system:

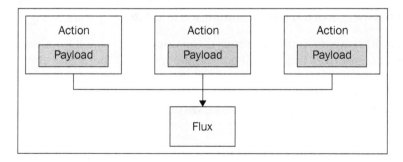

This diagram might give the impression that actions are external to Flux, when in fact they're an integral part of the system. The reason this perspective is valuable is because it forces us to think about actions as the only means to deliver new data into the system.

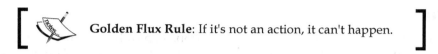

Golden Flux Rule: If it's not an action, it can't happen.

Dispatcher

The dispatcher in a Flux architecture is responsible for distributing actions to the store components (we'll talk about stores next). A dispatcher is actually kind of like a broker—if actions want to deliver new data to a store, they have to talk to the broker, so it can figure out the best way to deliver them. Think about a message broker in a system like RabbitMQ. It's the central hub where everything is sent before it's actually delivered. Here is a diagram depicting a Flux dispatcher receiving actions and dispatching them to stores:

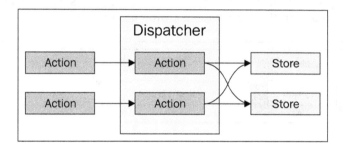

The earlier section of this chapter—"simple architectural layers"—didn't have an explicit layer for dispatchers. That was intentional. In a Flux application, there's only one dispatcher. It can be thought of more as a pseudo layer than an explicit layer. We know the dispatcher is there, but it's not essential to this level of abstraction. What we're concerned about at an architectural level is making sure that when a given action is dispatched, we know that it's going to make it's way to every store in the system.

Having said that, the dispatcher's role is critical to how Flux works. It's the place where store callback functions are registered and it's how data dependencies are handled. Stores tell the dispatcher about other stores that it depends on, and it's up to the dispatcher to make sure these dependencies are properly handled.

Golden Flux Rule: The dispatcher is the ultimate arbiter of data dependencies.

Store

Stores are where state is kept in a Flux application. Typically, this means the application data that's sent to the frontend from the API. However, Flux stores take this a step further and explicitly model the state of the entire application. If this sounds confusing or like a generally bad idea, don't worry — we'll clear this up as we make our way through subsequent chapters. For now, just know that stores are where state that matters can be found. Other Flux components don't have state — they have implicit state at the code level, but we're not interested in this, from an architectural point of view.

Actions are the delivery mechanism for new data entering the system. The term *new data* doesn't imply that we're simply appending it to some collection in a store. All data entering the system is new in the sense that it hasn't been dispatched as an action yet — it could in fact result in a store changing state. Let's look at a visualization of an action that results in a store changing state:

The key aspect of how stores change state is that there's no external logic that determines a state change should happen. It's the store, and only the store, that makes this decision and then carries out the state transformation. This is all tightly encapsulated within the store. This means that when we need to reason about particular information, we need not look any further than the stores. They're their own boss — they're self-employed.

 Golden Flux Rule: Stores are where state lives, and only stores themselves can change this state.

View

The last Flux component we're going to look at in this section is the view, and it technically isn't even a part of Flux. At the same time, views are obviously a critical part of our application. Views are almost universally understood as the part of our architecture that's responsible for displaying data to the user—it's the last stop as data-flows through our information architecture. For example, in MVC architectures, views take model data and display it. In this sense, views in a Flux-based application aren't all that different from MVC views. Where they differ markedly is with regard to handling events. Let's take a look at the following diagram:

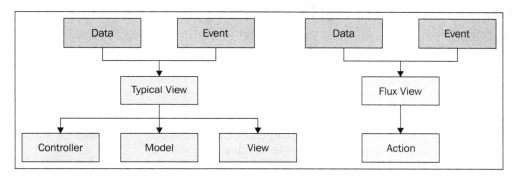

Here we can see the contrasting responsibilities of a Flux view, compared with a view component found in your typical MVC architecture. The two view types have similar types of data flowing into them—application data used to render the component and events (often user input). What's different between the two types of view is what flows out of them.

The typical view doesn't really have any constraints in how its event handler functions communicate with other components. For example, in response to a user clicking a button, the view could directly invoke behavior on a controller, change the state of a model, or it might query the state of another view. On the other hand, the Flux view can only dispatch new actions. This keeps our single entry point into the system intact and consistent with other mechanisms that want to change the state of our store data. In other words, an API response updates state in the exact same way as a user clicking a button does.

Given that views should be restricted in terms of how data-flows out of them (besides DOM updates) in a Flux architecture, you would think that views should be an actual Flux component. This would make sense insofar as making actions the only possible option for views. However, there's also no reason we can't enforce this now, with the benefit being that Flux remains entirely focused on creating information architectures.

Keep in mind, however, that Flux is still in it's infancy. There's no doubt going to be external influences as more people start adopting Flux. Maybe Flux will have something to say about views in the future. Until then, views exist outside of Flux but are constrained by the unidirectional nature of Flux.

 Golden Flux Rule: The only way data-flows out of a view is by dispatching an action.

Installing the Flux package

We'll close the first chapter by getting our feet wet with some code, because everyone needs a hello world application under their belt. We'll also get some of our boilerplate code setup tasks out of the way too, since we'll be using a similar setup throughout the book.

 We'll skip going over Node + NPM installation since it's sufficiently covered in great detail all over the Internet. We'll assume Node is installed and ready to go from this point forward.

The first NPM package we'll need installed is Webpack. This is an advanced module bundler that's well suited for modern JavaScript applications, including Flux-based applications. We'll want to install this package globally so that the webpack command gets installed on our system:

```
npm install webpack -g
```

With Webpack in place, we can build each of the code examples that ship with this book. However, our project does require a couple of local NPM packages, and these can be installed as follows:

```
npm install flux babel-core babel-loader babel-preset-es2015 --save-dev
```

The --save-dev option adds these development dependencies to our file, if one exists. This is just to get started—it isn't necessary to manually install these packages to run the code examples in this book. The examples you've downloaded already come with a package.json, so to install the local dependencies, simply run the following from within the same directory as the package.json file:

```
npm install
```

Now the `webpack` command can be used to build the example. This is the only example in the first chapter, so it's easy to navigate to within a terminal window and run the `webpack` command, which builds the `main-bundle.js` file. Alternatively, if you plan on playing with the code, which is obviously encouraged, try running `webpack --watch`. This latter form of the command will monitor for file changes to the files used in the build, and run the build whenever they change.

This is indeed a simple hello world to get us off to a running start, in preparation for the remainder of the book. We've taken care of all the boilerplate setup tasks by installing Webpack and its supporting modules. Let's take a look at the code now. We'll start by looking at the markup that's used.

```html
<!doctype html>
<html>
  <head>
    <title>Hello Flux</title>
    <script src="main-bundle.js" defer></script>
  </head>
  <body></body>
</html>
```

Not a lot to it is there? There isn't even content within the `body` tag. The important part is the `main-bundle.js` script—this is the code that's built for us by Webpack. Let's take a look at this code now:

```javascript
// Imports the "flux" module.
import * as flux from 'flux';

// Creates a new dispatcher instance. "Dispatcher" is
// the only useful construct found in the "flux" module.
const dispatcher = new flux.Dispatcher();

// Registers a callback function, invoked every time
// an action is dispatched.
dispatcher.register((e) => {
  var p;

  // Determines how to respond to the action. In this case,
  // we're simply creating new content using the "payload"
  // property. The "type" property determines how we create
  // the content.
  switch (e.type) {
    case 'hello':
      p = document.createElement('p');
```

```
        p.textContent = e.payload;
        document.body.appendChild(p);
        break;
      case 'world':
        p = document.createElement('p');
        p.textContent = `${e.payload}!`;
        p.style.fontWeight = 'bold';
        document.body.appendChild(p);
        break;
      default:
        break;
    }
});

// Dispatches a "hello" action.
dispatcher.dispatch({
  type: 'hello',
  payload: 'Hello'
});

// Dispatches a "world" action.
dispatcher.dispatch({
  type: 'world',
  payload: 'World'
});
```

As you can see, there's not much to this hello world Flux application. In fact, the only Flux-specific component this code creates is a dispatcher. It then dispatches a couple of actions and the handler function that's registered to the store processes the actions.

Don't worry that there's no stores or views in this example. The idea is that we've got the basic Flux NPM package installed and ready to go.

Summary

This chapter introduced you to Flux. Specifically, we looked at both what Flux is and what it isn't. Flux is a set of architectural patterns that, when applied to our JavaScript application, help with getting the data-flow aspect of our architecture right. Flux isn't yet another framework used for solving specific implementation challenges, be it browser quirks or performance gains — there's a multitude of tools already available for these purposes. Perhaps the most important defining aspect of Flux are the conceptual problems it solves — things like unidirectional data flow. This is a major reason that there's no de facto Flux implementation.

We wrapped the chapter up by walking through the setup of our build components used throughout the book. To test that the packages are all in place, we created a very basic hello world Flux application.

Now that we have a handle on what Flux is, it's time for us to look at why Flux is the way it is. In the following chapter, we'll take a more detailed look at the principles that drive the design of Flux applications.

2
Principles of Flux

In the previous chapter, you were introduced at a 10,000 foot level to some of the core Flux principles. For example, unidirectional data-flow is central to Flux's existence. The aim of this chapter is to go beyond the simplistic view of Flux principles.

We'll kick things off with a bit of an MVC retrospective — to identify where it falls apart when we're trying to scale a frontend architecture. Following this, we'll take a deeper look at at unidirectional data-flow and how it solves some of the scaling issues we've identified in MVC architectures.

Next, we'll address some high-level compositional issues faced by Flux architectures, such as making everything explicit and favoring layers over deep hierarchies. Finally, we'll compare the various kinds of state found in a Flux architecture and introduce the concept of an update round.

Challenges with MV*

MV* is the prevailing architectural pattern of frontend JavaScript applications. We're referring to this as MV* because there's a number of accepted variations on the pattern, each of which have models and views as core concepts. For our discussions in this book, they can all be considered the same style of JavaScript architecture.

MV* didn't gain traction in the development community because it's a terrible set of patterns. No, MV* is popular because it works. Although Flux can be thought of as a sort of MV* replacement, there's no need to go out and tear apart a working application.

There's no such thing as a perfect architecture, and Flux is by no means immune to this fact. The goal of this section isn't to downplay MV* and all the things it does well, but rather to look at some of the MV* weaknesses and see how Flux steps in and improves the situation.

Separation of concerns

One thing MV* is really good at is establishing a clear separation of concerns. That is, a component has one responsibility, while another component is responsible for something else, and so on, all throughout the architecture. Complementary to the *separation of concerns* principle is the *single responsibility* principle, which enforces a clear separation of concerns.

Why do we care though? The simple answer is that when we separate responsibilities into different components, different parts of the system are naturally decoupled from one another. This means that we can change one thing without necessarily impacting the other. This is a desired trait of any software system, regardless of the architecture. But, is this really what we get with MV*, and is this actually something we should shoot for?

For example, maybe there's no clear advantage in dividing a feature into five distinct responsibilities. Maybe the decoupling of the feature's behavior doesn't actually achieve anything because we would have to touch all five components every time we want to change something anyway. So rather than help us craft a robust architecture, the separation of concerns principle has amounted to nothing more than needles indirection that hampers productivity. Here's an example of a feature that's broken down into several pieces of focused responsibility:

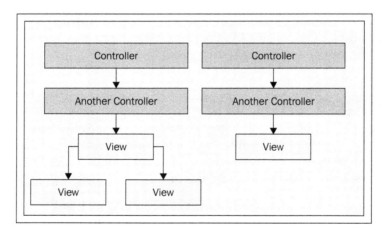

Anytime a developer needs to pull apart a feature so that they can understand how it works, they end up spending more time jumping between source code files. The feature feels fragmented, and there's no obvious advantage to structuring the code like this. Here's a look at the moving parts that make up a feature in a Flux architecture:

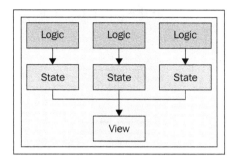

The Flux feature decomposition leaves us with a feeling of predictability. We've left out the potential ways in which the view itself could be decomposed, but that's because the views are outside Flux. All we care about in terms of our Flux architecture is that the correct information is always passed to our views when state changes occur.

You'll note that the logic and state of a given Flux feature are tightly coupled with one another. This is in contrast to MV*, where we want application logic to be a standalone entity that can operate on any data. The opposite is true with Flux, where we'll find the logic responsible for change state in close proximity to that state. This is an intentional design trait, with the implication being that we don't need to get carried away with separating concerns from one another, and that this activity can sometimes hurt rather than help.

As we'll see in the coming chapters, this tight coupling of data and logic is characteristic of Flux stores. The preceding diagram shows that with complex features, it's much easier to add more logic and more state, because they're always near the surface of the feature, rather than buried in a nested tree of components.

Cascading updates

It's nice when we have a software component that *just works*. This could mean any number of things, but it's meaning is usually centered around automatically handling things for us. For instance, instead of manually having to invoke this method, followed by that method, and so on, everything is handled by the component for us. Let's take a look at the following illustration:

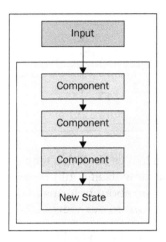

When we pass input into a larger component, we can expect that it will do the right thing automatically for us. What's compelling about these types of components is that it means less code for us to maintain. After all, the component knows how to update itself by orchestrating the communication between any subcomponents.

This is where the cascading effect begins. We tell one component to perform some behavior. This, in turn, causes another component to react. We give it some input, which causes another component to react, and so on. Soon, it's very difficult to comprehend what's going on in our code. This is because the things that are *taken care of* for us are hidden from view. Intentional by design, with unintended consequences.

The previous diagram isn't too bad. Sure, it might get a little difficult to follow depending on how many subcomponents get added to the larger component, but in general, it's a tractable problem. Let's look at a variation of this diagram:

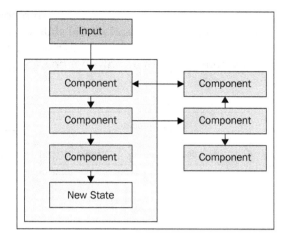

What just happened? Three more boxes and four more lines just happened, resulting in an explosion of cascading update complexity. The problem is no longer tractable because we simply cannot handle this type of complexity, and most MV* applications that rely on this type of automatic updating have way more than six components. The best we can hope for is that once it works the way we want it to, it keeps working.

This is the naive assumption that we make about automatically updating components — this is something we want to encapsulate. The problem is that this generally isn't true, at least not if we ever plan to maintain the software. Flux sidesteps the problem of cascading updates because only a store can change it's own state, and this is always in response to an action.

Model update responsibilities

In an MV* architecture, state is stored within models. To initialize model state, we could fetch data from the backend API. This is clear enough: we create a new model, then tell that model to go fetch some data. However, MV* doesn't say anything about who is responsible for updating these models. One might think it's the controller component that should have total control over the model, but does this ever happen in practice?

For example, what happens in view event handlers, called in response to user interactivity? If we only allow controllers to update the state of our models, then the view event handler functions should talk directly to the controller in question. The following diagram is a visualization of a controller changing the state of models in different ways:

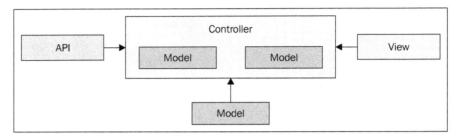

At first glance, this controller setup makes perfect sense. It acts as a wrapper around the models that store state. It's a safe assumption the anything that wants to mutate any of these models needs to go through the controller. That's its responsibility after all — to control things. Data that comes from the API, events triggered by the user and handled by the view, and other models — these all need to talk to the controller if they want to change the state of the models.

As our controller grows, making sure that model state changes are handled by the controller will produce more and more methods that change the model state. If we step back and look at all of these methods as they accumulate, we'll start to notice a lot of needless indirection. What do we stand to gain by proxying these state changes?

Another reason the controller is a dead-end for trying to establish consistent state changes in MV* is the changes that models can make to themselves. For example, setting one property in a model could end up changing other model properties as a side-effect. Worse, our models could have listeners that respond to state changes, somewhere else in the system (the cascading updates problem).

Flux stores deal with the cascading updates problem by only allowing state changes via actions. This same mechanism solves the MV* challenges discussed here; we don't have to worry about views or other stores directly changing the state of our store.

Unidirectional data

A cornerstone of any Flux architecture is unidirectional data-flow. The idea being data flows from point A to point B, or from point A to B to C, or from point A to C. It's the direction that's important with unidirectional data-flow, and to a lesser extent, the ordering. So when we say that our architecture uses a unidirectional data-flow, we can say that data never flows from point B to point A. This is an important property of Flux architectures.

As we saw in the previous section, MV* architectures have no discernible direction with their data-flows. In this section, we'll talk though some of the properties that make a unidirectional data-flow worth implementing. We'll begin with a look at the starting points and completion points of our data-flows, and then we'll think about how side-effects can be avoided when data flows in one direction.

From start to finish

If data-flows in only one direction, there has to be both a starting point and a finish point. In other words, we can't just have an endless stream of data, which arbitrarily affects the various components the data-flows through. When data-flows are unidirectional with clearly defined start and finish points, there's no way we can have circular flows. Instead, we have one big data-flow cycle in Flux, as visualized here:

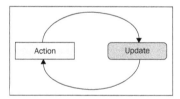

This is obviously an over-simplification of any Flux architecture, but it does serve to illustrate the start and finish points of any given data-flow. What we're looking at is called an **update round**. A round is atomic in the sense that it's run-to-completion—there's no way to stop an update round from completing (unless an exception is thrown).

JavaScript is a run-to-completion language, meaning that once a block of code starts running, it's going to finish. This is good because it means that once we start updating the UI, there's no way a callback function can interrupt our update. The exception to this is when our own code interrupts the updating process. For example, our store logic that's meant to mutate the state of the store dispatches an action. This would be bad news for our Flux architecture because it would violate the unidirectional data-flow. To prevent this, the dispatcher can actually detect when a dispatch takes place inside of an update round. We'll have more on this in later chapters.

Update rounds are responsible for updating the state of the entire application, not just the parts that have subscribed to a particular type of action. This means that as our application grows, so do our update rounds. Since an update round touches every store, it may start to feel as though the data is flowing sideways through all of our stores. Here's an illustration of the idea:

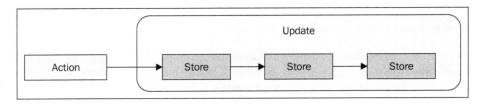

From the perspective of unidirectional data-flow, it doesn't actually matter how many stores there are. The important thing to remember is that the updates will not be interrupted by other actions being dispatched.

No side-effects

As we saw with MV* architectures, the nice thing about automatic state changes is also their demise. When we program by hidden rules, we're essentially programming by stitching together a bunch of side-effects. This doesn't scale well, mainly due to the fact that it's impossible to hold all these hidden connections in our head at a given point in time. Flux likes to avoid side-effects wherever possible.

Let's think about stores for a moment. These are the arbiters of state in our application. When something changes state, it has the potential to cause another piece of code to run in response. This does indeed happen in Flux. When a store changes state, views may be notified about the change, if they've subscribed to the store. This is the only place where side-effects happen in Flux, which is inevitable since we do need to update the DOM at some point when state changes. But what's different about Flux is how it avoids side-effects when there's data dependencies involved. The typical approach to dealing with data dependencies in user interfaces is to notify the dependent model that something has happened. Think cascading updates, as illustrated here:

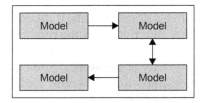

When there's a dependency between two stores in Flux, we just need to declare this dependency in the dependent store. What this does is it tells the dispatcher to make sure that the store we depend on is always updated first. Then, the dependent store can just directly use the store data it depends on. This way, all of the updates can still take place within the same update round.

Explicit over implicit

With architectural patterns, the tendency is to make things easier by veiling them behind abstractions that grow more elaborate with time. Eventually, more and more of the system's data changes automatically and developer convenience is superseded by hidden complexity.

This is a real scalability issue, and Flux handles it by favoring explicit actions and data transformations over implicit abstractions. In this section, we'll explore the benefits of explicitness along with the trade-offs to be made.

Updates via hidden side-effects

We've seen already, in this chapter, how difficult it can be to deal with hidden state changes that hide behind abstractions. They help us avoid writing code, but they also hurt by making it difficult to comprehend an entire work-flow when we come back and look at the code later. With Flux, state is kept in a store, and the store is responsible for changing its own state. What's nice about this is that when we want to inquire about how a given store changes state, all the state transformation code is there, in one place. Let's look at an example store:

```
// A Flux store with state.
class Store {
  constructor() {

    // The initial state of the store.
    this.state = { clickable: false };

    // All of the state transformations happen
    // here. The "action.type" property is how it
    // determines what changes will take place.
    dispatcher.register((e) => {

      // Depending on the type of action, we
      // use "Object.assign()" to assign different
      // values to "this.state".
      switch (e.type) {
```

```
      case 'show':
        Object.assign(this.state, e.payload,
          { clickable: true });
        break;
      case 'hide':
        Object.assign(this.state, e.payload,
          { clickable: false });
        break;
      default:
        break;
      }
    });
  }
}

// Creates a new store instance.
var store = new Store();

// Dispatches a "show" action.
dispatcher.dispatch({
  type: 'show',
  payload: { display: 'block' }
});

console.log('Showing', store.state);
// → Showing {clickable: true, display: "block"}

// Dispatches a "hide" action.
dispatcher.dispatch({
  type: 'hide',
  payload: { display: 'none' }
});

console.log('Hiding', store.state);
// → Hiding {clickable: false, display: "none"}
```

Here, we have a store with a simple state object. In the constructor, the store registers a callback function with the dispatcher. All state transformations take place, explicitly, in one function. This is where data turns into information for our user interface. We don't have to hunt down the little bits and pieces of data as they change state across multiple components; this doesn't happen in Flux.

So the question now becomes, how do views make use of this monolithic state data? In other types of frontend architecture, the views get notified whenever any piece of state changes. In the preceding example, a view gets notified when the `clickable` property changes, and again when the `display` property changes. The view has logic to render these two changes independently of one another. However, views in Flux don't get fine-grained updates like these. Instead, they're notified when the store state changes and the state data is what's given to them.

The implication here is that we should lean toward view technology that's good at re-rendering whole components. This is what makes React a good fit for Flux architectures. Nonetheless, we're free to use any view technology we please, as we'll see later on in the book.

Data changes state in one place

As we saw in the preceding section, the store transformation code is encapsulated within the store. This is intentional. The transformation code that mutates a store's state is supposed to live nearby. Close proximity drastically reduces the complexity of figuring out where state changes happen as systems grow more complex. This makes state changes explicit, instead of abstract and implicit.

One potential trade-off with having a store manage all of the state transformation code is that there could be a lot of it. The code we looked at used a single `switch` statement to handle all of the state transform logic. This would obviously cause a bit of a headache later on when there's a lot of cases to handle. We'll think about this more later in the book, when the time comes to consider large, complex stores. Just know that we can re-factor our stores to elegantly handle a large number of cases, while keeping the coupling of business logic and state tight.

This leads us right back to the separation of concerns principle. With Flux stores, the data and the logic that operates on it isn't separated at all. Is this actually a bad thing though? An action is dispatched, a store is notified about it, and it changes its state (or does nothing, ignoring the action). The logic that changes the state is located in the same component because there's nothing to gain by moving it somewhere else.

Too many actions?

Actions make everything that happens in a Flux architecture explicit. By everything, I mean everything—if it happens, it was the result of an action being dispatched. This is good because it's easy to figure out where actions are dispatched from. Even as the system grows, action dispatches are easy to find in our code, because they can only come from a handful of places. For example, we won't find actions being dispatched within stores.

Any feature we create has the potential to create dozens of actions, if not more. We tend to think that more means bad, from an architectural perspective. If there's more of something, it's going to be more difficult to scale and to program with. There's some truth to this, but if we're going to have a lot of something, which is unavoidable in any large system, it's good that it's actions. Actions are relatively lightweight in that they describe something that happens in our application. In other words, actions aren't heavyweight items that we need to fret over having a lot of.

Does having a lot of actions mean that we need to cram them all into one huge monolithic actions module? Thankfully, we don't have to do this. Just because actions are the entry point into any Flux system, doesn't mean that we can't modularize them to our liking. This is true of all the Flux components we develop, and we'll keep an eye open for ways that we can keep our code modular as we progress through the book.

Layers over hierarchies

User interfaces are hierarchical in nature, partly because HTML is inherently hierarchical and partly because of the way that we structure the information presented to users. For example, this is why we have nested levels of navigation in some applications—we can't possibly fit everything on the screen at once. Naturally, our code starts to reflect this hierarchical structure by becoming a hierarchy itself. This is good in the sense that it reflects what the user sees. It's bad in the sense that deep hierarchies are difficult to comprehend.

In this section, we'll look at hierarchical structures in frontend architectures and how Flux is able to avoid complex hierarchies. We'll first cover the idea of having several top-level components, each with their own hierarchies. Then, we'll look at the side-effects that happen within hierarchies and how data-flows through Flux layers.

Multiple component hierarchies

A given application probably has a handful of major features. These are often implemented as the top-level components or modules in our code. These aren't monolithic components; they're decomposed into smaller and smaller components. Perhaps some of these components share the smaller multipurpose components. For example, a top-level component hierarchy might be composed of models, views, and controllers as is illustrated here:

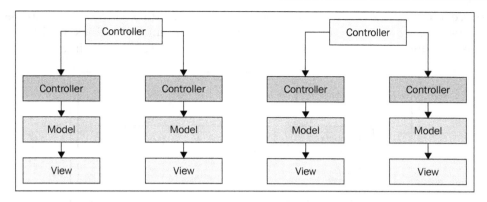

This makes sense in terms of the structure of our application. When we look at pictures of component hierarchies, it's easy to see what our application is made of. Each of these hierarchies, with the top-level component as their root, are like a little universes that exist independently of one anothers. Again, we're back to the notion of separation of concerns. We can develop one feature without impacting another.

The problem with this approach is that user interface features often depend on other features. In other words, the state of one component hierarchy will likely depend on the state of another. How do we keep these two component trees synchronized with one another when there's no mechanism in place to control when state can change? What ends up happening is that a component in one hierarchy will introduce an arbitrary dependency to a component in another hierarchy. This serves a single purpose, so we have to keep introducing new inter-hierarchy dependencies to make sure everything is synchronized.

Hierarchy depth and side-effects

One challenge with hierarchies is depth. That is, how far down will a given hierarchy extend? The features of our application are constantly changing and expanding in scope. This can lead to our component trees growing taller. But they also grow wider. For example, let's say that our feature uses a component hierarchy that's three levels deep.

Then, we add a new level. Well, we'll probably have to add several new components to this new level and in higher levels. So to build upon our hierarchies, we have to scale in multiple directions—horizontally and vertically. This idea is illustrated here:

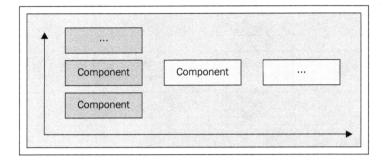

Scaling components in multiple directions is difficult, especially in component hierarchies where there's no data-flow direction. That is, input that ends up changing the state of something can enter the hierarchy at any level. Undoubtedly, this has some sort of side-effect, and if we're dependent on components in other hierarchies, all hope is lost.

Data-flow and layers

Flux has distinct architectural layers, which are more favorable to scaling architectures than hierarchies are. The reason is simple—we only need to scale components horizontally, within each layer of the architecture. We don't need to add new components to a layer and add new layers. Let's take a look at what scaling a Flux architecture looks like in the following diagram:

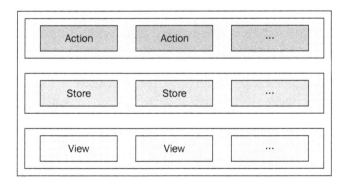

No matter how large an application gets, there's no need to add new architectural layers. We simply add new components to these layers. The reason we're able to do this without creating a tangled mess of component connections within a given layer is because all three layers play a part in the update round. An update round starts with an action and completes with the last view that is rendered. The data-flows through our application from layer to layer, in one direction.

Application data and UI state

When we have a separation of concerns that sticks presentation in one place and application data in another, we have two distinct places where we need to manage state. Except in Flux, the only place where there's state is within a store. In this section, we'll compare application data and UI data. We'll then address the transformations that ultimately lead to changes in the user interface. Lastly, we'll discuss the feature-centric nature of Flux stores.

Two of the same thing

Quite often, application data that's fetched from an API is fed into some kind of view layer. This is also known as the presentation layer, responsible for transforming application data into something of value for the user — from data to information in other words. In these layers, we end up with state to represent the UI elements. For example, is the checkbox checked? Here is an illustration of how we tend to group the two types of state within our components:

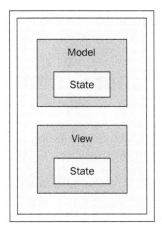

This doesn't really fit well with Flux architectures, because stores are where state belongs, including the UI. So, can a store have both application and UI state within it? Well, there isn't a strong argument against it. If everything that has a state is self-contained within a store, it should be fairly simple to discern between application data and state that belongs to UI elements. Here's an illustration of the types of state found in Flux stores:

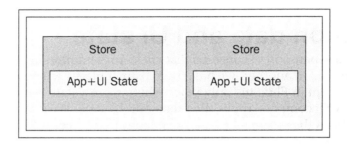

The fundamental misconception with trying to separate UI state from other state is that components often depend on UI state. Even UI components in different features can depend on each other's state in unpredictable ways. Flux acknowledges this and doesn't try to treat UI state as something special that should be split off from application data.

The UI state that ultimately ends up in a store can be derived from a number of things. Generally, two or more items from our application data could determine a UI state item. A UI state could be derived from another UI state, or from something more complex, like a UI state and other application data. In other cases, the application data is simple enough that it can be consumed directly by the view. The key is that the view has enough information that it can render itself without having to track its own state.

Tightly coupled transformations

Application data and UI state are tightly coupled together in Flux stores. It only makes sense that the transformations that operate on this data be tightly coupled to the store as well. This makes it easy for us to change the state of the UI based on other application data or based on the state of other stores.

If our business logic code wasn't in the store, then we'd need to start introducing dependencies to the components containing the logic needed by the store. Sure, this would mean generic business logic that transforms the state, and this could be shared in several stores, but this seldom happens at a high level. Stores are better off keeping their business logic that transforms the state of the store tightly coupled. If we need to reduce repetitive code, we can introduce smaller, more fine-grained utility functions to help with data transformations.

We can get generic with our stores as well. These stores are abstract and don't directly interface with views. We'll go into more detail on this advanced topic later in the book.

Feature centric

If the data transformations that change the state of a store are tightly coupled to the store itself, does this mean that the store is tailored for a specific feature? In other words, do we care about stores being reused for other features? Sure, in some cases we have generic data that doesn't make much sense in repeating several times across stores. But generally speaking, stores are feature specific. Features are synonymous with domains in Flux parlance—everyone divides up the capabilities of their UI in different ways.

This is a departure from other architectures that base their data models on the data model of the API. Then, they use these models to create more specific view models. Any given MV* framework will have loads of features in their model abstractions, things like data bindings and automatic API fetching. They're only worried about storing state and publishing notifications when this state changes.

When stores encourage us to create and store new state that's specific to the UI, we can more easily design for the user. This is the fundamental difference between stores in Flux and models in other architectures—the UI data model comes first. The transformations within stores exist to ensure that the correct state is published to views—everything else is secondary.

Summary

This chapter introduced you to the driving principles of Flux. These should be in the back your mind as you work on any Flux architecture. We started the chapter off with a brief retrospective of MV* style architectures that permeate frontend development. Some challenges with this style of architecture include cascading model updates and a lack of data-flow direction. We then looked at the prize concept of Flux—unidirectional data-flow.

Next, we covered how Flux favors explicit actions over implicit abstractions. This makes things easier to comprehend when reading Flux code, because we don't have to go digging around for the root cause of a state change. We also looked at how Flux utilizes architectural layers to visualize how data-flows in one direction through the system.

Finally, we compared application data with state that's generally considered specific to UI elements. Flux stores tend to focus on state that's relevant to the feature it supports, and doesn't distinguish between application data and UI state. Now that we have a handle on the principles that drive Flux architectures, it's time for us to code one. In the next chapter, we'll implement our skeleton Flux architecture, allowing us to focus on information design.

3
Building a Skeleton Architecture

The best way to think in Flux is to write code in Flux. This is why we want to start building a **skeleton architecture** as early as possible. We call this phase of building our application the skeleton architecture because it isn't yet the full architecture. It's missing a lot of key application components, and this is on purpose. The aim of the skeleton is to keep the moving parts to a minimum, allowing us to focus on the information our stores will generate for our views.

We'll get off the ground with a minimalist structure that, while small, doesn't require a lot of work to turn our skeleton architecture into our code base. Then, we'll move on to some of the information design goals of the skeleton architecture. Next, we'll dive into implementing some aspects of our stores.

As we start building, we'll begin to get a sense of how these stores map to domains — the features our users will interact with. After this, we'll create some really simple views, which can help us ensure that our data flows are in fact reaching their final destination. Finally, we'll end the chapter by running through a checklist for each of the Flux architectural layers, to make sure that we've validated our skeleton before moving on to other development activities.

General organization

As a first step in building a skeleton Flux architecture, we'll spend a few minutes getting organized. In this section, we'll establish a basic directory structure, figure out how we'll manage our dependencies, and choose our build tools. None of this is set in stone — the idea is to get going quickly, but at the same time, establish some norms so that transforming our skeleton architecture into application code is as seamless as possible.

Directory structure

The directory structure used to start building our skeleton doesn't need to be fancy. It's a skeleton architecture, not the complete architecture, so the initial directory structure should follow suit. Having said that, we also don't want to use a directory structure that's difficult to evolve into what's actually used in the product. Let's take a look at the items that we'll find in the root of our project directory:

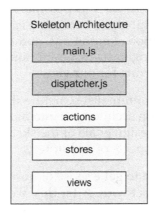

Pretty simple right? Let's walk through what each of these items represent:

- `main.js`: This is the main entry point into the application. This JavaScript module will bootstrap the initial actions of the system.

- `dispatcher.js`: This is our dispatcher module. This is where the Flux dispatcher instance is created.

- `actions`: This directory contains all our action creator functions and action constants.

- `stores`: This directory contains our store modules.
- `views`: This directory contains our view modules.

This may not seem like much, and this is by design. The directory layout is reflective of the architectural layers of Flux. Obviously there will be more to the actual application once we move past the skeleton architecture phase, but not a whole lot. We should refrain from adding any extraneous components at this point though, because the skeleton architecture is all about information design.

Dependency management

As a starting point, we're going to require the basic Facebook Flux dispatcher as a dependency of our skeleton architecture—even if we don't end up using this dispatcher in our final product. We need to start designing our stores, as this is the most crucial and the most time-consuming aspect of the skeleton architecture; worrying about things like the dispatcher at this juncture simply doesn't pay off.

We need to start somewhere and the Facebook dispatcher implementation is good enough. The question is, will we need any other packages? In *Chapter 1, What is Flux?* we walked through the setup of the Facebook Flux NPM package and used Webpack to build our code. Can this work as our eventual production build system?

Not having a package manager or a module bundler puts us at a disadvantage, right from the onset of the project. This is why we need to think about dependency management as a first step of the skeleton architecture, even though we don't have many dependencies at the moment. If this is the first time we're building an application that has a Flux architecture behind it, the way we handle dependencies will serve as a future blueprint for subsequent Flux projects.

Is it a bad idea to add more module dependencies during the development of our skeleton architecture? Not at all. In fact, it's better that we use a tool that's well suited for the job. As we're implementing the skeleton, we'll start to see places in our stores where a library would be helpful. For example, if we're doing a lot of sorting and filtering on data collections and we're building higher-order functions, using something like lodash for this is perfect.

On the other hand, pulling in something like ReactJS or jQuery at this stage doesn't make a whole lot of sense because we're still thinking about the information and not how to present it in the DOM. So that's the approach we're going to use in this book—NPM as our package manager and Webpack as our bundler. This is the basic infrastructure we need, without much overhead to distract us.

Information design

We know that the skeleton architecture we're trying to build is specifically focused on getting the right information into the hands of our users. This means that we're not paying much attention to user interactivity or formatting the information in a user-friendly way. It might help if we set some rough goals for ourselves—how do we know we're actually getting anywhere with our information design?

In this section, we'll talk about the negative influence API data models can have on our user interface design. Then, we'll look at mapping data to what the user sees and how these mappings should be encouraged throughout our stores. Finally, we'll think about the environment we find ourselves working in.

Users don't understand models

Our job as user interface programmers is to get the right information to the user at the right time. How do we do this? Conventional wisdom revolves around taking some data that we got from the API and then rendering it as HTML. Apart from semantic markup and some styles, nothing much has changed with the data since it arrived from the API. We're saying *here's the data we have, let's make it look nice for the user*. Here's an illustration of this idea:

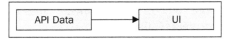

There's no data transformation taking place here, which is fine, so long as the user is getting what they need. The problem this picture paints is that the data model of the API has taken the UI feature development hostage. We must heed everything that's sent down to us from the backend. The reason this is a problem is because we're limited in what we can actually do for the user. Something we can do is have our own models enhance the data that's sent back from the API. This means that if we're working on a feature that would require information that isn't exactly as the API intended it, we can fabricate it as a frontend model, as shown here:

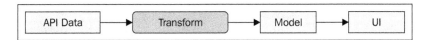

This gets us slightly closer to our goal in the sense that we can create a model of the feature we're trying to implement and put it in front of the user. So while the API might not deliver exactly what we want to display on the screen, we can use our transformation functions to generate a model of the information we need.

During the skeleton architecture phase of our design process, we should think about stores independent of API's as much as possible. Not completely independently; we don't want to go way out into left field, jeopardizing the product. But the idea of producing a Flux skeleton architecture is to ensure that we're producing the right information, first and foremost. If there's no way the API can support what we're trying to do, then we can take the necessary steps, before spending a lot of time implementing full-fledged features.

Stores map to what the user sees

State isn't the only thing that's encapsulated by the stores found in our Flux architecture. There's also the data transformations that map old state to new state. We should spend more time thinking about what the user needs to see and less time thinking about the API data, which means that the store transformation functions are essential.

We need to embrace data transformations in Flux stores, because they're the ultimate determinant of how things change in front of the user's eyes. Without these transformations, the user would only be able to view static information. Of course, we could aim to design an architecture that only uses the data that's passed into the system "as-is", without transforming it. This never works out as we intend, for the simple reason that we're going to uncover dependencies with other UI components.

What should our early goals be with stores and how we transform their state? Well, the skeleton architecture is all about experimentation, and if we start writing transformation functionality upfront, we're likely to discover dependencies sooner. Dependencies aren't necessarily a bad thing, except when we find a lot of them late in the project, well after we've completed the skeleton architecture phase. Of course, new features are going to add new dependencies. If we can use state transformations early on to identify potential dependencies, then we can avoid future headaches.

What do we have to work with?

The last thing we'll need to consider before we roll up our sleeves and start implementing this skeleton Flux architecture is what's already in place. For example, does this application already have an established API and we're re-architecting the frontend? Do we need to retain the user experience of an existing UI? Is the project completely greenfield with no API or user experience input?

The following diagram illustrates how these external factors influence the way we treat the implementation of our skeleton architecture:

There's nothing wrong with having these two factors shape our Flux architecture. In the case of existing APIs, we'll have a starting point from which we can start writing our state transformation functions, to get the user the information that they need. In the case of keeping an existing user experience, we already know what the shape of our target information looks like, and we can work the transformation functions from a different angle.

When the Flux architecture is completely greenfield, we can let it inform both the user experience and the APIs that need to be implemented. It's highly unlikely that any of the scenarios in which we find ourselves building a skeleton architecture will be cut-and-dried. These are just the starting points that we may find ourselves in. Having said that, it's time to start implementing some skeleton stores.

Putting stores into action

In this section, we're going to implement some stores in our skeleton architecture. They won't be complete stores capable of supporting end-to-end work-flows. However, we'll be able to see where the stores fit within the context of our application.

We'll start with the most basic of all store actions, which are populating them with some data; this is usually done by fetching it via some API. Then, we'll discuss changing the state of remote API data. Finally, we'll look at actions that change the state of a store locally, without the use of an API.

Fetching API data

Regardless of whether or not there's an API with application data ready to consume, we know that eventually this is how we'll populate our store data. So it makes sense that we think about this as the first design activity of implementing skeleton stores.

Let's create a basic store for the homepage of our application. The obvious information that the user is going to want to see here is the currently logged-in user, a navigation menu, and perhaps a summarized list of recent events that are relevant to the user. This means that fetching this data is one of the first things our application will have to do. Here's our first implementation of the store:

```
// Import the dispatcher, so that the store can
// listen to dispatch events.
import dispatcher from '../dispatcher';

// Our "Home" store.
class HomeStore {
  constructor() {

    // Sets a default state for the store. This is
    // never a bad idea, in case other stores want to
    // iterate over array values - this will break if
    // they're undefined.
    this.state = {
      user: '',
      events: [],
      navigation: []
    };

    // When a "HOME_LOAD" event is dispatched, we
    // can assign "payload" to "state".
    dispatcher.register((e) => {
      switch (e.type) {
        case 'HOME_LOAD':
          Object.assign(this.state, e.payload);
          break;
      }
    });
  }
}

export default new HomeStore();
```

This is fairly easy to follow, so lets point out the important pieces. First, we need to import the dispatcher so that we can register our store. When the store is created, the default state is stored in the state property. When the HOME_LOAD action is dispatched, we change the state of the store. Lastly, we export the store instance as the default module member.

As the action name implies, HOME_LOAD is dispatched when data for the store has loaded. Presumably, we're going to pull this data for the home store from some API endpoints. Let's go ahead and put this store to use in our main.js module—our application entry point:

```javascript
// Imports the "dispatcher", and the "homeStore".
import dispatcher from './dispatcher';
import homeStore from './stores/home';

// Logs the default state of the store, before
// any actions are triggered against it.
console.log(`user: "${homeStore.state.user}"`);
// → user: ""

console.log('events:', homeStore.state.events);
// → events: []

console.log('navigation:', homeStore.state.navigation);
// → navigation: []

// Dispatches a "HOME_LOAD" event, when populates the
// "homeStore" with data in the "payload" of the event.
dispatcher.dispatch({
  type: 'HOME_LOAD',
  payload: {
    user: 'Flux',
    events: [
      'Completed chapter 1',
      'Completed chapter 2'
    ],
    navigation: [
      'Home',
      'Settings',
      'Logout'
    ]
  }
});

// Logs the new state of "homeStore", after it's
// been populated with data.
console.log(`user: "${homeStore.state.user}"`);
// → user: "Flux"
```

```
console.log('events:', homeStore.state.events);
// → events: ["Completed chapter 1", "Completed chapter 2"]

console.log('navigation:', homeStore.state.navigation);
// → navigation: ["Home", "Settings", "Logout"]
```

This is some fairly straightforward usage of our home store. We're logging the default state of the store, dispatching the HOME_LOAD action with some new payload data, and logging the state again to make sure that the state of the store did in fact change. So the question is, what does this code have to do with the API?

This is a good starting point for our skeleton architecture because there's a number of things to think about before we even get to implementing API calls. We haven't even started implementing actions yet, because if we did, they'd just be another distraction. And besides, actions and real API calls are easy to implement once we flesh out our stores.

The first question that comes to mind about the main.js module is the location of the dispatch() call to HOME_LOAD. Here, we're bootstrapping data into the store. Is this the right place to do this? When the main.js module runs will we always require that this store be populated? Is this the place where we'll want to bootstrap data into all of our stores? We don't need immediate answers to these questions, because that would likely result in us dwelling on one aspect of the architecture for far too long, and there are many other issues to think about.

For example, does the coupling of our store make sense? The home store we just implemented has a navigation array. These are just simple strings right now, but they'll likely turn into objects. The bigger issue is that the navigation data might not even belong in this store—several other stores are probably going to require navigation state data too. Another example is the way we're setting the new state of the store using the dispatch payload. Using Object.assign() is advantageous, because we can dispatch the HOME_LOAD event with a payload with only one state property and everything will continue to function the same. Implementing this store took us very little time at all, but we've asked some very important questions and learned a powerful technique for assigning new store state.

This is the skeleton architecture, and so we're not concerned with the mechanics of actually fetching the API data. We're more concerned about the actions that get dispatched as a result of API data arriving in the browser; in this case, it's HOME_LOAD. It's the mechanics of information flowing through stores that matters in the context of a skeleton Flux architecture. And on that note, let's expand the capabilities of our store slightly:

```
// We need the "dispatcher" to register our store,
// and the "EventEmitter" class so that our store
// can emit "change" events when the state of the
// store changes.
import dispatcher from '../dispatcher';
import { EventEmitter } from 'events';

// Our "Home" store which is an "EventEmitter"
class HomeStore extends EventEmitter {
  constructor() {

    // We always need to call this when extending a class.
    super();

    // Sets a default state for the store. This is
    // never a bad idea, in case other stores want to
    // iterate over array values - this will break if
    // they're undefined.
    this.state = {
      user: '',
      events: [],
      navigation: []
    };

    // When a "HOME_LOAD" event is dispatched, we
    // can assign "payload" to "state", then we can
    // emit a "change" event.
    dispatcher.register((e) => {
      switch (e.type) {
        case 'HOME_LOAD':
          Object.assign(this.state, e.payload);
          this.emit('change', this.state);
          break;
      }
    });
  }
}

export default new HomeStore();
```

The store still does everything it did before, only now the store class inherits from `EventEmitter`, and when the `HOME_LOAD` action is dispatched, it emits a `change` event using the store state as the event data. This gets us one step closer to having a full work-flow, as views can now listen to the `change` event to get the new state of the store. Let's update our main module code to see how this is done:

```
// Imports the "dispatcher", and the "homeStore".
import dispatcher from './dispatcher';
import homeStore from './stores/home';

// Logs the default state of the store, before
// any actions are triggered against it.
console.log(`user: "${homeStore.state.user}"`);
// → user: ""

console.log('events:', homeStore.state.events);
// → events: []

console.log('navigation:', homeStore.state.navigation);
// → navigation: []

// The "change" event is emitted whenever the state of The
// store changes.
homeStore.on('change', (state) => {
  console.log(`user: "${state.user}"`);
  // → user: "Flux"

  console.log('events:', state.events);
  // → events: ["Completed chapter 1", "Completed chapter 2"]

  console.log('navigation:', state.navigation);
  // → navigation: ["Home", "Settings", "Logout"]
});

// Dispatches a "HOME_LOAD" event, when populates the
// "homeStore" with data in the "payload" of the event.
dispatcher.dispatch({
  type: 'HOME_LOAD',
  payload: {
    user: 'Flux',
    events: [
      'Completed chapter 1',
      'Completed chapter 2'
    ],
```

```
        navigation: [
          'Home',
          'Settings',
          'Logout'
        ]
      }
    });
```

This enhancement to the store in our skeleton architecture brings about yet more questions, namely, about setting up event listeners on our stores. As you can see, we have to make sure that the handler is actually listening to the store before any actions are dispatched. All of these concerns we need to address, and we've only just begun to design our architecture. Let's move on to changing the state of backend resources.

Changing API resource state

After we've set the initial store state by asking the API for some data, we'll likely end up needing to change the state of that backend resource. This happens in response to user activity. In fact, the common pattern looks like the following diagram:

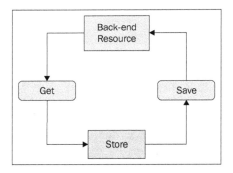

Let's think about this pattern in the context of a Flux store. We've already seen how to load data into a store. In the skeleton architecture we're building, we're not actually making these API calls, even if they exist—we're focused solely on the information that's produced by the frontend right now. When we dispatch an action that changes the state of a store, we'll probably need to update the state of this store in response to successful completion of the API call. The real question is, what does this entail exactly?

For example, does the call we make to change the state of the backend resource actually respond with the updated resource, or does it respond with a mere success indication? These types of API patterns have a dramatic impact on the design of our stores because it means the difference between having to always make a secondary call or having the data in the response.

Let's look at some code now. First, we have a user store as follows:

```
import dispatcher from '../dispatcher';
import { EventEmitter } from 'events';

// Our "User" store which is an "EventEmitter"
class UserStore extends EventEmitter {
  constructor() {
    super();
    this.state = {
      first: '',
      last: ''
    };

    dispatcher.register((e) => {
      switch (e.type) {
        // When the "USER_LOAD" action is dispatched, we
        // can assign the payload to this store's state.
        case 'USER_LOAD':
          Object.assign(this.state, e.payload);
          this.emit('change', this.state);
          break;

        // When the "USER_REMOVE" action is dispatched,
        // we need to check if this is the user that was
        // removed. If so, then reset the state.
        case 'USER_REMOVE':
          if (this.state.id === e.payload) {
            Object.assign(this.state, {
              id: null,
              first: '',
              last: ''
            });

            this.emit('change', this.state);
          }

          break;
      }
    });
  }
}

export default new UserStore();
```

We'll assume that this singular user store is for a page in our application where only a single user is displayed. Now, let's implement a store that's useful for tracking the state of several users:

```
import dispatcher from '../dispatcher';
import { EventEmitter } from 'events';

// Our "UserList" store which is an "EventEmitter"
class UserListStore extends EventEmitter {
  constructor() {
    super();

    // There's no users in this list by default.
    this.state = []

    dispatcher.register((e) => {
      switch (e.type) {

        // The "USER_ADD" action adds the "payload" to
        // the array state.
        case 'USER_ADD':
          this.state.push(e.payload);
          this.emit('change', this.state);
          break;

        // The "USER_REMOVE" action has a user id as
        // the "payload" - this is used to locate the
        // user in the array and remove it.
        case 'USER_REMOVE':
          let user = this.state.find(
            x => x.id === e.payload);

          if (user) {
            this.state.splice(this.state.indexOf(user), 1);
            this.emit('change', this.state);
          }

          break;
      }
    });
  }
}

export default new UserListStore();
```

Let's now create the `main.js` module that will work with these stores. In particular, we want to see how interacting with the API to change the state of a backend resource will influence the design of our stores:

```
import dispatcher from './dispatcher';
import userStore from './stores/user';
import userListStore from './stores/user-list';

// Intended to simulate a back-end API that changes
// state of something. In this case, it's creating
// a new resource. The returned promise will resolve
// with the new resource data.
function createUser() {
  return new Promise((resolve, reject) => {
    setTimeout(() => {
      resolve({
        id: 1,
        first: 'New',
        last: 'User'
      });
    }, 500);
  });
}

// Show the user when the "userStore" changes.
userStore.on('change', (state) => {
  console.log('changed', `"${state.first} ${state.last}"`);
});

// Show how many users there are when the "userListStore"
// changes.
userListStore.on('change', (state) => {
  console.log('users', state.length);
});

// Creates the back-end resource, then dispatches actions
// once the promise has resolved.
createUser().then((user) => {

  // The user has loaded, the "payload" is the resolved data.
  dispatcher.dispatch({
    type: 'USER_LOAD',
    payload: user
  });
```

```
    // Adds a user to the "userListStore", using the resolved
    // data.
    dispatcher.dispatch({
      type: 'USER_ADD',
      payload: user
    });

    // We can also remove the user. This impacts both stores.
    dispatcher.dispatch({
      type: 'USER_REMOVE',
      payload: 1
    });
  });
```

Here, we can see that the `createUser()` function serves as a proxy for the actual API implementation. Remember, this is a skeleton architecture where the chief concern is the information constructed by our stores. Implementing a function that returns a promise is perfectly acceptable here because this is very easy to change later on once we start talking to the real API.

We're on the lookout for interesting aspects of our stores—their state, how that state changes, and the dependencies between our stores. In this case, when we create the new user, the API returns the new object. Then, this is dispatched as a USER_LOAD action. Our `userStore` is now populated. We're also dispatching a USER_ADD action so that the new user data can be added to this list. Presumably, these two stores service different parts of our application, and yet the same API call that changes the state of something in the backend is relevant.

What can we learn about our architecture from all of this? For starters, we can see that the promise callback is going to have to dispatch multiple actions for multiple stores. This means that we can probably expect more of the same with similar API calls that create resources. What about calls that modify users, would the code look similar?

Something that we're missing here is an action to update the state of a user object within the array of users in `userListStore`. Alternatively, we could have this store also handle the USER_LOAD action. Any approach is fine, it's the exercise of building the skeleton architecture that's supposed to help us find the approach that best fits our application. For example, we're dispatching a single USER_REMOVE action here too, and this is handled easily by both our stores. Maybe this is the approach we're looking for?

Local actions

We'll close the section on store actions with a look at local actions. These are actions that have nothing to do with the API. Local actions are generally in response to user interactions, and dispatching them will have a visible effect on the UI. For example, the user wants the toggle the visibility of some component on the page.

The typical application would just execute a jQuery one-liner to locate the element in the DOM and make the appropriate CSS changes. This type of thing doesn't fly in Flux architectures, and it's the type of thing we should start thinking about during the skeleton architecture phase of our application. Let's implement a simple store that handles local actions:

```
import dispatcher from '../dispatcher';
import { EventEmitter } from 'events';

// Our "Panel" store which is an "EventEmitter"
class PanelStore extends EventEmitter {
  constructor() {

    // We always need to call this when extending a class.
    super();

    // The initial state of the store.
    this.state = {
      visible: true,
      items: [
        { name: 'First', selected: false },
        { name: 'Second', selected: false }
      ]
    };

    dispatcher.register((e) => {
      switch (e.type) {

        // Toggles the visibility of the panel, which is
        // visible by default.
        case 'PANEL_TOGGLE':
          this.state.visible = !this.state.visible;
          this.emit('change', this.state);
          break;

        // Selects an object from "items", but only
        // if the panel is visible.
```

```
        case 'ITEM_SELECT':
          let item = this.state.items[e.payload];

          if (this.state.visible && item) {
            item.selected = true;
            this.emit('change', this.state);
          }

          break;
      }
    });
  }
}

export default new PanelStore();
```

The PANEL_TOGGLE action and the ITEM_SELECT action are two local actions handled by this store. They're local because they're likely triggered by the user clicking a button or selecting a checkbox. Let's dispatch these actions so we can see how our store handles them:

```
import dispatcher from './dispatcher';
import panelStore from './stores/panel';

// Logs the state of the "panelStore" when it changes.
panelStore.on('change', (state) => {
  console.log('visible', state.visible);
  console.log('selected', state.items.filter(
    x => x.selected));
});

// This will select the first item.
dispatcher.dispatch({
  type: 'ITEM_SELECT',
  payload: 0
});
// → visible true
// → selected [ { name: First, selected: true } ]

// This disables the panel by toggling the "visible"
// property value.
dispatcher.dispatch({ type: 'PANEL_TOGGLE' });
// → visible false
// → selected [ { name: First, selected: true } ]
```

```
// Nothing the second item isn't actually selected,
// because the panel is disabled. No "change" event
// is emitted here either, because the "visible"
// property is false.
dispatcher.dispatch({
  type: 'ITEM_SELECT',
  payload: 1
});
```

This example serves as an illustration as to why we should consider all things state-related during the skeleton architecture implementation phase. Just because we're not implementing actual UI components right now, doesn't mean we can't guess at some of the potential states of common building blocks. In this code, we've discovered that the `ITEM_SELECT` action is actually dependent on the `PANEL_TOGGLE` action. This is because we don't actually want to select an item and update the view when the panel is disabled.

Building on this idea, should other components be able to dispatch this action in the first place? We've just found a potential store dependency, where the dependent store would query the state of `panelStore` before actually enabling UI elements. All of this from local actions that don't even talk to APIs, and without actual user interface elements. We're probably going to find many more items like this throughout the course of our skeleton architecture, but don't get hung up on finding everything. The idea is to learn what we can, while we have an opportunity to, because once we start implementing real features, things become more complicated.

Stores and feature domains

With more traditional frontend architectures, models that map directly to what's returned from the API provide a clear and concise data model for our JavaScript components to work with. Flux, as we now know, leans more in the direction of the user, and focuses on the information that they need to see and interact with. This doesn't need to be a gigantic headache for us, especially if we're able to decompose our user interface into domains. Think of a domain as a really big feature.

In this section, we'll talk about identifying the top-level features that form the core of our UI. Then, we'll work on shedding irrelevant API data from the equation. We'll finish the section with a look at the structure of our store data, and the role it plays in the design of our skeleton architecture.

Identifying top-level features

During the skeleton architecture phase of our Flux project, we should jump in and start writing store code, just as we've done in this chapter. We've been thinking about the information the user is going to need and how we can best get this information to the user. Something we didn't spend a lot of time on upfront was trying to identify the top level features of the application. This is fine, because the exercises we've performed so far in this chapter are often a prerequisite for figuring out how to organize our user interface.

However, once we've identified how we're going to implement some of the low-level store mechanisms that get us the information we're after, we need to start thinking about these top-level features. And there's a good reason for this—the stores we ultimately maintain will map to these features. When we say top-level, it's tempting to use the navigation as the point of reference. There's actually nothing wrong with using the page navigation as a guide; if it's big enough for the main navigation, it's probably a top-level feature that's worthy of its own Flux store.

In addition to being a top-level feature, we need to think about the role of the store— why does it exist? What value does this add for the user? The reason these questions are important is because we could end up having six pages that all could have used the same store. So it's a balance between consolidating value into one store and making sure that the store isn't to large and general-purpose.

Applications are complex, with lots of moving parts that drive lots of features. Our user interface probably has 50 awesome features. But this is unlikely to require 50 awesome top-level navigation links and 50 Flux stores. Our stores will have to represent the complex intricacies of these features in their data, at some point. This comes later though, for now we just need to get a handle on approximately how many stores we're working with, and how many dependencies we have between them.

Irrelevant API data

Use it or lose it—the mantra of Flux store data. The challenge with API data is that it's a representation of a backend resource—it's not going to return data that's specifically required for our UI. An API exists so that more than one UI can be built on it. However, this means that we often end up with irrelevant data in our stores. For example, if we only need a few properties from an API resource, we don't want to store 36 properties. Especially when some of these can themselves be collections. This is wasteful in terms of memory consumption, and confusing in terms of their existence. It's actually the latter point that's more concerning because we can easily mislead other programmers working on this project.

One potential solution is to exclude these unused values from the API response. Many APIs today support this, by letting us opt-in to the properties we want returned. And this is probably a good idea if it means drastically reduced network bandwidth. However, this approach can also be error-prone because we have to perform this filtering at the ajax call level, instead of at the store level. Let's look at an example that takes a different approach, by specifying a store record:

```
import dispatcher from '../dispatcher';
import { EventEmitter } from 'events';

class PlayerStore extends EventEmitter {
  constructor() {
    super();

    // The property keys in the default state are
    // used to determine the allowable properties
    // used to set the state.
    this.state = {
      id: null,
      name: ''
    };

    dispatcher.register((e) => {
      switch (e.type) {
        case 'PLAYER_LOAD':

          // Make sure that we only take payload data
          // that's already a state property.
          for (let key in this.state) {
            this.state[key] = e.payload[key];
          }

          this.emit('change', this.state);
          break;
      }
    });
  }
}

export default new PlayerStore();
```

In this example, the default `state` object plays an important role, other than providing default state values. It also provides the store record. In other words, the property keys used by the default state determine the allowable values when the `PLAYER_LOAD` action is dispatched. Let's see if this works as expected:

```
import dispatcher from './dispatcher';
import playerStore from './stores/player';

// Logs the state of the player store when it changes.
playerStore.on('change', (state) => {
  console.log('state', state);
});

// Dispatch a "PLAYER_LOAD" action with more payload
// data than is actually used by the store.
dispatcher.dispatch({
  type: 'PLAYER_LOAD',
  payload: {
    id: 1,
    name: 'Mario',
    score: 527,
    rank: 12
  }
});
// → state {id: 1, name: "Mario"}
```

Structuring store data

All of the examples shown so far in this chapter have relatively simple state objects within stores. Once we build the skeleton architecture up, these simple objects will turn into something more complicated. Remember, the state of a store reflects the state of the information that the user is looking at. This includes the state of some of the elements on the page.

This is something we need to keep an eye on. Just because we're through performing the skeleton architecture exercise doesn't mean an idea will hold up as we start to implement more elaborate features. In other words, if a store state becomes too large—too nested and deep—then it's time to consider moving our stores around a little bit.

The idea is that we don't want too many stores driving our views, because they're more like models from an MVC architecture at this point. We want the stores to represent a specific feature of the application. This doesn't always work out, because we could end up having some complex and convoluted state in the store for the feature. In this case, our top-level feature needs to be split somehow.

This will no doubt happen at some point during our time with Flux, and there's no rule in place that says when it's time to refactor stores. Instead, if the state data stays at a size where it feels comfortable to work with, you're probably fine with the store as it is.

Bare bone views

We've made some progress with our skeleton stores to the point where we're ready to start looking at skeleton views. These are simple classes, much in the same spirit as stores are, except we're not actually rendering anything to the DOM. The idea with these bare bone views is to affirm the sound infrastructure of our architecture, and that these view components are in fact getting the information they expect. This is crucial because the views are the final item in the Flux data-flow, so if they're not getting what they need, when they need it, we need to go back and fix our stores.

In this section, we'll discuss how our bare-boned views can help us more quickly identify when stores are missing a particular piece of information. Then, we'll look at how these views can help us identify potential actions in our Flux application.

Finding missing data

The first activity we'll perform with our bare bone views is figuring out whether or not the stores are passing along all the essential information required by the view. By essential, we're talking about things that would be problematic for the user were they not there. For example, we're looking at a settings page, and there's a whole section missing. Or, there's a list of options to select from, but we don't actually have the string labels to show because they're part of some other API.

Once we figure out that these critical pieces of information are missing from the store, the next step is to determine if they're a possibility, because if they're not, we've just avoided spending an inordinate amount of time implementing a full-fledged view. However, these are the rare cases. Usually, it isn't a big deal to go back to the store in question and add the missing transformation that will compute and set the missing state we're looking for.

How much time do we need to spend on these bare bone views? Think of it this way — as we start implementing the actual views that render to the DOM for us, we'll discover more missing state from the store. These, however, are superficial and easy to fix. With the bare bone views, we're more concerned with teasing out the critical parts that are missing. What can we do with these views when we're done with them? Are they garbage? Not necessarily, depending on how we want to implement our production views, we could either adjust them to become ReactJS components or we could embed the actual view inside the bare-bone view, making it more of a container.

Identifying actions

As we saw earlier in the chapter, the first set of actions to be dispatched by a given Flux architecture are going to be related to fetching data from the backend API. Ultimately, these are the start of the data-flows that end with the views. Sometimes, these are merely *load* type actions, where we're explicitly saying to go fetch the resource and populate our store. Other times, we might have more abstract actions that describe the action taken by the user, resulting in several stores being populated from many different API endpoints.

This gets the user to a point where we can start thinking about how they're going to want to interact with this information. The only way they do so is by dispatching more actions. Let's create a view with some action methods. Essentially, the goal is to have access our views from the browser JavaScript console. This lets us view the state information associated with the view at any given point, as well as call the method to dispatch the given action.

To do this, we need to adjust our Webpack configuration slightly:

```
output: {
  ...
  library: 'views'
}
```

This one line will export a global `views` variable in the browser window, and its value will be whatever our `main.js` module exports. Let's have a look at this now:

```
import settingsView from './views/settings';
export { settingsView as settings };
```

Well, this looks interesting. We're simply exporting our view as settings. So, as we're creating our bare bone views in the skeleton architecture, we simply follow this pattern in main.js to keep adding views to the browser console to experiment with. Let's now take a look at the settings view itself:

```
import dispatcher from '../dispatcher';
import settingsStore from '../stores/settings';

// This is a "bare bones" view because it's
// not rendering anything to the DOM. We're just
// using it to validate our Flux data-flows and
// to think about potential actions dispatched
// from this view.
class SettingsView {
  constructor() {

    // Logs the state of "settingsStore" when it
    // changes.
    settingsStore.on('change', (state) => {
      console.log('settings', state);
    });

    // The initial state of the store is logged.
    console.log('settings', settingsStore.state);
  }

  // This sets an email value by dispatching
  // a "SET_EMAIL" action.
  setEmail(email) {
    dispatcher.dispatch({
      type: 'SET_EMAIL',
      payload: 'foo@bar.com'
    });
  }

  // Do all the things!
  doTheThings() {
    dispatcher.dispatch({
      type: 'DO_THE_THINGS',
      payload: true
    })
  }
}
```

```
// We don't need more than one of these
// views, so export a new instance.
export default new SettingsView();
```

The only thing left to do now is to see what's available in the browser console when we load this page. We should have a global `views` variable, and this should have each of our view instances as properties. Now, we get to play around with actions dispatched by views as though we're users clicking around in the DOM. Let's see how this looks:

```
views.settings.setEmail()
// → settings {email: "foo@bar.com", allTheThings: false}

views.settings.doTheThings()
// → settings {email: "foo@bar.com", allTheThings: true}
```

End-to-end scenarios

At some point, we're going to have to wrap up the skeleton architecture phase of the project and start implementing real features. We don't want the skeleton phase to drag on for too long because then we'll start making too many assumptions about the reality of our implementation. At the same time, we'll probably want to walk through a few end-to-end scenarios before we move on.

The aim of this section is to provide you with a few high-level points to be on the lookout for in each architectural layer. These aren't strict criteria, but they can certainly help us formulate our own measurements that determine whether or not we've adequately answered our questions about the information architecture by building a skeleton. If we're feeling confident, it's time to go full steam and flesh out the application detail—the subsequent chapters in this book dive into the nitty-gritty of implementing Flux.

Action checklist

The following items are worth thinking about when we're implementing actions:

- Do our features have actions that bootstrap store data by fetching it from the API?

- Do we have actions that change the state of backend resources? How are these changes reflected in our frontend Flux stores?

- Does a given feature have any local actions, and are they distinct from actions that issue API requests?

Store checklist

The following items are worth thinking about when implementing stores:

- Does the store map to a top-level feature in our application?
- How well does the data structure of the store meet the needs of the views that use it? Is the structure too complex? If so, can we refactor the store into two stores?
- Do the stores discard API data that isn't used?
- Do the stores map API data to relevant information that the user needs?
- Is our store structure amenable to change once we start adding more elaborate view functionality?
- Do we have too many stores? If so, do we need to rethink the way we've structured the top-level application features?

View checklist

The following items are worth thinking about when implementing views:

- Does the view get the information it needs out of the store?
- Which actions result in the view rendering?
- Which actions does the view dispatch, in response to user interaction?

Summary

This chapter was about getting started with a Flux architecture by building some skeleton components. The goal being to think about the information architecture, without the distraction of other implementation issues. We could find ourselves in a situation where the API is already defined for us, or where the user experience is already in place. Either of these factors will influence the design of our stores, and ultimately the information we present to our users.

The stores we implemented were basic, loading data when the application starts and updating their state in response to an API call. We did, however, learn to ask the pertinent questions about our stores, such as the approach taken with parsing the new data to set as the store's state, and how this new state will affect other stores.

Then, we thought about the top-level features that form the core of our application. These features give a good indication of the stores that our architecture will need. Toward the end of the skeleton architecture phase, we want to walk through a few end-to-end scenarios to sanity-check our chosen information design. We looked at a few high-level checklist items to help ensure we didn't leave anything important out. In the following chapter, we'll take a deeper look at actions and how they're dispatched.

4
Creating Actions

In the previous chapter, we worked on building a skeleton architecture for our Flux application. The actions were directly dispatched by the dispatcher. Now that we have a skeleton Flux architecture under our belts, it's time to look more deeply into actions, and in particular, how actions are created.

We'll start by talking about the names we give actions and the constants used to identify the available actions in our system. Then, we'll implement some action creator functions, and we'll think about how we can keep these modular. Even though we might be done with implementing our skeleton architecture, we may still have a need to mock some API data—we'll go over how this is done with action creator functions.

Typical action creator functions are stateless—data in, data out. We'll cover some scenarios where action creators actually depend on state, such as when long-running connections are involved. We'll wrap the chapter up with a look at parameterized action creators, allowing us to reuse them for different purposes.

Action names and constants

Any large Flux application will have a lot of actions. This is why having action constants and sensible action names matter. The focus of this section is to discuss possible naming conventions for actions and to get organized with our actions. Constants help with reducing repetitive strings that are error-prone, but we'll also need to think about the best way to organize our constants. We'll also look at static action data—this will also help us reduce the amount of action dispatch code we have to write.

Action name conventions

All actions in a Flux system have a name. The name is important because it tells whoever is looking at it a lot about what it does. An application where there are less than ten actions is unlikely to have a strong naming convention requirement, because we can easily figure out what these actions do. However, it's equally unlikely we'd use Flux to implement a small application—Flux is for systems that need to scale. This means that there's a strong likelihood of many actions.

Action names can be divided into two segments—the *subject* and the *operation*. For example, having an action named ACTIVATE wouldn't be terribly helpful—what are we activating? Adding a subject to the name is often all it takes to provide some much needed context. Here are some examples:

- ACTIVATE_SETTING
- ACTIVATE_USER
- ACTIVATE_TAB

The subject is just an abstract type of thing in our system—it doesn't even have to correspond to a concrete software entity. However, if there are a lot of subjects in our system with similar actions, we might want to change up the format of our action names, like this for example:

- SETTING_ACTIVATE
- USER_ACTIVATE
- TAB_ACTIVATE

At the end of the day, this is really a personal (or team) preference, just as long as the name is descriptive enough to provide meaning for someone who's looking at the code. What if the subject and the operation aren't enough? For example, there could be several subjects that are similar, and this could cause confusion. Then, we could add another layer of subject to the name—think of this as namespacing the action.

 Try not to go beyond three segments in a Flux action name. If you feel the need to do this, there's probably somewhere else in your architecture that needs attention.

Static action data

Some actions are very similar to other actions, similar in the sense, that the payload data that's sent to the stores has many of the same properties. If we were to directly dispatch these actions, using the dispatcher instance, then we'd usually have to repeat object literal code. Let's take a look at an action creator function:

```
import dispatcher from '../dispatcher';

// The action name.
export const SORT_USERS = 'SORT_USERS';

// This action creator function hard-codes
// the action payload.
export function sortUsers() {
  dispatcher.dispatch({
    type: SORT_USERS,
    payload: {
      direction: 'asc'
    }
  });
}
```

The aim of this action is pretty straightforward—sort the list of users that are presumably UI components. The only payload data that's required is a sort direction, which is specified in the `direction` property. The problem with this action creator function is that this payload data is hard-coded. For example, the payload data in question here seems fairly generic, and other action creator functions that sort data should follow this pattern. But, this also means that they'll each have their own hard-coded values.

One thing we can do about this is to create a module within the `actions` directory that exports any default payload data that can be shared amongst several action creator functions. Carrying on with the sorting example, the module might start off looking something like this:

```
// This object is used by several action
// creator functions as part of the action
// payload.
export const PAYLOAD_SORT = {
  direction: 'asc'
};
```

This is easy to build on. We can extend PAYLOAD_SORT, as new properties are needed and when old defaults need to change. It's also easy to add new default payloads as they're needed. Let's take look at another action creator function that uses this default payload:

```
import dispatcher from '../dispatcher';
import { PAYLOAD_SORT } from './payload-defaults';

// The action name.
export const SORT_TASKS = 'SORT_TASKS';

// This action creator function is using
// the "PAYLOAD_SORT" default object as the
// payload.
export function sortTasks() {
  dispatcher.dispatch({
    type: SORT_TASKS,
    payload: PAYLOAD_SORT
  });
}
```

As we can see, the PAYLOAD_SORT object is used by the sortTasks() function, rather than hard-coding the payload within the action creator. This reduces the amount of code we need to write, and it puts common payload data in a central place, making it easy for us to change the behavior of many action creator functions.

You may have noticed that the default payload object is being passed to dispatch() as is. More often than not, we'll have part of the payload object that's common across several functions and part of the payload object that's dynamic. We'll build in the examples from this section in the last section of the chapter, when it's time to think about parameterized action creator functions.

Now, let's take a look at both of these action creator functions in use, to make sure we're getting what we expect. Rather than setting up stores for this, we'll just listen to the dispatcher directly:

```
import dispatcher from './dispatcher';

// Gets the action constant and creator function
// for "SORT_USERS".
import {
  SORT_USERS,
  sortUsers
```

```
} from './actions/sort-users';

// Gets the action constant and creator function
// for "SORT_TASKS".
import {
  SORT_TASKS,
  sortTasks
} from './actions/sort-tasks';

// Listen for actions, and log some information
// depending on which action was dispatched.
// Note that we're using the action name constants
// here, so there's less chance of human error.
dispatcher.register((e) => {
  switch (e.type) {
    case SORT_USERS:
      console.log(`Sorting users "${e.payload.direction}"`);
      break;
    case SORT_TASKS:
      console.log(`Sorting tasks "${e.payload.direction}"`);
      break;
  }
});

sortUsers();
// → Sorting users "asc"

sortTasks();
// → Sorting tasks "asc"
```

Organizing action constants

You may have noticed that there's already a hint of organization with the action constants used in the previous example. For example, the SORT_USERS constant was defined in the same module as the sortUsers() action creator function. This is generally a good idea because these two things are closely related to one another. There is a downside to this though. Imagine a more complex store that needs to handle a lot of actions. If each individual action constant is declared in its own module, the store would have to perform a lot of imports just to get these constants. If there's a number of complex stores that each need access to lots of actions, the number of imports starts to really add up. This problem is illustrated here:

```
import { ACTION_A } from '../actions/action-a';
import { ACTION_B } from '../actions/action-b';
import { ACTION_C } from '../actions/action-c';
// …
```

If we find ourselves in a situation like this one, where several stores need access to several modules, maybe we need a `constants.js` module in the `actions` directory. This module would expose every action in the system. Here's an example of what this module might look like:

```
export { ACTION_A } from './action-a';
export { ACTION_B } from './action-b';
export { ACTION_C } from './action-c';
```

As our system grows and new actions are added, this is where we would centralize the action constants for easy access by stores that require many of them. They're not defined here; this is just a proxy that reduces the number of imports from stores, because the stores never need the action creator functions. Let's see if the situation has improved from the perspective of a store that requires action constants:

```
import {
  ACTION_A,
  ACTION_B,
  ACTION_C
} from './actions/constants';

console.log(ACTION_A);
// → ACTION_A

console.log(ACTION_B);
// → ACTION_B

console.log(ACTION_C);
// → ACTION_C
```

That's better. Only one `import` statement gets us everything we need, and it's still nice and legible. There are several ways we could spin this approach to better suit our needs. For example, maybe instead of one big constants module, we want to group our actions into logical modules that more closely resemble our features, and likewise for our action creator functions. We'll discuss action modularity as it relates to our application features in the next section.

Feature action creators

Action creator functions need to be organized, just as action constants are. In the preceding code examples of this chapter, we've organized both our action constants and our action creator functions into modules. This keeps our action code clean and easy to traverse. In this section, we'll build on this idea from the feature point of view. We'll look at why this is worth thinking about in the first place, then we'll talk about how these ideas make the architecture as a whole more modular.

When modularity is needed

Do we need to think deeply about modular action creator functions at the beginning of our Flux project? While the project is still small in size, it's okay if all action creator functions are part of one monolithic action creator module—there's simply no meaningful impact on the architecture. It's when we have more than a dozen or so actions that we need to start thinking about modularity and, in particular, features.

We can split our action creator module into several smaller modules, each with their own action creator function. This is certainly a step in the right direction, but in essence, we're just moving the problem to the directory level. So instead of a monolithic module, we now have a monolithic directory with lots of files in it. This directory is illustrated here:

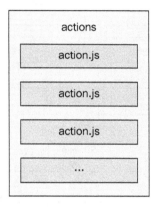

There's nothing inherently wrong with this layout—it's just that there's no indication of which feature a given action is part of. This may not even be necessary, but when the architecture grows to be a certain size, it's usually helpful to group action modules by features. This concept is illustrated here:

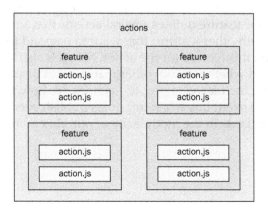

Once we're able to get the actions of the system organized in such a way that they reflect the behavior of any given feature, we can start thinking about other architectural challenges related to modularity. We'll discuss these next.

Modular architecture

It's a good thing when the modules in a Flux architecture start taking the shape of the features our application provides. This has implications elsewhere in the architecture as well. For example, if we're organizing the actions by features, then should we not also organize the stores and the views by feature as well? Stores are easy — they're not exactly decomposable into smaller stores; they naturally represent the feature in its entirety. Views, on the other hand, could potentially have many JavaScript modules to organize within a feature. Here's a potential directory structure of a Flux feature:

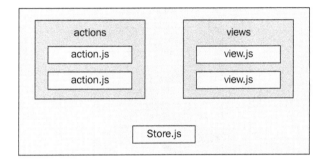

This is a cohesive structure — everything the views need to dispatch these actions are in the same parent directory. Likewise, the store that notifies the views about state changes is in the same place. We can get away with following a similar pattern for all of our features, which has the added benefit of promoting consistency.

We'll revisit structuring feature modules toward the end of the book. For now, our main concern is the dependencies that other features might have with a given set of actions. For example, our feature defines several actions that are dispatched by views. What should happen with other features that want to respond to these actions — do they need to depend on this feature for the action? There's also the matter of the action creators themselves, and whether or not other features can dispatch them. The answer is a resounding yes, and the reason is simple — actions are how things happen in Flux architectures. There's no event bus where modules publish events in a fire-and-forget way. Actions play a vital role in the modularity of our Flux architecture.

Mocking data

The dispatcher in Flux architectures is the single point of entry for new data entering the system. This makes it easy to fabricate mock data to help us churn out features faster. In this section, we'll discuss mocking existing APIs, and whether or not this is worthwhile to build into the action creator functions that talk to them. Then, we'll go over implementing mocks for new APIs that doesn't yet exist, followed by a look at strategies to substitute mock action creators for the real deal.

Mocking existing APIs

In order to mock data in a Flux system, the actions that are dispatched need to deliver this mock data to the stores. This is done by creating an alternative implementation of the action creator function that dispatches the action. When there's already an API that an action creator can target, we don't necessarily need to mock the data during the development of a given feature—the data is already there. However, the existence of an API that's used by an action creator shouldn't rule out the existence of a mocked version.

The main reason we would want to do this is because at any given point during the lifetime of our product, there's going to be a missing API that we need. As we'll see in the next section, we'll obviously want to mock the data returned by this API, so we can continue implementing the feature we're working on. But do we really want to mock some actions and not others? The idea is illustrated here:

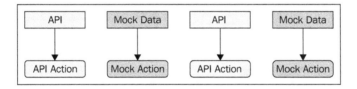

The challenge with this approach—mocking some actions while actually implementing others—is consistency. When we're mocking data that enters the system, we have to be cognizant of the relationships between one set of data and another. Look at it from the perspective of our stores—they'll likely have dependencies on one another. Can we capture these dependencies using a mixture of mock data and actual data? Here is an illustration of actions that mock the entirety of the system:

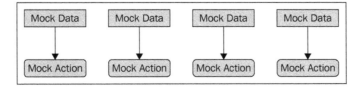

It's better to have total control over the data that's used when we experiment with new functionality. This eliminates the possibility of errant behavior because of some inconsistency in our data. It takes more effort to construct mock data like this, but it pays off in the end when we're adding new features and we only have to mock one new action at a time, as it's added into the system. As we'll see later in this section, it's easy to substitute mock action creators for production action creators.

Mocking new APIs

Once we reach the point during the implementation of a new feature where we're missing API functionality, we'll have to mock it. We can use this new mock with the other mocks we've created to support other features in the application. The advantage of doing this is that it allows us to create something without delay, something we can demonstrate to stakeholders. Another benefit of mocking APIs as action creator functions is that they can help steer the API in the right direction. Without a UI, the API has nothing to base its design on, so this is a good opportunity to solicit a design that works best with the application we're building.

Let's take a look at some action creator functions that mock the data that's dispatched as action payloads. We'll start with a basic loader function that bootstraps some data into the store for us:

```
import dispatcher from '../dispatcher';

// The action identifier...
export const LOAD_TASKS = 'LOAD_TASKS';

// Immediately dispatches the action using an array
// of task objects as the mock data.
export function loadTasks() {
  dispatcher.dispatch({
    type: LOAD_TASKS,
    payload: [
      { id: 1, name: 'Task 1', state: 'running' },
      { id: 2, name: 'Task 2', state: 'queued' },
      { id: 3, name: 'Task 3', state: 'finished'}
    ]
  });
}
```

This is quite simple. The data we want to mock is part of the function, as the action payload. Let's look at another mock action creator now, one that manipulates the state of a store after the data has already been bootstrapped:

```
import dispatcher from '../dispatcher';

// The action identifier...
export const RUN_TASK = 'RUN_TASK';

// Uses "setTimeout()" to simulate latency we'd
// likely see in a real network request.
export function runTask() {
  setTimeout(() => {
    dispatcher.dispatch({
      type: RUN_TASK,

      // Highly-specific mock payload data. This
      // mock data doesn't necessarily have to
      // be hard-coded like this, but it does make
      // experimentation easy.
      payload: {
        id: 2,
        state: 'running'
      }
    });
  }, 1000);
}
```

Once again, we have very specific mock data we're using here, which is fine because it's directly coupled to the action creator function that's dispatching the action—this is the only way this data can enter the system too. Something else that's different about this function is that it's simulating latency by not dispatching the action until the `setTimeout()` callback triggers after one second.

 We'll take a more detailed look at asynchronous actions, including latency, promises, and multiple API endpoints in a later chapter.

At this point, we have two mock action creator functions available for use. But before we start using these functions, let's create a task store so that we can make sure the correct information is being stored:

```
import EventEmitter from 'events';
import dispatcher from '../dispatcher';
import { LOAD_TASKS } from '../actions/load-tasks';
import { RUN_TASK } from '../actions/run-task';

// The store for tasks displayed in the application.
class TaskStore extends EventEmitter {
  constructor() {
    super();

    this.state = [];

    dispatcher.register((e) => {
      switch(e.type) {

        // In the case of "LOAD_TASKS", we can use the
        // "payload" as the new store state.
        case LOAD_TASKS:
          this.state = e.payload;
          this.emit('change', this.state);
          break;

        // In the case of "RUN_TASK", we need to look
        // up a specific task object and change it's state.
        case RUN_TASK:
          let task = this.state.find(
            x =>x.id === e.payload.id);

          task.state = e.payload.state;

          this.emit('change', this.state);

          break;
      }
    });
  }
}

export default new TaskStore();
```

Now that we have a store to handle both actions we've just implemented, let's put the store and the actions to use in the main.js module of the application:

```
import taskStore from './stores/task';
import { loadTasks } from './actions/load-tasks';
import { runTask } from './actions/run-task';

// Logs the state of the store, as a mapped array
// of strings.
taskStore.on('change', (state) => {
  console.log('tasks',
    state.map(x => `${x.name} (${x.state})`));
});

loadTasks();
// →
// tasks [
//    "Task 1 (running)",
//    "Task 2 (queued)",
//    "Task 3 (finished)"
// ]

runTask();
// →
// tasks [
//    "Task 1 (running)",
//    "Task 2 (running)",
//    "Task 3 (finished)"
// ]
```

As you can see, the tasks were successfully bootstrapped into the store with the call to loadTasks(), and the state of the second task was updated when we called runTask(). This latter update isn't logged till one second has elapsed.

Replacing action creators

At this point, we have a working action creator function that dispatches actions with mock payload data into the system. Recall that we don't necessarily want to get rid of these action creator functions, because when it's time to implement something new, we'll want to use these mocks again.

What we really need is a global switch that toggles the mock mode of the system, and this would change the implementation of the action creator function that's used. Here's a diagram that shows how this might work:

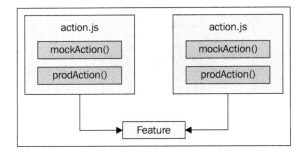

The idea here is that there's a mock version and a production version of the same action creator function within the module. This is the easy part; the tricky part is going to be implementing a global mock switch so that the correct function is exported, depending on the mode of the application:

```javascript
import { MOCK } from '../settings';
import dispatcher from '../dispatcher';

// The action identifier...
export const LOAD_USERS = 'LOAD_USERS';

// The mock implementation of the action creator.
function mockLoadUsers() {
  dispatcher.dispatch({
    type: LOAD_USERS,
    payload: [
      { id: 1, name: 'Mock 1' },
      { id: 2, name: 'Mock 2' }
    ]
  });
}

// The production implementation of the action creator.
function prodLoadUsers() {
  dispatcher.dispatch({
    type: LOAD_USERS,
    payload: [
      { id: 1, name: 'Prod 1' },
      { id: 2, name: 'Prod 2' }
    ]
```

```
    });
}

// Here's where the "loadUsers" value is determined, based
// on the "MOCK" setting. It's always going to be exported
// as "loadUsers", meaning that no other code needs to change.
const loadUsers = MOCK ? mockLoadUsers : prodLoadUsers;
export { loadUsers as loadUsers };
```

This is very handy during development, because the extent of our mocked functions is limited to the action creator modules and is controlled by one setting. Let's see how this action creator function is used, regardless of whether the mock or the production implementation is exported:

```
import dispatcher from './dispatcher';

// This code never has to change, although the actual
// function that's exported will change, depending on
// the "MOCK" setting.
import { loadUsers } from './actions/load-users';

dispatcher.register((e) => {
  console.log('Users', e.payload.map(x =>x.name));
});

loadUsers();
// → Users ["Mock 1", "Mock 2"]
// When the "MOCK" setting is set to true...
// → Users ["Prod 1", "Prod 2"]
```

Stateful action creators

The action creator functions we've looked at so far in this chapter have been relatively simple—they dispatch some action when called. But before that happens, these action creators will typically reach out to some API endpoint to retrieve some data, then dispatch the action, using the data as the payload. These are called stateless action creator functions because there's no intermediary state about them—no lifecycle in other words.

In this section, we'll think about things that are stateful and how we might go about integrating these into our Flux architecture. Another challenge we could face is integrating our Flux application into another architecture. First, we'll cover some basic ground on stateful action creators, then we'll look at a concrete example using web sockets.

Integrating with other systems

Most of the time, Flux applications are standalone in the browser. That is, they're not a cog in a larger machine. We will, however, come up against cases where our Flux architecture needs to fit into something bigger. For example, if we need to interface with components that use a completely different framework, then we need to come up with a way to embed our software without compromising the Flux patterns. Or perhaps the coupling between our application and the one we're integrating with is a little looser, as when communicating with another browser tab. Whatever the case may be, we have to be able to send messages to this external system and we need to be able to consume messages from it, translating them into actions. Here is an illustration of this idea:

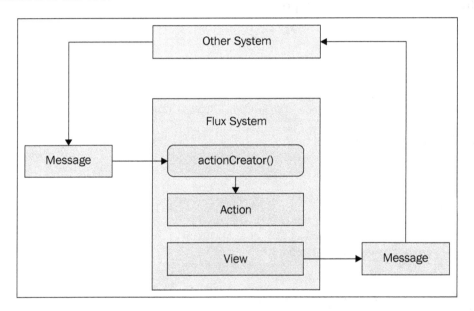

As you can see, the Flux architecture depicted here isn't a closed system. The main implication is that the typical action creator functions that we're used to working with aren't necessarily called within the system. That is, they're handling a stream of external messages, using a stateful connection to the other system. This is just how web sockets work. We'll look at these stateful action creators next.

Web socket connectivity

Web socket connectivity is growing to the point of pervasiveness in modern web applications, and if we're building a Flux architecture, there's a good chance we're going to need to build web socket support. When something changes state in the backend, web socket connections are a great way to notify clients about such a change. For example, imagine a Flux store is managing the state of some piece of backend data, and something causes its state to change—wouldn't we want the store to know about it?

The challenge is that we need a stateful connection in order to receive web socket messages and translate them into Flux actions. This is how web socket data enters the system. Let's take a look at some socket listener code:

```
// Get the action constants and action functions
// that we need.
import { ONE, one } from './one';
import { TWO, two } from './two';
import { THREE, three } from './three';

var ws;
var actions = {};

// Create a mapping of constants to functions
// that the web socket handler can use to call
// the appropriate action creator.
actions[ONE] = one;
actions[TWO] = two;
actions[THREE] = three;

// Connects the web socket...
export default function connect() {
  ws = new WebSocket('ws://127.0.0.1:8000');

  ws.addEventListener('message', (e) => {

    // Parses the message data and uses the
    // "actions" map to call the corresponding
    // action creator function.
    let data = JSON.parse(e.data);
    actions[data.task](data.value);
  });
}
```

All we're doing here is creating a simple `actions` map. This is how we call the correct action creator function based on the `task` property of the message that was received. What's nice about this approach is that there's very little additional functionality required to make this work; the preceding code is the extent of it. The actual action creator functions, constants, and so on, are just typical Flux items. Let's look at the server code that generates these web socket messages, so we have an idea of what's actually being passed to the socket listener code:

```javascript
// The HTTP server...
var server = require('http').createServer();

// The web socket server...
var ws = new require('ws').Server({
  server: server,
});

// Makes life worth living...
var express = require('express');
var app = express();

// So we can serve "index.html"...
app.use(express.static(__dirname));

// Handler for when a client connects via web socket.
ws.on('connection', function connection(ws) {
  let i = 0;
  const names = [ null, 'one', 'two', 'three' ];

  // Sends the client 3 messages, spaced by 1 second
  // intervals.
  function interval() {
    if (++i< 4) {
      ws.send(JSON.stringify({
        value: i,
        task: names[i]
      }));

      setTimeout(interval, 1000);
    }
  }

  setTimeout(interval, 1000);
});
```

```
// Fire up the HTTP and web socket servers.
server.on('request', app);
server.listen(8000, () => {
  console.log('Listening on', server.address().port)
});
```

Over the course of three seconds, we'll see three web socket messages delivered to the client. Each message has a `task` property, and this is the value we're using to determine which action is dispatched. Let's take a look at the `main.js` frontend module and make sure everything's working as expected:

```
import dispatcher from './dispatcher';
import connect from './actions/socket-listener';
import { ONE } from './actions/one';
import { TWO } from './actions/two';
import { THREE } from './actions/three';

// Logs the web socket messages that have been
// dispatched as Flux actions.
dispatcher.register((e) => {
  switch (e.type) {
    case ONE:
      console.log('one', e.payload);
      break;
    case TWO:
      console.log('two', e.payload);
      break;
    case THREE:
      console.log('three', e.payload);
      break;
  }
});
// →
// one 1
// two 2
// three 3

// Establishes the web socket connection. Note
// that it's important to connect after everything
// with the Flux dispatcher is setup.
connect();
```

As you can see, the connect() function is responsible for establishing the web socket connection. This is a simple implementation, lacking several production-grade capabilities, such as reconnecting dropped connections. However, the important thing to note here is that this listener is actually located in the same directory as the other action modules. We actually want a tight coupling here because the main goal of the socket listener is to dispatch actions, by translating web socket messages.

Parameterized action creators

The final section of this chapter focuses on parameterized action creators. All the action creator functions we've looked at so far in the chapter have been basic functions that don't accept any arguments. This is fine, except for when we start to accumulate several unique actions that are nearly identical. Without parameterized action creator functions, we'll soon have an endless proliferation of functions; this does not scale.

First, we'll establish the goals of passing arguments to action creator functions, followed by some example code that implements generic action creator functions. We'll then look into creating partial functions to further reduce repetitiveness by composing action creators.

Removing redundant actions

Action creators are plain JavaScript functions. This means that they can accept zero or more arguments when called. The whole point of implementing a function, regardless of whether or not it's in the context of Flux, is to reduce the amount of code we have to write. Action creators in a Flux application are likely to accumulate because they drive the behavior of our application. If anything happens, it can be traced back to an action. So it's easy to introduce several new actions over the course of a day.

Once our application has several features implemented, we're bound to have a lot of actions. Some of these actions will serve a distinct purpose, while other actions will be very similar to each other. In other words, some actions will start to feel redundant. The goal is to remove redundant action creator functions by introducing parameters.

We should exercise caution in how we go about refactoring our action creator functions. There's a strong argument in favor of keeping a dedicated function for each type of action in the system. That is, one action creator function should only ever dispatch one type of action, not one of several options. Otherwise, the traceability of our code will be diminished. We should aim to reduce the total number of actions in the system altogether.

Keeping actions generic

When actions are generic, the architecture requires less of them. This is a good thing because it means there's less knowledge to keep in our heads as we're writing code. Let's take a look at a couple of actions that do essentially the same thing; in other words, they're not generic at all. The first action is as follows:

```
import dispatcher from '../dispatcher';
import sortBy from 'lodash/sortBy';

// The action identifier...
export const FIRST = 'FIRST';

export function first() {

  // The payload data.
  let payload = [ 20, 10, 30 ];

  // Dispatches the "FIRST" action with
  // the payload sorted in ascending order.
  dispatcher.dispatch({
    type: FIRST,
    payload: sortBy(payload)
  });
}
```

Simple enough—it's using the lodash `sortBy()` function to sort the payload before dispatching the action.

 Note that we wouldn't actually sort payload data like this in the action creator function. Think of this as an API mock. The point is that action creator function is asking something outside of Flux for data.

Let's look at another similar but distinct action:

```
import dispatcher from '../dispatcher';
import sortBy from 'lodash/sortBy';

// The action identifier...
export const SECOND = 'SECOND';

export function second() {

  // The payload data.
```

```
let payload = [ 20, 10, 30 ];

// Dispatches the action, with the
// payload sorted in descending order.
dispatcher.dispatch({
  type: SECOND,
  payload: sortBy(payload, x => x * -1)
});
}
```

The only difference here is how we're sorting the data. If this were a production action creator function, we would tell the API to sort the data in descending order instead of using lodash to do it in the action creator. Do we need two distinct actions for these two sort directions? Or can we eliminate both of them in favor of a generic action that accepts a sort direction parameter? Here's a generic implementation of the action:

```
import dispatcher from '../dispatcher';
import sortBy from 'lodash/sortBy';

// The action identifier...
export const THIRD = 'THIRD';

// Accepts a sort direction, but defaults
// to descending.
export function third(dir='desc') {

  // The payload data.
  let payload = [ 20, 10, 30 ];

  // The iteratee function that's passed
  // to "sortBy()".
  let iteratee;

  // Sets up the custom "iteratee" if we
  // want to sort in descending order.
  if (dir === 'desc') {
    iteratee = x => x * -1;
  }

  // Dispatches the action, sorting the payload
  // based on "dir".
  dispatcher.dispatch({
    type: THIRD,
    payload: sortBy(payload, iteratee)
  });
}
```

Here are all three actions being used. Note that the third action covers both cases, and yet the fundamental sort action is the same no matter what arguments are passed. You can see in the dispatcher callback function that stores would have an easier time listening to one action instead of two or more:

```
import dispatcher from './dispatcher';
import { FIRST, first } from './actions/first';
import { SECOND, second } from './actions/second';
import { THIRD, third } from './actions/third';

// Logs the specific action payloads as
// they're dispatched.
dispatcher.register((e) => {
  switch(e.type) {
    case FIRST:
      console.log('first', e.payload);
      break;
    case SECOND:
      console.log('second', e.payload);
      break;
    case THIRD:
      console.log('third', e.payload);
      break;
  }
});

first();
// → first [10, 20, 30]

second();
// → second [30, 20, 10]

third();
// → third [30, 20, 10]

third('asc');
// → third [10, 20, 30]
```

Creating action partials

In some cases, function arguments are straightforward — as in there are one or two of them. In others, the argument lists can be daunting, especially when we're calling them repeatedly using the same handful of arguments. Action creators in Flux applications are no different. There will be cases where we have a generic function that supports the odd case where, instead of a new action creator function, we simply supply a different parameter. But in the most common case, where the same parameters have to be supplied all the time, this can get repetitive to the point where it defeats the purpose of having generic functions.

Let's look at a generic action creator function that accepts a variable number of arguments. Since the same arguments are passed to the function in the most common case, we'll also export a partial version of the function where these arguments have been partially applied.

 Default parameters in ES2015 syntax are a good alternative to creating partial functions, but only when the number of arguments is fixed.

```
import dispatcher from '../dispatcher';
import partial from 'lodash/partial';

// The action identifier...
export const FIRST = 'FIRST';

// The generic implementation of the action creator.
export function first(...values) {

  // The payload data.
  let defaults = [ 'a', 'b', 'c' ];

  // Dispatches the "FIRST" action with
  // the "values" array concatenated to
  // the "defaults" array.
  dispatcher.dispatch({
    type: FIRST,
    payload: defaults.concat(values)
  });
}

// Exports a common version of "first()" with
// the common arguments already applied.
export const firstCommon = partial(first, 'd', 'e', 'f');
```

Now let's see how these two versions of the same action creator are used:

```
import dispatcher from './dispatcher';
import { FIRST, first, firstCommon } from './actions/first';

// Logs the specific action payloads as
// they're dispatched.
dispatcher.register((e) => {
  switch(e.type) {
    case FIRST:
      console.log('first', e.payload);
      break;
  }
});

// Calls the action creator with a common set
// of arguments. This is the type of code we
// want to avoid repeating all over the place.
first('d', 'e', 'f');
// → first ["a", "b", "c", "d", "e", "f"]

// The exact same thing as the "fist()" call above.
// The common arguments have been partially-applied.
firstCommon();
// → first ["a", "b", "c", "d", "e", "f"]
```

> It's important to note that the first() and firstCommon() functions are the same action creator, and this is why they're defined in the same module. If we were to define firstCommon() in another action module, this would lead to confusion, because they both use the same action type—FIRST.

Summary

In this chapter, you learned about the action creator functions that Flux applications utilize in order to dispatch actions. Without action creator functions, we'd have to directly interface with the dispatcher in our code, which makes the architecture more difficult to reason about.

We started off by thinking about action naming conventions and the general organization of our action modules. Grouping action creators by feature has implications for modularity as well, especially in how this influences modularity in other areas of the architecture.

Next, we discussed mocking data using action creator functions. Mocking data in Flux applications is easy to do and encouraged. Actions are the only way for data to enter the system, making it easy for us to switch between mocked action data and our production implementations. We wrapped the chapter up with a look at stateful action creators that listen to things such as web socket connections, and a look at parameterized action creators that keep repetitive code to a minimum.

In the next chapter, we'll address another key aspect of action creator functions—asynchronicity.

5
Asynchronous Actions

In *Chapter 4*, *Creating Actions*, we examined Flux actions in detail—action creator functions in particular. One aspect of action creators we didn't cover was asynchronous behavior. Asynchronicity is central to any web application, and in this chapter, we'll think about what this means for a Flux architecture.

We'll start by covering the synchronous nature of Flux, as breaking this synchronicity breaks the whole architecture. Next, we'll dive into some code that makes API calls and some action creators that need to synchronize multiple API calls before actually dispatching the action. Then, we'll introduce promises as return values from action creator functions.

Keeping Flux synchronous

It may sound strange that we would want to keep an architecture synchronous—especially on the web. What about the laggy user experience that happens when everything is performed synchronously?

It's just the Flux data-flow that's synchronous, not the entire application. In this section, we'll touch upon why keeping the core data-flow mechanisms of our architecture synchronous is a good idea. Next, we'll talk about how we should encapsulate asynchronous behavior in our application. Finally, we'll go over the general semantics of how asynchronous action creator functions work.

Why synchronicity?

The simple answer is that anything that's asynchronous introduces a level of uncertainty that wouldn't otherwise be there. It can be tempting, given all the new hotness in web browsers, to make everything happen in parallel—to leverage as many concurrent web requests and as many processor cores as we possibly can. Once we go down this path, it's hard to turn back, and the further down we go, the more tangled the synchronization semantics get.

Let's think about the DOM API for a moment. JavaScript applications use this API to change the state of elements on the page. When these changes happen, the browser's rendering engine kicks in and performs an update to the screen so that the user can actually see the changes. The DOM API doesn't directly interface with what's displayed on screen—there's a whole bunch of nasty details taken care of for us by the rendering engine. This idea is illustrated here:

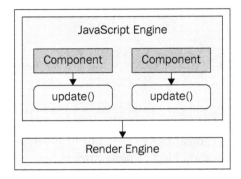

The takeaway here is that it's not the individual updates made by our components that cause the rendering engine to update the screen. The JavaScript engine is run-to-completion, meaning that it waits for all these components to finish making their calls to update the DOM (and any other code they're running) before handing off control to the rendering engine. This means that any updates the user sees are fundamentally synchronous—all the concurrent code in the world doesn't change the synchronous communication path between the JavaScript engine and the render engine.

You might be wondering what this has to do with Flux at this point. It's actually very relevant because the authors of Flux understand this synchronous DOM update mechanism, so rather than fight it with complex asynchronous code everywhere, they came up with data-flow semantics that embrace the synchronous nature of updating the DOM.

The core abstraction Flux uses for synchronous data-flow is the **update round**, which was introduced in *Chapter 2, Principles of Flux*. Nothing can interrupt an update round because every component that takes part in it has no asynchronous behavior. If Flux has a killer feature, this is it. The update round is such a critical property of Flux architectures that we have to be especially careful to maintain it. It's like an umbrella concept—dozens of little edge cases caused by asynchronous behavior fall outside of it.

Encapsulating asynchronous behavior

With Flux update rounds being synchronous, where should we put our asynchronous code? Let's think about this for a moment. Flux architecture aside, any asynchronous behavior is going to update the state of the system in some way when the action completes and is synchronized with the rest of our code. In some architectures, this happens all over the place and there's nothing guarding against these types of asynchronous actions from being called from places where they shouldn't.

For example, a Flux update round should never result in new asynchronous behavior running. We know that update rounds are synchronous, so this is a non-starter. We do need to encapsulate our asynchronous behavior somehow though. This is what action creator functions are really good at—performing the asynchronous work and managing the action dispatches once the asynchronous portion has completed. Here is a visualization of action creator functions encapsulating asynchronous calls:

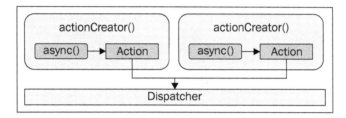

Keeping asynchronous behavior in the action creator functions does two things for us. First, we know there's no synchronization semantics involved in calling the action creator—this is all handled within the function for us. The second advantage is that all of our asynchronous behavior can be found within a single architectural layer. That is, if there's something that's asynchronous, such as making an API call, we know where to look for this code.

Asynchronous action semantics

It's up to our action creator functions to perform any synchronizations before dispatching any actions. There are two parts to a given action creator function. The first is the asynchronous calls, if any, while the second part is the actual dispatching of the action. The job of these action creator functions is to synchronize the async call with the Flux dispatcher, meaning that the function will have to wait for some kind of response before the action can be dispatched.

This is because the asynchronous action has payload data. Let's take a look at an example, shall we? Here's an action creator function that calls an API to load a list of user objects:

```
import dispatcher from '../dispatcher';

// The action identifier...
export const LOAD_USERS = 'LOAD_USERS';

// Performs some asynchronous behavior, and once
// complete, dispatches the action.
export function loadUsers() {

  // Creates a new promise, intended to simulate
  // a call to some API function, which would likely
  // also return a promise.
  let api = new Promise((resolve, reject) => {

    // Resolves the promise with some data after half
    // a second.
    setTimeout(() => {
      resolve([
        { id: 1, name: 'User 1' },
        { id: 2, name: 'User 2' },
        { id: 3, name: 'User 3' }
      ]);
    }, 500);
  });

  // When the promise resolves, the callback that's
  // passed to "then()" is called with the resolved
  // value. This is the payload that's dispatched.
  api.then((response) => {
    dispatcher.dispatch({
      type: LOAD_USERS,
      payload: response
    });
  });
}
```

As you can see, we're using a promise in place of an actual API call. Generally speaking, our application will probably have an API function call that returns a promise. This is exactly what we're doing here—making it seem like we're talking with an API when in reality, it's just a promise. The mechanics are the same, regardless of whether `setTimeout()` or an actual AJAX response resolves the promise.

The important thing to note is that it's the `loadUsers()` function that takes care of dispatching the action after the promise has resolved. Think of it this way — the dispatcher is never invoked unless we have new data for the system. The waiting part falls outside of the Flux update round, which is why it's nice to keep everything together in a function like this. Here's how we use the `loadUsers()` function:

```
import dispatcher from './dispatcher';
import {
  LOAD_USERS,
  loadUsers
} from './actions/load-users';

// Logs the specific action payloads as
// they're dispatched.
dispatcher.register((e) => {
  switch(e.type) {
    case LOAD_USERS:
      console.log('users', e.payload.map(x =>x.id));
      break;
  }
});

loadUsers();
// → users [1, 2, 3]
```

 Something that you may have noticed is missing from this example is any kind of error handling. For example, it would be unpleasant to call `loadUsers()` and have it fail silently because something's wrong with the API. We'll cover error-handling in more depth in the final section of this chapter.

Making API calls

In this section, well go over the common case for asynchronous behavior in Flux architectures — making API calls over the network. Then, we'll discuss some the implications of asynchronous behavior in the context of user interactivity and the Flux tools available to deal with them.

APIs are the common case

Flux architecture is for the frontend of web applications. That said, there's going to be a lot of network communication between some components of our architecture and the backend API. This is the common case for asynchronous behavior, not just in Flux, but in the majority of JavaScript applications. Therefore, this is where the emphasis should be when designing action creators that directly communicate asynchronously with these API endpoints. Here's what the most common communication paths look like in Flux applications:

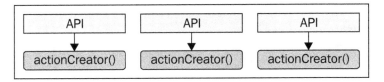

The stores need to be populated with data, and this is the most common way to get data—by fetching it from the API. In fact, the user is likely going to spend more time consuming information than interacting with UI elements. As you saw in the last section, synchronizing the response with the dispatcher isn't difficult to do with promises.

These types of API calls aren't the only source of asynchronous data in Flux architectures. For example, reading a file using the file API requires the use of an asynchronous function call. Interacting with web workers is another asynchronous form of communication—you ask the worker to compute something and get a response in the form of a callback function. Although less common than HTTP calls, these asynchronous interfaces may be treated in the same way, as illustrated here:

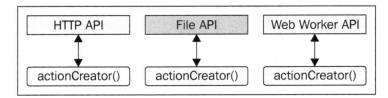

The same synchronization mechanism—promises—can be used for all of these types of asynchronous communication channels. As far as the action creator functions are concerned, they all have the same interface—a promised value that's resolved at a later time. The dispatcher semantics are the same here as well.

There's no asynchronous behavior entering the Flux update round because it's all encapsulated within the action creator functions themselves. Additionally, it could take more than one API to get all the data needed for an action payload. We'll look at this shortly. For now, let's turn our attention to how asynchronous action creators impact user interactivity.

API calls and user interactivity

The main challenge with asynchronous calls and user interface elements is that we have to manage the state of the request, which in turn reflects the state of the UI elements. For example, when the user submits a form, we have to give some sort of visual indication that the request has been made and that it's being processed. Moreover, we also need to prevent the user from interacting with certain UI elements until a response comes back with the state of the request.

The stores in a Flux architecture contain all application state, including the state of any network requests we want to track. This can help us coordinate the state of relevant UI elements with a given request. Let's look at an action creator that sends an asynchronous API request to start something:

```
import dispatcher from '../dispatcher';

// The action identifier...
export const START = 'START';

export function start() {

  // Simulate an async API call that starts
  // something. The promise resolves after
  // one second.
  let api = new Promise((resolve, reject) => {
    setTimeout(resolve, 1000);
  });

  // Dispatches the action after the promise
  // has resolved.
  api.then((response) => {
    dispatcher.dispatch({ type: START });
  });
}
```

As you can see, the `start()` function dispatches the START action after the promise resolves. Just like a real API call, this delay allows the user ample time to interact with the UI before the call returns. So, we have to take steps to prevent this from happening. Let's look at another action creator function that tells the system about the state of the API request we just made:

```
import dispatcher from '../dispatcher';

export const STARTING = 'STARTING';

export function starting() {
  dispatcher.dispatch({ type: STARTING });
}
```

By calling `starting()`, we can inform any stores that might be listening that we're about to make an API call to start something. This could be what we need to take care of handling the state of UI elements to inform the user that the request is in progress, and to disable elements the user shouldn't touch while the request is happening. Let's take a look at a store that processes these types of actions.

 The store also processes STOP and STOPPING actions. These modules aren't listed separately here because they're nearly identical to the START and STARTING actions, respectively.

```
import dispatcher from '../dispatcher';
import {
  START,
  STARTING,
  STOP,
  STOPPING
} from '../actions/constants';

import { EventEmitter } from 'events';

class MyStore extends EventEmitter {
  constructor() {
    super();

    this.state = {
      startDisabled: false,
      stopDisabled: true
    };
```

```
dispatcher.register((e) => {
  switch(e.type) {

    // If starting or stopping, we don't want any
    // buttons enabled.
    case STARTING:
    case STOPPING:
      this.state.startDisabled = true;
      this.state.stopDisabled = true;
      this.emit('change', this.state);
      break;

    // Disable the stop button after being started.
    case START:
      this.state.startDisabled = true;
      this.state.stopDisabled = false;
      this.emit('change', this.state);
      break;

    // Disabled the start button after being stopped.
    case STOP:
      this.state.startDisabled = false;
      this.state.stopDisabled = true;
      this.emit('change', this.state);
      break;
  }
});
  }
}

export default new MyStore();
```

The store has a clear representation of the disabled state for both a start and a stop button. If the STARTING or STOPPING action is dispatched, then we can mark both buttons as disabled. In the case of START or STOP, we can mark the appropriate button as disabled and the other as enabled. Now that the stores have all the state that they need, let's now look at a view that actually renders the button elements.

You might be wondering why we've separated these two actions into two action creator functions—start() and starting(). The reason is simple: one action creator dispatches one action. However, this isn't set in stone and is a matter of personal preference. For example, start() could have dispatched the STARTING action before actually making the API call. The upside here is that there's only one function that takes care of everything. On the downside, we lose the one-to-one correspondence between action creator and action, raising the potential for confusion.

```
import myStore from '../stores/mystore';
import {
  start,
  starting,
  stop,
  stopping
} from '../actions/functions';

class MyView {
  constructor() {

    // The elements our view interacts with...
    this.start = document.getElementById('start');
    this.stop = document.getElementById('stop');

    // The start button was clicked. Dispatch the
    // "STARTING" action, and the "START" action
    // once the asynchronous call resolves.
    this.start.addEventListener('click', (e) => {
      starting();
      start();
    });

    // The stop button was clicked. Dispatch the
    // "STOPPING" action, and the "STOP" action
    // once the asynchronous call resolves.
    this.stop.addEventListener('click', (e) => {
      stopping();
      stop();
    });

    // When the store state changes, update the UI
    // by enabling or disabling the buttons,
    // depending on the store state.
    myStore.on('change', (state) => {
      this.start.disabled = state.startDisabled;
      this.stop.disabled = state.stopDisabled;
    });
  }
}

export default new MyView();
```

Note that the main job of the click handlers is to call action creator functions. They're not performing extra state checking to make sure that the actions can be called, and so on. This sort of thing doesn't belong in views, it belongs in a store. We're following this tactic here, where we disable the buttons in the store by change a particular piece of state. If we check for this sort of thing in view event handlers, we end up decoupling the state from the logic that operates on it, and in Flux this is not a good thing.

Combining API calls

As development moves forward and features become more involved, we're inevitably faced with complex API scenarios. This means that there's no longer a simple API endpoint that delivers everything the feature needs with one call. Instead, our code has to stitch together two or more resources from different endpoints just to get the data needed by the feature.

In this section, we'll look at action creator functions that fetch data from multiple asynchronous resources and pass them to stores as payload data. These stores then convert these to information required by features. Then, we'll look at an alternative approach, where we compose action creator functions out of smaller action creator functions, each pulling data from their own asynchronous resource.

Complex action creators

Sometimes, a single API endpoint doesn't have all of the data we need for a given store. This means that we have to fetch data from multiple API endpoints. The challenge is that these are asynchronous resources, and they need to be synchronized before passing them to stores by dispatching them as action payloads. Let's take a look at an action creator that fetches data from three asynchronous API endpoints. But first, here's the API functions we'll use to simulate asynchronous network calls:

```
// API helper function - resolves the given
// "data" after the given MS "delay".
function api(data, delay=1000) {
  return new Promise((resolve, reject) => {
    setTimeout(() => {
      resolve(data);
    }, delay);
  });
}

// The first API...
export function first() {
```

```
    return api([ 'A', 'B', 'C' ], 500);
}

// The second API...
export function second() {
  return api([ 1, 2, 3 ]);
}

// The third API...
export function third() {
  return api([ 'D', 'E', 'F' ], 1200);
}
```

So we have consistent return values from these API functions—promises. Each promise that's returned from a given function is responsible for synchronizing that one API call. But what about when our store needs to combine all of these resolved values to form the state of a store? Let's now look at an action creator function that handles this:

```
import dispatcher from '../dispatcher';

// The mock API functions we need.
import {
  first,
  second,
  third
} from './api';

// The action identifier...
export constMY_ACTION = 'MY_ACTION';

export function myAction() {

  // Calls all three APIs, which all resolve
  // after different delay times. The "Promise.all()"
  // method synchronizes them and returns a new promise.
  Promise.all([
    first(),
    second(),
    third()
  ]).then((values) => {

    // These are the resolved values...
    let [ first, second, third ] = values;
```

```
      // All three API calls have resolved, meaning we
      // can now dispatch "MY_ACTION" with the three
      // resolved async values as the payload.
      dispatcher.dispatch({
        type: MY_ACTION,
        payload: {
          first: first,
          second: second,
          third, third
        }
      });
    });
}
```

The action MY_ACTION is only dispatched once all three asynchronous values have resolved, because the store depends on all three. All three values are available to the store within a single update round when the action is dispatched. Something less obvious about this code, but important nonetheless, is the fact that we're not performing any data transformations inside the action creator function before dispatching the payload. Instead, we provide the resolved API data as is, in the form of payload properties. This ensures that the store is the sole component responsible for the state of its information. Let's look at how a store is now able to use this payload:

```
import { EventEmitter } from 'events';
import dispatcher from '../dispatcher';
import { MY_ACTION } from '../actions/myaction';

class MyStore extends EventEmitter {
  constructor() {
    super();

    this.state = [];

    dispatcher.register((e) => {
      switch(e.type) {
        case MY_ACTION:

          // Get the resolved async values from the
          // action payload.
          let { first, second, third } = e.payload;

          // Zip the three arrays and set the resulting
          // array as the store state.
          this.state = first.map((item, i) =>
```

```
                [ item, second[i], third[i] ]);

            this.emit('change', this.state);
            break;
        }
    });
    }
}

export default new MyStore();
```

As you can see, the store has everything it needs in the payload to perform the necessary transformations. Let's call the action creator function and see if this store behaves as expected:

```
import { myAction } from './actions/myaction';
import myStore from './stores/mystore';

myStore.on('change', (state) => {
  console.log('changed', state);
});

myAction();
// → changed
// [
//   [ 'A', 1, 'D' ],
//   [ 'B', 2, 'E' ],
//   [ 'C', 3, 'F' ]
// ]
```

Composing action creators

As you saw earlier in the chapter, our action creator function calls can get quite verbose when user interactivity is involved. This is because we have to make two or more calls to action creator functions. One call ensures that the UI elements are in a state that's appropriate while the user waits for the asynchronous action to complete. The other call invokes the asynchronous behavior. To avoid having to make two calls everywhere, we could just have the action creator function dispatch two actions. However, this isn't always ideal because we might need to call the first action creator without the second action creator at some point. It's a granularity problem more than anything.

The easy solution is to compose a function out of the two. This way, we keep the granularity intact, while reducing the number of functions to call in many places. Let's revisit our code from earlier, where we had to manually call `starting()` then `start()`:

```
import { start as _start } from './start';
import { starting } from './starting';
import { stop as _stop } from './stop';
import { stopping } from './stopping';

// The "start()" function now automatically
// calls "starting()".
export function start() {
  starting();
  _start();
}

// The "stop()" function now automatically
// calls "stopping()"
export function stop() {
  stopping();
  _stop();
}

// Export "starting()" and "stopping()" so
// that they can still be used on their
// own, or composed into other functions.
export { starting, stopping };
```

Now our views can simply call `start()` or `stop()` and the necessary state changes are applied to the relevant UI elements. This works because the first action creator function is synchronous—meaning that the full Flux update round takes place before the asynchronous call is made. This behavior is consistent, no matter what. Where we start running into problems is when we start composing functions out of several asynchronous action creators, as visualized here:

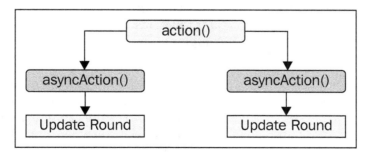

The problem here is that each of these `asyncAction()` functions we've used to compose `action()` results in an update round. The update round that happens first is a race condition. We can't combine them into a single action creator that makes requests to multiple API endpoints because they service two different stores. Flux is all about predictable data flows, and this means always knowing the order of update rounds. In the next section, we'll revisit promises in action creator functions to help us get around these tricky asynchronous action creator scenarios.

Returning promises

None of the action creator functions we've looked at so far in this chapter have returned any values. That's because their main job is to dispatch actions, while at the same time hiding any concurrency synchronization semantics. On the other hand, action creator functions could return a promise so that we could compose more complex asynchronous behavior that spans multiple stores. In the last section, we saw that composing asynchronous behavior using action creator functions can be difficult if not impossible to do.

In this section, we'll revisit the challenges posed by asynchronous behavior in the context of composing larger functionality. Then, we'll create an example implementation with action creators that return promises and use them to synchronize with one another. Finally, we'll see whether returning promises from action creators can help us deal with errors that happen in the asynchronous resources we're communicating with.

Synchronizing without promises

One nice aspect of a Flux architecture is the fact that a lot of it is synchronous. For example, when we call the dispatcher with a new action and a new payload, we can rest assured that the call will block until the update round has completed, and everything in the UI is reflecting the current state of things. With asynchronous behavior, things are different—especially in a Flux architecture where this type of thing is strictly confined to action creator functions. Therefore, we face the inevitable challenge of trying to piece together complex systems from an abundance of asynchronous resources.

We saw how to get partway there earlier in the chapter. A single action creator function can combine the resolved values of several asynchronous resources into a single action and a payload. Then the logic within the store can figure out how to make use of the data and update its state. This works fine when single stores are in play, but falters when we're trying to synchronize resources across several stores and features.

This is when being able to synchronize the async data and the Flux update round becomes important. To do so, our action creator functions need to return promises that resolve when both have completed. Here's an illustration of what we need to accomplish:

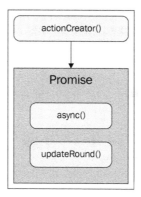

Composing asynchronous behavior

The way to get around these tricky asynchronous action creator scenarios is to have these functions return promises that are resolved after the asynchronous behavior and the update round have completed. This lets the caller know that the update round is complete and that anything we call now will take place afterward. Consistency is what we're after here, so let's take a look at an action creator function that returns a promise:

```
// The action identifier...
export const FIRST = 'FIRST';

// The API function that returns a promise that's
// resolved after 1.5 seconds.
function api() {
  return new Promise((resolve, reject) => {
    setTimeout(() => {
      resolve({ first: 'First Name' });
    }, 1500);
  });
}

export function first() {

  // Returns a promise so that the caller
```

```
      // knows when the update round is complete,
      // regardless of the asynchronous behavior
      // that takes place before the action is dispatched.
      return new Promise((resolve, reject) => {
        api().then((response) => {

          // Action is dispatched after the asynchronous
          // value is resolved.
          dispatcher.dispatch({
            type: FIRST,
            payload: response
          });

          // Resolve the promise returned by "first()",
          // after the update round.
          resolve();
        });
      });
    }
```

So this action creator calls an asynchronous API that resolves after 1.5 seconds, at which point the action payload is dispatched and the returned promise is resolved. Let's take a look at another action creator that uses a different API function:

```
import dispatcher from '../dispatcher';

// The action identifier...
export const LAST = 'LAST';

// The API function that returns a promise that's
// resolved after 1.5 seconds.
function api() {
  return new Promise((resolve, reject) => {
    setTimeout(() => {
      resolve({ last: 'Last Name' });
    }, 1000);
  });
}

export function last() {
  return new Promise((resolve, reject) => {
    api().then((response) => {
      dispatcher.dispatch({
```

```
        type: LAST,
        payload: response
    });

    resolve();
  });
});
}
```

You can see that the two action creator functions—`first()` and `last()`—follow an identical strategy by returning promises. The API function, however, resolves different data, and it takes only 1 second to do so. Let's see what happens when we try to use these two functions together:

```
import dispatcher from './dispatcher';
import { FIRST, first } from './actions/first';
import { LAST, last } from './actions/last';

// Logs the payload as actions are dispatched...
dispatcher.register((e) => {
  switch (e.type) {
    case FIRST:
      console.log('first', e.payload.first);
      break;
    case LAST:
      console.log('last', e.payload.last);
      break;
  }
});

// Order of update rounds isn't guaranteed here.
first();
last();
// →
// last Last Name
// first First Name

// With promises, update round order is consistent.
first().then(last);
// →
// first First Name
// last Last Name
```

Handling errors

What happens when the API that Flux action creators interact with fails? Generally speaking, when we make AJAX calls, we supply both success and error callback functions. This way, we can fail in a graceful manor. We have to be careful about how we handle failure in Flux action creators because, just as stores want to know about actions, they want to know about failures too.

So the question is—what do we do differently in our action creator functions? Do we just dispatch some sort of error action from within the action creator when the API fails? We do want to dispatch an error action so that the stores can adjust their state accordingly, but what about the caller of the action creator? For example, we could have a generic action creator function that's used in many places, and the error-handling could be context dependent.

The answer is to have the promise that's returned by the action creator reject. This allows the caller to specify their own behavior in the event of a failed API call. Let's look at an action creator function that handles errors this way:

```
import dispatcher from '../dispatcher';

// The action identifier...
export const UPDATE_TASK = 'UPDATE_TASK';

// The action error identifier...
export const UPDATE_TASK_ERROR = 'UPDATE_TASK_ERROR';

// Returns a promise that's rejected with an error
// message after 0.5 seconds.
function api() {
  return new Promise((resolve, reject) => {
    setTimeout(() => {
      reject('Failed to update task');
    }, 500);
  });
}

export function updateTask() {
  return new Promise((resolve, reject) => {

    // Dispatches the "UPDATE_TASK" action as usual
    // when the promise resolves. Then resolves
    // the promise returned by "updateTask()".
    api().then((response) => {
```

```
      dispatcher.dispatch({
        type: UPDATE_TASK
      });

      resolve();

      // If the API promise rejects, reject the promise
      // returned by "updateTask()" as well.
    }, (error) => {
      reject(error);
    });
  });
}


// A basic helper action creator for when the
// "updateTask()" function is rejected.
export function updateTaskError(error) {
  dispatcher.dispatch({
    type: UPDATE_TASK_ERROR,
    payload: error
  });
}
```

Now let's call this `updateTask()` function and see if we can assign error handling behavior to it:

```
import dispatcher from './dispatcher';
import {
  UPDATE_TASK,
  UPDATE_TASK_ERROR,
  updateTask,
  updateTaskError
} from './actions/update-task';

// Logs the payload as actions are dispatched...
dispatcher.register((e) => {
  switch (e.type) {
    case UPDATE_TASK:
      console.log('task updated');
      break;
    case UPDATE_TASK_ERROR:
      console.error(e.payload);
      break;
  }
```

```
});

// We can tell "updateTask()" how to respond when
// the underlying API call fails.
updateTask().catch(updateTaskError);
// → Failed to update task
```

Summary

This chapter focused on asynchronous action creators in Flux architectures. These are functions that need to dispatch actions, but before they can, they have to wait for some asynchronous resource to resolve. We looked at the synchronous update round concept, which is central to any Flux architecture. Then, we discussed how action creators encapsulate asynchronous behavior in such a way that they preserve the synchronous update rounds.

Network calls are the most common form of asynchronous communication in JavaScript applications, including Flux architectures. We covered the difference between these and other asynchronous channels, and how promises can be used to bridge the gap between them. We also looked at how promises can be utilized by action creator functions to allow for the composition of more complex functionality.

In the next chapter, we'll take a deeper look at stores and everything they have to do to maintain consistent state in our Flux architectures.

6

Changing Flux Store State

This chapter is about the continuing evolution of our Flux stores, as the application features we implement drive architectural improvements. In fact, this is something Flux architectures excel at—adapting to changes influenced by the application as they happen. This chapter dives into changing the design of stores and hammers home the idea that stores will change often. Higher-level changes to our stores might be necessary, such as introducing generic stores that are shared by several other stores that target specific features. As stores evolve, so do the dependencies between them; we'll look at how to manage inter-store dependencies using the dispatcher. We'll close the chapter with a discussion on keeping store complexity at bay.

Adapting to changing information

Earlier in the book, I mentioned that stores aren't models from MV* architectures. They're different from a number of perspectives, including their ability to cope with changing schemas in other architectural areas, such as the API and changing feature requirements. In this section, we'll look at the Flux store's ability to adapt to changing APIs. We'll also address the opposite direction of change, when views that consume store data have changing requirements. Finally, we'll talk about other components that might change as the direct result of a store's ongoing evolution.

Changing API data

API data changes, especially during the early stages of development. Even though we tell ourselves that a given API is going to stabilize over time, this rarely works out in practice. Or if an API does become stable and unchanging, we end up having to use a different API. The safe assumption is that this data is going to change, and our stores will need to adapt to such changes.

The beautiful part of Flux stores is the fact that they're feature driven more than they're API driven. This means that changes in API data have less of an impact on stores because their job is to transform the API data into information required by the feature. Here is a visualization of this idea:

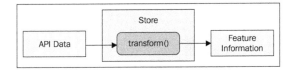

Unlike models, we're not trying to represent the API data in stores as is. Stores hold on to state that serves as information consumed by the features our customers use. This means that when changes happen in the API data that a given store depends on, we just have to revisit the transformation functions that create the feature information. On the other hand, models that are used by many different views in many different features of the application have a much harder time coping with API data changes such as these. It's because these components have dependencies with the schema of the API data, and not with the actual state that's relevant for the UI elements we need to render.

Can we always recreate the feature information that is used in our architecture after an API change has taken place? Not always. And this requires that we revisit how our views interact with the store. For example, if properties are removed entirely from a given API schema, this will likely require more than a simple transform update in our store. But this is a rare case; the most common case is that Flux stores can easily adapt to changing API data.

Changing feature functionality

Stores change and evolve through changing API data. This can impact the information that's available to the features that rely on the store. As our application grows, stores can feel pressure in the opposite direction—changing feature functionality often requires new information. This concept is illustrated in the following diagram:

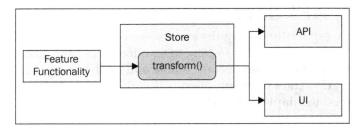

Instead of the API data alone dictating what happens in the `transform()` function, it's the other way around. The feature and the information that drives it serve as input to the design of the store transformation. This can actually be more difficult than adapting to changing API data. There are two main reasons for this.

First, there's the information itself. The store can transform resources into whatever the feature needs. But stores aren't magical—the API data needs to provide at least the basic necessities in terms of data; otherwise, we're at a dead end. Second, there are the UI elements themselves, some of which have state that needs to be captured by the store. Combining these two factors can make for a challenge.

It's good to get these difficult feature-related questions about information answered sooner rather than later. Being able to work in this direction means that we're letting the information that users care about drive the design, rather than letting the available API dictate what's possible.

Impacted components

As we saw earlier in this section, stores transform their data sources into information that's consumable by user features. This is a great architectural characteristic of Flux, because it means that the views that listen to these stores aren't constantly having to change as a result of changes made to the API. We do, however, need to stay conscious of the impact to other components when stores evolve.

Let's think about actions for a moment. When the API data changes, is this likely to result in new actions that we need to dispatch? No, because we're likely dealing with existing entry points into the system—these actions already exist. What about feature functionality—does this result in new actions? This is likely, because we could see new user interactivity introduced into a feature or new data and APIs. Existing action payloads can evolve as well, in response to changing UI elements, for example.

Something else to consider is the effect a changing store has on other stores that depend on it. Will it still be able to get the information it needs after the change? Views aren't the only Flux components that have store dependencies. We'll look at inter-store dependencies in more depth later in the chapter.

Reducing duplicate store data

Stores help us separate the state found in our architectures into features. This works out well because we can have drastically different data structures from one feature to the next. Alternatively, we could find that, as new features are introduced, a lot of the same data starts to appear in different stores. Nobody wants to repeat themselves— it's inefficient, and we can do better.

In this section, we'll introduce the notion of **generic stores**. These types of stores aren't necessarily used by views, but by other stores as a sort of repository for common data. We'll then walk through the basic setup of a generic store and how we can put generic stores to use in our more specialized stores.

Generic store data

Generic stores are similar to parent classes in a class hierarchy. A parent class has the common behavior and properties found in several children. However, unlike class hierarchies, we don't have several levels of structure. The aim of generic stores in Flux architectures is pretty simple—remove duplication where possible. Here is an illustration of a generic store:

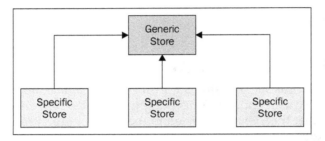

This allows for the state and transformations that are common to stores that serve specific features to share state that's also common. Otherwise, every update round will have to perform the same update on a different store. It's better to keep the update in one place to let stores query the generic store to compute their own state.

It's important to point out that specific stores don't actually inherit anything from generic stores in the way that a child class would inherit properties from its parent. Think of generic stores as instances, just like any other store. Also just like any other store, generic stores receive actions from the dispatcher to compute state changes.

Registering generic stores

With data dependencies, such as those we'll eventually find with the stores in our Flux architectures, order matters. For example, if a specific store is processed before a store that it depends on in an update round, we could end up with unexpected results. The generic store always needs to process actions first so that it has an opportunity to perform any transformations and set its state before any dependent stores access it.

Let's look at an example. First, we'll implement a generic store that takes a collection of document objects and maps it to a collection of document names:

```
import { EventEmitter } from 'events';
import dispatcher from '../dispatcher';
import { LOAD_DOC } from '../actions/load-doc';

// The generic "Docs" store keeps an index
// of document names, since they're used
// by many other stores.
class Docs extends EventEmitter {
  constructor() {
    super();

    this.state = [];

    dispatcher.register((e) => {
      switch(e.type) {
        case LOAD_DOC:

          // When a "LOAD_DOC" action is dispatched,
          // we take the "payload.docs" data and
          // transform it into the generic state that's
          // required by many other stores.
          for (let doc of e.payload.docs) {
            this.state[doc.id] = doc.name;
          }

          this.emit('change', this.state);
          break;
      }
    });
  }
}

export default new Docs();
```

Next, we'll implement a specific store that depends on this generic Docs store. It will be a specific document, which is used by a page that displays the name of the document. This store will have to locate the name based on the id property, in the generic store:

```
import { EventEmitter } from 'events';
import dispatcher from '../dispatcher';
import docs from './docs';
import { LOAD_DOC } from '../actions/load-doc';

// The specific store that depends on the generic
// "docs" store.
class Doc extends EventEmitter {
```

```
    constructor() {
      super();

      this.state = {
        name: ''
      };

      dispatcher.register((e) => {
        switch(e.type) {
          case LOAD_DOC:

            // The "id" of the document...
            let { id } = e.payload;

            // Here's where the generic store data
            // comes in handy - we only care about
            // the document name. We can use the "id"
            // to look this up from the generic store.
            this.state.name = docs.state[id];

            this.emit('change', this.state);
            break;
        }
      });
    }
  }

  export default new Doc();
```

Let's stop for a moment and think about what we've done here and why we're doing it. This generic Docs store implements a transformation that maps a collection of document data to an array of names. We're doing this because we have several other stores that need to look up a document name by id. If it were just the Doc store that needed this data, this would hardly be worth implementing. The idea is to reduce duplication, not to introduce indirection.

With that said, let's take a look at an action creator function that both of these stores will listen to:

```
  import dispatcher from '../dispatcher';

  // The action identifier...
  export constLOAD_DOC = 'LOAD_DOC';

  // Loads the name of a specific document.
```

```
export function loadDoc(id) {

  // The API data resolves raw document data...
  new Promise((resolve, reject) => {
    resolve([
      { id: 1, name: 'Doc 1' },
      { id: 2, name: 'Doc 2' },
      { id: 3, name: 'Doc 3' }
    ]);
  }).then((docs) => {

    // The payload contains both the raw document
    // collection and the specific document "id".
    // The generic "docs" store uses the raw
    // "docs" data while the specific store depends
    // on this generic collection.
    dispatcher.dispatch({
      type: LOAD_DOC,
      payload: {
        id: id,
        docs: docs
      }
    });
  });
}
```

As you can see, this function takes a document `id` as a parameter and makes an asynchronous call to load all the documents. Once they're loaded, the `LOAD_DOC` action is dispatched and the two stores can set their state. The challenge then becomes — how do we ensure that the generic store is updated before any stores that depend on it? Let's take a look at the `main.js` module and see this action creator, along with the two stores, put to work:

```
// We have to import the generic "docsStore", even though
// we're not using it here, so that it can register with
// the dispatcher and respond to "LOAD_DOC" actions.
import docsStore from './stores/docs';
import docStore from './stores/doc';
import { loadDoc } from './actions/load-doc';

// Logs the data our specific store gets from
// the generic store.
docStore.on('change', (state) => {
  console.log('name', `"${state.name}"`);
```

```
  });

  // Load the document with an id of 2.
  loadDoc(2);
  // → name "Doc 2"
```

When `loadDoc(2)` is called, the specific store gets its state set as we expect. This only works because of the order in which we're importing the two stores into `main.js`. In fact, if we were to swap the order, and import `docStore` before `docsStore`, then we wouldn't see the results we expect. The reason is simple—the order in which the stores are registered with the dispatcher determines the order in which they process actions. Later in the chapter, we'll look at a less cumbersome approach to handling store dependencies.

Combining generic and specific data

What's nice about generic stores is that they can be used directly by views. That is, they're not some abstract concept. These same stores can also be used by more specific stores to extend their data and transform their state into something that's required by other views. Let's look at an example where a specific store combines the state of a more general store with its own state. We'll start by looking at a generic group's store:

```
import { EventEmitter } from 'events';
import dispatcher from '../dispatcher';
import { LOAD_GROUPS } from '../actions/load-groups';

// A generic store for user groups...
class Groups extends EventEmitter {
  constructor() {
    super();

    this.state = [];

    dispatcher.register((e) => {
      switch(e.type) {

        // Stores the payload of a group array "as-is".
        case LOAD_GROUPS:
          this.state = e.payload;
          this.emit('change', this.state);
          break;
      }
    });
```

```
    }
  }

export default new Groups();
```

There isn't much going on here in the way of state transformation—the store just sets the payload as its state. Now, we'll look at the more specific users store, which depends on the groups store:

```
import { EventEmitter } from 'events';
import dispatcher from '../dispatcher';
import groups from './groups';
import { LOAD_USERS } from '../actions/load-users';


// A users store that depends on the generic
// groups store so that it can perform the necessary
// state transformations.
class Users extends EventEmitter {
  constructor() {
    super();

    this.state = [];

    dispatcher.register((e) => {
      switch(e.type) {
        case LOAD_USERS:

          // We only want to keep enabled users.
          let users = e.payload.filter(
            x => x.enabled);

          // Maps to a new users array, each user object
          // containing a new "groupName" property. This
          // comes from the generic group store, and is
          // looked up by id.
          this.state = users.map(
            x =>Object.assign({
              groupName: groups.state.find(
                y =>y.id === x.group
              ).name
            }, x));

          this.emit('change', this.state);
          break;
      }
```

```
    });
  }
}

export default new Users();
```

The state transformation that happens in this store is a little more involved. The LOAD_ USERS payload is an array of user objects, each with a group property. However, the views that observe this store have a specific need for the name of the group, not the id. So, it is here that we perform the mapping that creates a new array of user objects, this one with the groupName property required by our views. Here's a look at the loadUsers() action creator function:

```
import dispatcher from '../dispatcher';

// The action identifier...
export constLOAD_USERS = 'LOAD_USERS';

// Dispatches a "LOAD_USERS" action once the
// asynchronous data has resolved.
export function loadUsers() {
  new Promise((resolve, reject) => {
    resolve([
      { group: 1, enabled: true, name: 'User 1' },
      { group: 2, enabled: false, name: 'User 2' },
      { group: 2, enabled: true, name: 'User 3' }
    ]);
  }).then((users) => {
    dispatcher.dispatch({
      type: LOAD_USERS,
      payload: users
    });
  });
}
```

And here's how we load the generic group's data, followed by the users data which depends on it:

```
import groupsStore from './stores/groups';
import usersStore from './stores/users';
import { loadGroups } from './actions/load-groups';
import { loadUsers } from './actions/load-users';

// Log the state of the "usersStore" to make
// sure that includes data from the generic
```

```
// "groupsStore"
usersStore.on('change', (state) => {
  state.forEach(({ name, groupName }) => {
    console.log(`${name} (${groupName})`);
  });
});

// We always load the generic data first. Especially
// if it doesn't change often.
loadGroups();
loadUsers();
// →
// User 1 (Group 1)
// User 3 (Group 2)
```

Generic store data like this is especially useful if it's used by plenty of other specific stores, and if its state doesn't change often. For example, loading this generic store data could be part of the application initialization activities, and it doesn't need to be touched after that.

Handling store dependencies

So far in this book, we've treated our Flux store dependencies implicitly. The order in which we imported the store modules determined the order in which actions were handled, which has implications if something we depend on hasn't been updated yet. It's time to start treating our store dependencies with a little more rigor.

In this section, we'll introduce the waitFor() mechanism of the Flux dispatcher to manage store dependencies. Then, we'll talk about two types of store dependencies we might have. The first type of dependency is strictly related to application data. The second type of dependency is related to UI elements.

Waiting for stores

The dispatcher has a built-in mechanism that allows us to explicitly resolve store dependencies. What's more, dependencies are declared right in the callback function, where the dependency is actually used. Let's look at an example that highlights the improved code for dealing with store dependencies. First, we have a basic store that doesn't do much:

```
import { EventEmitter } from 'events';
import dispatcher from '../dispatcher';
import { MY_ACTION } from '../actions/my-action';
```

```
class Second extends EventEmitter {
  constructor() {
    super();

    // Registering a callback with the dispatcher
    // returns an identifier...
    this.id = dispatcher.register((e) => {
      switch(e.type) {
        case MY_ACTION:
          this.emit('change');
          break;
      }
    });
  }
}

export default new Second();
```

You'll notice something about this store looks slightly different. We're assigning the return value of `dispatcher.register()` to the `id` property of the store. This value is used to identify the callback function that we've just registered within the dispatcher. Now, let's define a store that depends on this one so that we can see why this `id` property is relevant:

```
import { EventEmitter } from 'events';
import dispatcher from '../dispatcher';
import { MY_ACTION } from '../actions/my-action';
import second from './second';

class First extends EventEmitter {
  constructor() {
    super();

    // Registering a callback with the dispatcher
    // returns an identifier...
    this.id = dispatcher.register((e) => {
      switch(e.type) {
        case MY_ACTION:

          // This tells the dispatcher to process any
          // callback functions that were registered
          // to "second.id" before continuing here.
          dispatcher.waitFor([ second.id ]);
          this.emit('change');
          break;
      }
    });
```

```
    }
}

export default new First();
```

The `id` property is used by the call to `dispatcher.waitFor()`. This method of the dispatcher forces actions to be dispatched to the stores that we depend on before we continue with making state transformations. This ensures that we're always working with the most up-to-date data in the stores that we depend on. Let's see the `myAction()` function in use, and whether the dependency management between our two stores is working as expected:

```
// The order of store imports no longer matters,
// since the stores use the dispatcher to
// explicitly handle dependency resolution.
import first from './stores/first';
import second from './stores/second';
import { myAction } from './actions/my-action';

// The first store changed...
first.on('change', () => {
  console.log('first store changed');
});

// The second store changed...
second.on('change', () => {
  console.log('second store changed');
});

// Dispatches "MY_ACTION"...
myAction();
```

It no longer matters which order things happen in `main.js`, or anywhere else in the architecture for that matter. The dependency is declared where it matters, close to the code that's using the dependent data. This is enforced by the dispatcher component.

> Note that the `waitFor()` method accepts an array of IDs. This means that in more complex scenarios where we depend on the state of more than one store, we can pass in each store ID that we depend on. However, the more common case is to depend on the state of one store. If there are multi-store dependencies all over the architecture, it's a sign of too much complexity.

Data dependencies

There are two types of dependencies worth thinking about in Flux stores. The most common are data dependencies. This is the type of dependency in place when a specific store depends on a generic store—it has some generic data that several stores need to access. This application data usually comes from an API and is ultimately rendered by a view. However, we're not restricted to generic stores when we're talking about data dependencies.

For example, let's say that we have a user interface and the main layout is separated by tabs. The stores in our Flux architecture are, unsurprisingly, aligned with these tabs. If one of these stores makes an API call, then performs some data transformations to set its state, can another store depend on this store to use this data? It would make sense to share data like this, otherwise, we'd have to repeat the same API request, data transforms, and so on—this gets repetitive and we'd like to avoid it.

However, when stores that explicitly model top-level features such as tabs, we start to notice other dependencies that aren't strictly data-related. These are UI dependencies, and it's perfectly feasible to have these. For example, what the user sees in one tab could depend on the state of a checkbox in another tab. Here's an illustration of the two types of store dependencies:

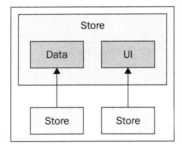

UI dependencies

In typical frontend architectures, the state of UI elements is probably the single most error-prone aspect of state modeling. The main problem with UI elements is that when we don't explicitly model their states, we have a hard time grasping cause and effect when those states change. This gets particularly troublesome when the state of one UI element depends on the state of another UI element. We end up with code that implicitly ties these items together.

Flux stores are better at dealing with this type of dependency because in a store, a UI dependency is the same as a data dependency—it's all just state. It's a good thing that we're easily able to do this in Flux architectures, because these types of dependencies tend to grow complex rather quickly. To illustrate how Flux deals with UI dependencies, let's look at an example. We'll create two stores for different sections of the UI: one for checkboxes and one for labels. The idea is that the labels depend on the state of the checkboxes, because their style changes as the checkboxes change.

First, we have the store representing the checkbox elements:

```
import { EventEmitter } from 'events';
import dispatcher from '../dispatcher';
import { FIRST } from '../actions/first';
import { SECOND } from '../actions/second';

class Checkboxes extends EventEmitter {
  constructor() {
    super();

    this.state = {
      first: true,
      second: true
    };

    // Sets the dispatch id of this store
    // so that other stores can depend on it.
    // Depending on the action, this handler
    // changes the boolean UI state of a given
    // checkbox.
    this.id = dispatcher.register((e) => {
      switch(e.type) {
        case FIRST:
          this.state.first = e.payload;
          this.emit('change', this.state);
          break;
        case SECOND:
          this.state.second = e.payload;
          this.emit('change', this.state);
          break;
      }
    });
  }
}

export default new Checkboxes();
```

There are two checkbox elements modeled by this store—first and second. The state is Boolean, true when checked, false when unchecked. By default, both checkboxes are checked, and when either the FIRST or the SECOND actions are dispatched, the state of the respective checkbox is updated to reflect the payload. Now let's look at the Labels store, which depends on the state of the Checkboxes store:

```
import { EventEmitter } from 'events';
import dispatcher from '../dispatcher';
import { FIRST } from '../actions/first';
import { SECOND } from '../actions/second';
import checkboxes from './checkboxes';

class Labels extends EventEmitter {
  constructor() {
    super();

    // The initial state of this store depends
    // on the initial state of the "checkboxes"
    // store.
    this.state = {
      first: checkboxes.state.first ?
        'line-through' : 'none',
      second: checkboxes.state.second ?
        'line-through' : 'none'
    };

    this.id = dispatcher.register((e) => {
      switch(e.type) {

        // The "FIRST" action was dispatched, so wait
        // for the "checkboxes" UI state, then update
        // the UI state of the "first" label.
        case FIRST:
          dispatcher.waitFor([ checkboxes.id ]);

          this.state.first = checkboxes.state.first ?
            'line-through' : 'none';

          this.emit('change', this.state);
          break;

        // The "SECOND" action was dispatched, so wait
        // for the "checkboxes" UI state, then update
        // the UI state of the "second" label.
```

```
    case SECOND:
      dispatcher.waitFor([ checkboxes.id ]);

      this.state.second = checkboxes.state.second ?
        'line-through' : 'none';

      this.emit('change', this.state);
      break;
    }
  });
  }
}


export default new Labels();
```

You can see here that even the initial state of this store is dependent on the state of the Checkboxes store. The value of the first or second state properties in this store are actually CSS values. It's important that we model these values here, because this is state, after all—all state goes into a store. This means that later on something else can depend on these values. When everything is explicit, we know why the way things are the way they are, which translates to stable software.

Now, let's look at the views that use these stores to render the UI elements and to respond to user input. First, the Checkboxes view:

```
import checkboxes from '../stores/checkboxes';
import { first } from '../actions/first';
import { second } from '../actions/second';

class Checkboxes {
  constructor() {

    // The DOM elements our view manipulates (these
    // are checkboxes).
    this.first = document.getElementById('first');
    this.second = document.getElementById('second');

    // Dispatch the appropriate action when either
    // of the checkboxes change. The action payload
    // is the "checked" property of the UI element.
    this.first.addEventListener('change', (e) => {
      first(e.target.checked);
    });

    this.second.addEventListener('change', (e) => {
```

```
      second(e.target.checked);
    });

    // When the "checkboxes" store changes state,
    // render the view using the new state.
    checkboxes.on('change', (state) => {
      this.render(state);
    });

  }

  // Sets the "checked" properties of the checkbox
  // UI elements. By default, we use the initial
  // state of the "checkboxes" store. Otherwise,
  // we use whatever state is passed.
  render(state=checkboxes.state) {
    this.first.checked = state.first;
    this.second.checked = state.second;
  }
}

export default new Checkboxes();
```

There are two checkbox elements used here, and the first thing that's done in the view's constructor is to set up the change event handlers for the checkboxes. These handlers will dispatch the appropriate action—FIRST or SECOND—depending on the checkbox and its checked state. The render() function actually updates the DOM based on the state. Now. let's look at the Labels view:

```
import labels from '../stores/labels';

class Labels {
  constructor() {

    // The DOM elements this view manipulates (these
    // are labels).
    this.first = document.querySelector('[for="first"]');
    this.second = document.querySelector('[for="second"]');

    // When the "labels" store changes, render
    // the view using the new state.
    labels.on('change', (state) => {
      this.render(state);
    });
```

```
    }

    // Updates the "textDecoration" style of our
    // label UI elements, using the "labels" store
    // state as the default. Otherwise, we use whatever
    // state is passed in.
    render(state=labels.state) {
      this.first.style.textDecoration = state.first;
      this.second.style.textDecoration = state.second;
    }
  }

export default new Labels();
```

This view works similarly to the Checkboxes view. The main differences are that there's no user interactivity here, and that the changes made to the UI elements are style property values that were set in the Labels store. These ultimately depend on the state of the Checkboxes store, so as the user changes the state of checkbox, they'll see the corresponding label change its style.

If this feels like a lot of code to accomplish something simple, that's because it is. Remember, we've actually accomplished a lot more here than a simple checkbox toggle and label style update. We've established explicit UI state dependencies between two different sections of the UI. This is a victory for our architecture, because the first moment a given architecture struggles to scale is when we can't figure out why something happens. Throughout the lifetime of a Flux architecture, we actively take steps to make sure this doesn't happen, as we've just demonstrated here.

View update order

While it's nice to be able to explicitly control the dependencies of our stores using waitFor(), views don't have such luxuries. In this section, we'll look at the order in which our views render UI elements. First, we'll look at the role stores have to play in the order of view updates. Then, we'll go over the cases where view order actually affects the user experience versus those where the ordering doesn't matter.

Store registration order

The order in which actions are dispatched to stores matters. When a store transforms its state, it also notifies any views listening to the store. This means that if one view is listening to a store that was registered with the dispatcher first, this view will be rendered before any other views. The idea is illustrated here:

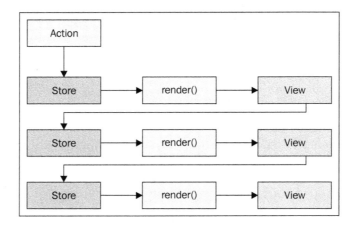

As you can see, the order of the store callback functions within the dispatcher clearly impacts the rendering order of views. Store dependencies can also impact the order of view rendering. For example, if store A depends on store B, then any views listening to store B will be rendered first. It could be that none of this matters or there could be some interesting side effects. We'll look at both outcomes next.

Prioritizing view rendering

Given that the stores that form the core of our Flux architecture can also determine the render order of our views, we have to take care to prioritize according to user experience. For example, we could have a store that represents the top header area of the page and another store that's for the main content area. Now, if the main content area renders first, leaving a noticeable gap near the top of the page, we'll want to fix that.

Seeing as how users will start at the top of the page and work their way down, we would have to make sure that the store for the header content is registered first. How do we do this? Once again, we're back to where we were when dealing with store dependencies. We have to take care to import our views in the correct order— an order that reflects the rendering order. As we saw with stores, this isn't an ideal situation to be in.

One answer is to introduce a store dependency. Even though the content store doesn't actually use any data from the header store, it could still depend on it for render ordering purposes. By using the `waitFor()` method, we'd know that any views that listen to the header store will be rendered first, eliminating the possibility of usability issues related to render order. The risk here, of course, is the same as any store dependency—complexity. When we reach the point where there are too many store dependencies to easily comprehend, it's time to rethink our store design.

Dealing with store complexity

The leading culprit of Flux store complexity is dependency management. Despite having the dispatcher as a tool to manage these dependencies, something is lost when there's too many of them. In this final section of the chapter, we'll discuss the consequences of having too many stores in our architecture and what can be done to remedy the situation.

Too many stores

The top-level features of our application do a decent job of providing a boundary for our stores and the state that they encapsulate. The challenge with stores is when there are too many of them. For example, as our applications grow over time, more features will be built which translates to more stores being tossed into the architecture. Additionally, the stores that already exist are apt to grow more complex as well, as they have to find ways to get along with all the other changing features of the application.

This makes for a complex scenario—growing complexity in stores and more stores overall. This almost certainly will lead to an explosion in dependencies, as we tease out all the edge cases of our user interface. Generic stores that are shared by many other specific stores can also be a source of trouble. For example, we could end up with way too many generic stores, eventually getting to the point where all our state data is indirect.

When we've reached the point where the sheer number of stores in our architecture is untenable, it's time to start rethinking what constitutes a feature.

Rethinking feature domains

Having top-level features map to our stores generally works well enough, until we have a lot of top-level features. At this point, it's time to re-evaluate the policy that a feature maps to a store. For example, if we have a lot of top-level features, odds are that there's a lot of similar data that could be folded into a single store that drives many features. Another potential effect of reducing the number of stores that power our features is the removal of generic stores. Generic stores are only good if we have too much duplicate data, which tends to be less of a problem when the number of stores shrinks. Here is a diagram that shows how a store could be the driver of more than one feature:

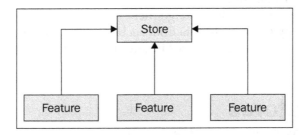

We might find ourselves in the opposite situation as well, whereby a store's complexity is simply too great, and we need to reduce its responsibilities by refactoring it into multiple stores. To fix this, we have to think about how one large feature can be turned into two smaller features. If we can't think of a good way to divide the feature, then maybe the complexity of the store is the best we can do, and it should be left alone.

Summary

In this chapter, we took a detailed look at stores in Flux architectures, starting with the aspects that are most likely to change once we've moved on from the skeleton architecture phase. We then introduced the notion of generic stores, the idea being to reduce the amount of state that individual stores have to keep. The awkward part of generic stores are the dependencies that they introduce, and to deal with them, you learned how to use the dispatcher's waitFor() mechanism.

Dependencies between stores come in two varieties, data dependencies and UI dependencies, and you learned that UI dependencies are a critical part of any Flux architecture. Finally, we discussed some of the ways that stores can grow out of hand in terms of complexity, and what can be done about it. In the following chapter, we'll look at view components in Flux architectures.

7
Viewing Information

The view layer is the last data flow stop in a Flux architecture. Views are the essence of our application because they provide information directly to the user and respond directly to user interactions. This chapter takes a detailed look at view components within the context of a Flux architecture.

We'll start with a discussion about getting views their data, and what they can do with it once they have it. Next, we'll look at some examples that emphasize the stateless nature of Flux views. Then, we'll review the responsibilities of views in Flux architectures, which are different from views in other types of frontend architectures.

We'll wrap the chapter up with a look at using ReactJS components as the view layer. Let's get started!

Passing views data

Views don't have their own data source that they can use to render UI elements. Instead, they rely on the state of Flux stores, and they listen for changes in state. In this section, we'll cover the change event that stores will emit to signify that views can render themselves. We'll also discuss the idea that it's ultimately up to the view to decide when and how to render the UI.

Data via the change event

The view components that we've seen so far in this book have all relied on the change event that stores emit when the state of a store has changed. This is how the view knows that it can render itself to the DOM—because there's new store state, meaning that there's probably a visual change that we want the user to see.

You may have noticed from the earlier examples that all the handler functions that listen for change events had a state parameter—this is the state of the store. The question is—why do we need to include this state data? Why can't the view just reference the store directly to reference the state data? This idea is illustrated here:

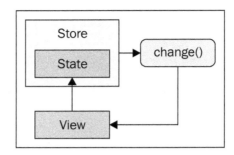

The change event is still necessary, even though the view is directly referencing the store's state—how else would it know to render? The change event is emitted, and the view then knows that the state it's referencing has changed as well. There's a potential issue with this approach, and it has to do with immutability. Let's look at some code to better understand the problem. Here's a store with a name property as its state:

```
import { EventEmitter } from 'events';
import dispatcher from '../dispatcher';
import { NAME_CAPS } from '../actions/name-caps';

class First extends EventEmitter {
  constructor() {
    super();

    // The default state is a "name" property
    // with a lower-case string.
    this.state = {
      name: 'foo'
    };

    this.id = dispatcher.register((e) => {
      switch(e.type) {

        // Mutates the "name" property, keeping
        // the "state" object intact.
        case NAME_CAPS:
          let { state } = this;
```

```
                    state.name = state.name.toUpperCase();
                    this.emit('change', state);
                    break;
                }
            });
        }
    }


    export default new First();
```

When this store responds to the NAME_CAPS action, its job is to transform the state of the name property, using a simple call to toUpperCase(). Then, the change event is emitted with the state as the event data. Let's look at another store that does the same thing, but using a different approach to updating the state object:

```
import { EventEmitter } from 'events';
import dispatcher from '../dispatcher';
import { NAME_CAPS } from '../actions/name-caps';

class Second extends EventEmitter {
    constructor() {
        super();

        // The defaul state is a name property
        // with a lower-case string.
        this.state = {
            name: 'foo'
        };

        this.id = dispatcher.register((e) => {
            switch(e.type) {

                // Assigns a new "state" object, invalidating
                // any references to any previous state.
                case NAME_CAPS:
                    this.state = {
                        name: this.state.name.toUpperCase()
                    };
                    this.emit('change', this.state);
                    break;
            }
        });
    }
}

export default new Second();
```

As you can see, the two stores are basically identical, and they produce the same result when the NAME_CAPS action is dispatched. However, note that this transformation doesn't mutate the state object. It replaces it instead. This approach keeps the state object immutable, meaning that the store will never change any of its properties. The difference is felt in the view layer, and it highlights the need for the state argument in the change event handler:

```
import first from './stores/first';
import second from './stores/second';
import { nameCaps } from './actions/name-caps';

// Setup references to the state of the
// two stores.
var firstState = first.state;
var secondState = second.state;

first.on('change', () => {
  console.log('firstState', firstState.name);
});
// → firstState FOO

second.on('change', () => {
  console.log('secondState', secondState.name);
});
// → secondState foo

second.on('change', (state) => {
  console.log('state', state.name);
});
// → state FOO

nameCaps();
```

This is why we can't make assumptions about the state of a store. In the preceding code, we just made a critical error in assuming that we could hold onto a secondStore.state reference. It turns out that this object is immutable, and so the only way for views to access the new state is through the state argument in the change handler.

Views decide when to render

The job of a Flux store is centered primarily on generating the correct information for views to consume. What isn't part of a store's job description is to know when a view actually needs to update or not. This means that it's up to the view to decide what happens when a store triggers a change event—it could be that nothing in the DOM needs to be updated. The question then becomes—why would a store emit a change event if nothing has changed?

The simple answer is that stores don't do enough bookkeeping to make a determination as to whether something has changed or not. The store knows how to perform the correct state transformations, but it doesn't necessarily keep track of previous states for diffing purposes—although it certainly could do that.

Let's look at a store that doesn't mutate its state. Instead, it creates new state when something is transformed:

```
import { EventEmitter } from 'events';
import dispatcher from '../dispatcher';
import { NAME_CAPS } from '../actions/name-caps';

class MyStore extends EventEmitter {
  constructor() {
    super();

    this.state = {
      name: 'foo'
    };

    this.id = dispatcher.register((e) => {
      switch(e.type) {
        case NAME_CAPS:

          // Convert to upper-case.
          let name = this.state.name.toUpperCase();

          // Only assign the new state object if
          // the "name" isn't already in upper-case.
          this.state = this.state.name === name ?
            this.state : {
              name: this.state.name.toUpperCase()
            };

          // Tell views about the state change, even
```

```
                    // if the state object is the same.
                    this.emit('change', this.state);
                    break;
                }
            });
        }
    }

    export default new MyStore();
```

This store is listening to the same NAME_CAPS message from the previous example. Its job is still the same—transform the name property to uppercase. However, this code works differently than in the last version of the store. It's immutable in that it doesn't mutate the state object—it replaces it. But it only does so if the value has actually changed. Otherwise, the state object stays the same. The idea here isn't to show that stores should detect state changes on individual properties, but rather that the change event can be emitted even when the state hasn't changed. In other words, our views shouldn't make the assumption that rendering to the DOM is necessary, just because of a change event.

Let's turn our attention to the view now. The plan is simple—don't render unless we have to:

```
    import myStore from '../stores/my-store';

class MyView {
    constructor() {

        // The view keeps a copy of the previous
        // store state.
        this.previousState = null;

        myStore.on('change', (state) => {

            // Make sure we have a new state before
            // rendering. If "state" is equal to
            // "previousState", then we know there's
            // nothing new to render.
            if (state !== this.previousState) {
                console.log('name', state.name);
            }

            // Keep a reference of the state, so that
            // we can use it in the next "change"
            // event.
```

```
        this.previousState = state;
    });
  }
}

export default new MyView();
```

You can see that the `previousState` property keeps a reference to the state of the store. But wait, isn't that a bad thing, according to the section before this one? Well, no, because we're not actually using the reference for anything other than strict equality checking. This is used to determine whether or not the view needs to render. Since the store state is immutable, we can assert that if the same reference is passed as an argument to the change event handler, nothing actually changed and we can safely ignore the event. Let's see what happens when we call the same action several times in succession:

```
import myView from './views/my-view';
import { nameCaps } from './actions/name-caps';

// Despite repeated calls to "nameCaps()",
// "myView" is only rendered once.
nameCaps();
nameCaps();
nameCaps();
// → name FOO
```

Later in this chapter when we look at ReactJS, we'll see more advanced scenarios of views that only render what they need to. Later in the book when we look at `Immutable.js`, we'll tackle more advanced state change detection.

Keeping views stateless

Views can't be completely stateless because they interact with the DOM, and the DOM elements associated with a view will always have a state. However, we can take steps to treat views as stateless entities within the context of our Flux architecture. In this section, we'll address two aspects of stateless views.

First, we'll go over the idea that all state in a Flux architecture belongs in a store, including any UI state that we might be tempted to keep in our view components. Second, we'll look at DOM querying and why we want to avoid doing this from within our Flux views.

UI state belongs in stores

As you learned in the previous chapter, UI state is just like state that's derived from application data — it all belongs in a store. UI state includes things such as the `disabled` property of a button or the name of a class that's applied to a `div`. The reason these bits of state belong in a store is that other stores might depend on them. This in turn affects the rendering outcome of other views. This type of dependency is visualized as follows:

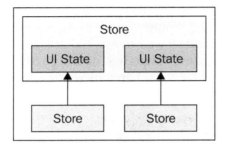

If the UI state that other stores might depend on isn't kept in a store, then they'd have to depend on the view or the DOM itself. This is inconsistent and goes against what Flux stands for — strict update ordering and keeping state confined.

No querying the DOM

When the UI state is kept in a Flux store, there's no need to query the DOM to figure out whether or not a button is disabled. Think about the jQuery approach to manipulating application state. First, we have to issue a DOM query that gets us the relevant DOM elements, and then we have to figure out whether they're in the appropriate state by reading some of their properties. Then, we can make changes elsewhere in the application. Or perhaps there's a blend of state that's kept directly in the DOM and some JavaScript objects.

It's the consistency that's the biggest difference maker in Flux architectures, because we don't have to query the DOM to get the `href` property of a link. The stores that hold onto UI state already have this information. This is always the case — it's never a matter of figuring out whether it's in the DOM or some other component.

Another advantage of having all the UI state that we need to make rendering decisions in our stores is that there's no performance bottleneck. Querying the DOM once or twice is not a big deal, and this does need to happen if we're going to display changes for the user. What we don't want is to have a long series of DOM query calls that don't even result in something being rendered. In other words, there's no need to query the DOM to extract information when it should already be in a store.

This is the same strategy used by virtual DOM tree technologies such as ReactJS, where the DOM data is all stored in JavaScript objects. Looking up some UI state from a JavaScript object is inherently faster than looking up DOM element properties, and this is how ReactJS is able to perform so well—by minimizing the number of DOM interactions for a given UI change.

View responsibilities

At this point in the book, you probably have a pretty good handle on the role of view components in a Flux architecture. Put simply, their job is to display store information for users by inserting it into the DOM. In this section, we'll break this core view concept into three parts.

First there's the input to the views—the store data. Next, we have the structure of the view itself, and the various ways that it can be decomposed into smaller views. Finally, there's the user interactivity. Each of these three areas of view components has a relation to the flow of data through our Flux architecture. Let's look at each of them now.

Rendering store data

If the store transforms data into information that the user needs, then why have views at all? Why not have the stores directly render the information to the DOM? We need views for a couple reasons. First of all, a store could actually be used in several places, rendered by several views. Second of all, Flux isn't necessarily concerned with the visual display of information. For example, if we were to design some view that's doesn't render HTML but some other display format, that would be perfectly fine.

Views don't keep any state or perform any transformations on store information. However, they do need to transform the information a little, to turn it into valid markup for display in the browser or any other display medium where our application runs. But aside from marking up the information returned from stores, views have little to do. It's the view technology, such as ReactJS, that does the majority of the legwork in terms of marking up JavaScript objects and inserting them into the DOM. Here is a diagram that shows the process:

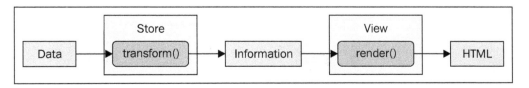

Subview structure

The aim of stores in Flux architectures is to structure them so that there's only one store per top-level feature. This gets us around the issues created by having massive hierarchies of data structures. Views, on the other hand, can benefit from a little bit of hierarchical structure. Just because a top-level feature is driven by information from a single store, it doesn't mean that only a single view can drive the user experience.

Earlier in the book, we discussed the notion of hierarchical structure and how it should be avoided in Flux architectures. This is still true to an extent with views, because no matter how you slice it, deep hierarchies are difficult to comprehend. Views do need to be decomposed to an extent, because otherwise we'll end of putting all the markup complexity in one place. HTML markup is hierarchical by nature, so to some degree our views should mimic this structure, as illustrated here:

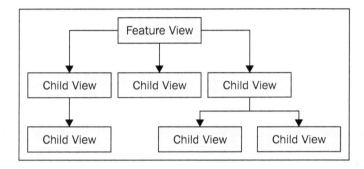

Just like stores can be generic, so can views. More than one feature can use generic components to present information using a common display pattern. For instance, think about some kind of expandable/collapsible panel that's used by all of our features—would it not make sense to plug this into our larger features rather than duplicate the functionality? The view technology that we're using is also a deciding factor in how we want to decompose our views into smaller reusable pieces, since this is easier to do with some frameworks than others. For example, we'll see in the next section that ReactJS makes it easy to compose coarse-grained views out of smaller more fine-grained views because they're largely self-contained.

Something to be aware of when composing view hierarchies like this—be mindful of the data-flow. For example, when a Flux store changes, it emits the change event so that the top-level view can render itself. Then it renders its immediate children, who render their immediate children, and so on. As the store state flows through these views, no data transformations should be happening along the way. Put another way, the leaf views in the tree should get the same information as the root view.

User interactivity

The final area of view responsibility we need to think about is user interactivity. Apart from passively watching the information on their screens change as the underlying stores of our architecture handle actions, they're going to need to do things. If nothing else, users need to be able to navigate around the application to use the various features we've implemented. To handle this sort of thing, the view components that render the UI should also intercept the DOM events as they're triggered. This generally results in a new action being dispatched, as we've already seen earlier in the book.

The key thing to remember about these event handlers is that they should have essentially one responsibility—calling the right action creator function. What these event handlers should avoid is trying to execute any logic—this belongs in a store, along with the state that the logic affects. This is so fundamental to Flux that it's quite possible I'll repeat it at least twelve more times in the book. Once we start introducing logic in places other than stores, we lose the ability to reason about the state of something—and the state largely determines what the user sees.

It's entirely plausible to pass action creator functions directly as event handlers to DOM nodes. This could actually help us, because it provides a very low chance of logic being introduced in the wrong place.

Using ReactJS with Flux

ReactJS is a library for creating view components. In fact, React doesn't even label itself as a view library—it's a set of tools for creating components that render UI elements. This simple premise is easy to understand and powerful—a perfect fit as the view technology in our Flux architecture.

In this section, we'll look at making ReactJS the technology of choice for views in our Flux applications, starting with passing state information from stores into React components. Next, we'll talk about the composition of views, and how Flux state flows from stores to parent views to child views. Lastly, we'll implement some event handling capabilities in our views using React mechanisms and a router using the react-router library.

Setting the view state

There are two ways to render React components based on the state of our Flux stores. These involve two different types of components—statefull and stateless—both of which we'll address here. First, let's take a look at the store containing the state that drives our views:

```
import { EventEmitter } from 'events';
import dispatcher from '../dispatcher';
import { ADD } from '../actions/add';

class MyStore extends EventEmitter {
  constructor() {
    super();

    // The "items" state is an empty array
    // by default...
    this.state = {
      items: []
    };

    this.id = dispatcher.register((e) => {
      switch(e.type) {

        // Push the "payload" to the "items"
        // array when the "ADD" action is
        // dispatched.
        case ADD:
          let { state } = this;
```

```
        state.items.push(e.payload);
        this.emit('change', state);
        break;
    }
  });
  }
}


export default new MyStore();
```

The idea here is simple—any time an ADD action is dispatched, we're pushing the action payload onto the items array. Any React components that wish to respond to this store state change can do so by listening for the change event. First, let's look at a stateful React component that renders the items list:

```
import { default as React, Component } from 'react';
import myStore from '../stores/my-store';

// A stateful React component that relies on
// it's on state in order to render updates.
export default class Stateful extends Component {
  constructor() {
    super();

    // When "myStore" changes, we set the state of
    // this component by calling "setState()", causing
    // a render to happen.
    myStore.on('change', (state) => {
      this.setState(state);
    });

    // The initial state of the component is
    // taken from the initial state of the Flux store.
    this.state = myStore.state;
  }

  // Renders a list of items.
  render() {
    return (
      <ul>
        {this.state.items.map(item =>
          <li key={item}>{item}</li>)}
      </ul>
    );
  }
}
```

This is a typical React component, created using the ES2015 class syntax and extending the base React `Component` class. This approach is necessary for stateful components. As you can see, the constructor of this component directly interacts with a Flux store. When the store changes, it calls `setState()`, which is how the component renders to reflect new store state. The constructor also sets the initial state by setting the `state` property. Next, we have the `render()` method, which returns React elements based on this state.

Note that our React component is using JSX syntax to define elements. We're not going to cover how this works in this book, nor will we cover other aspects of React in any level of detail. This is a book on Flux architecture, and we'll cover parts of React that are relevant in a Flux context. If you want more of a technical deep dive on React itself, there's plenty of free resources, as well as plenty of other books on the subject.

Now let's look at another implementation of the exact same component, meaning the exact same output. This is the stateless approach to React components/views:

```
import React from 'react';

// The stateless version of the React
// component is a much stripped-down
// version of a class component. Since
// it only relies on propertes passed
// into it, it can be a basic arrow function
// that returns a React element.
export default ({ items }) => (
  <ul>
    {items.map(item =>
      <li key={item}>{item}</li>)}
  </ul>
);
```

Wait, what? This is the exact same component, only it doesn't depend on state. This could be a good thing if we're implementing this as a view component inside our Flux architecture. The thing that stands out most about this implementation is that there are more comments than code, which is a good thing, allowing us to focus on the resulting DOM structure. You'll notice that there's no interaction with a Flux store in this module. Remember, this is a stateless React component, a simple arrow function, which means we don't have any life cycle methods to define, including the initial state. This is okay; let's see how we use both types of components in our `main.js` module:

```
import React from 'react';
import { render } from 'react-dom';
```

```
import Stateful from './views/stateful';
import Stateless from './views/stateless';
import myStore from './stores/my-store';
import { add } from './actions/add';

// These are the DOM element "containers" that
// our React components are rendered into.
var statefulContainer =
  document.getElementById('stateful');
var statelessContainer =
  document.getElementById('stateless');

// Sets up the store change listener for our
// "Stateless" React component. This is simple
// "render()" call, React efficiently handles
// the DOM diffing semantics.
myStore.on('change', (state) => {
  render(
    <Stateless items={myStore.state.items}/>,
    statelessContainer
  );
});

// Initial rendering of our two components.
render(
  <Stateful/>,
  statefulContainer
);

render(
  <Stateless items={myStore.state.items}/>,
  statelessContainer
);

// Dispatch some actions, causing our store to change,
// and our React components to re-render.
add('first');
add('second');
add('third');
```

The key difference here is that the Stateless view needs to have its interactions with the store set up manually here. The stateful component encapsulates this by setting up the change listener in the constructor.

Is one approach superior to the other? Within a Flux architecture, stateless React components tend to have an advantage over their stateful counterparts. This is due to the simple fact that they enforce the idea that state belongs in stores, nowhere else. When our React components are simple functions, we have no choice but to figure out the correct way to transform store state into something that can be consumed as simple immutable properties.

Composing views

Just as the state of our application is composed into stores, the views of that state are composed hierarchically to a degree. I say to a degree because we want to avoid decomposing the structure of our UI at a deep level, as this just makes it difficult to grasp. Where view composition really matters is when we have smaller parts that are used by many larger components. React is good at composing views without introducing too much complexity. In particular, stateless views are a good way to keep the vein of unidirectional data flow as it traverses the view levels. Let's look at an example. Here's a store with some initial state, which sorts this state upon a specific action:

```
import { EventEmitter } from 'events';
import dispatcher from '../dispatcher';
import { SORT_DESC } from '../actions/sort-desc';

class MyStore extends EventEmitter {
  constructor() {
    super();

    // The default store state has an array of
    // strings.
    this.state = {
      items: [
        'First',
        'Second',
        'Third'
      ]
    };

    this.id = dispatcher.register((e) => {
      switch(e.type) {

        // The "SORT_DESC" action sorts the
        // "items" array in descending order.
        case SORT_DESC:
```

```
        let { state } = this;

        state.items.sort().reverse();
        this.emit('change', state);
        break;
      }
    });
  }
}

export default new MyStore();
```

In this case, we would expect the array to be *Third*, *Second*, *First* (alphabetically) when the SORT_DESC action is dispatched. Now, let's look at the main view component that listens to this store:

```
import React from 'react';
import Item from './item';

// The application view. Renders a list of
// "Item" components.
export default ({ items }) => (
  <ul>
    {items.map(item =>
      <Item key={item}>{item}</Item>)}
  </ul>
);
```

Once again, we have a simple functional view that doesn't hold on to any state, because there's no need — all state is held in the Flux stores. Rather than use an li element here, we're using a custom Item React component that we've implemented for our application. This is part of the larger App view, and perhaps its part of other larger views. The result is code reuse and simplified aggregate views. Let's look at the Item component next:

```
import React from 'react';

// An "li" component with "strong" text.
export default (props) => (
  <li>
    <strong>{props.children}</strong>
  </li>
);
```

Not the most exciting view in the world, and in practice you'll find more complex atomic views than this. But the idea is the same—the value of `props.children` ultimately comes from a Flux store, and it traverses a parent view to get here. Let's see how all the pieces fit together in `main.js`:

```
import React from 'react';
import { render } from 'react-dom';

import myStore from './stores/my-store';
import App from './views/app';
import { sortDesc } from './actions/sort-desc';

// The containiner element for our application.
var appContainer = document.getElementById('app');

// Renders the "App" view component when
// the store state changes.
myStore.on('change', (state) => {
  render(
    <App {...state}/>,
    appContainer
  );
});

// Initial rendering...
render(
  <App {...myStore.state}/>,
  appContainer
);

// Perform the descending sort...
sortDesc();
```

Reacting to events

React components have their own event system baked into them. They're actually a wrapper around the DOM event system, making it easier for us to include event handling functions as part of the component JSX markup. This has implications for our Flux architecture too, because these events often translate directly to action creator function calls.

To get a feel for React events in a Flux context, let's build on the previous example. We'll add a button that toggles the sort order of our items. But first, we'll take a look at the store modifications required to support this new behavior:

```javascript
import { EventEmitter } from 'events';
import dispatcher from '../dispatcher';
import { SORT } from '../actions/sort';

// Constants for the direction label
// of the sort button.
const ASC = 'sort ascending';
const DESC = 'sort descending';

class MyStore extends EventEmitter {
  constructor() {
    super();

    // We have some "items", and a "direction"
    // as the default state of this store.
    this.state = {
      direction: ASC,
      items: [
        'Second',
        'First',
        'Third'
      ]
    };

    this.id = dispatcher.register((e) => {
      switch (e.type) {
        case SORT:
          let { state } = this;

          // The "items" are always sorted.
          state.items.sort()

          // If the current "direction" is ascending,
          // then update it to "DESC". Otherwise, it's
          // updated to "ASC" and the order is reversed.
          if (state.direction === ASC) {
            state.direction = DESC;
          } else {
            state.direction = ASC;
            state.items.reverse();
```

```
        }

        this.emit('change', state);
        break;
      }
    });
  }
}


export default new MyStore();
```

There's a new piece of state in MyStore—direction. It's relevant to both the sort direction of the items and the text content of the sort button in the view. Let's take a look at the new application view now:

```
import React from 'react';
import Sort from './sort';
import Item from './item';

// The application view. Renders a sort
// button and a list of "Item" components.
export default ({ items, direction }) => (
  <div>
    <Sort direction={direction}/>
    <ul>
      {items.map(item =>
        <Item key={item}>{item}</Item>) }
    </ul>
  </div>
);
```

You can see that the element returned by this stateless function is a div. Although not strictly necessary from a markup perspective, it is necessary from a React component perspective—rendering functions can only return one element. The Sort element we've added above the list represents the sort button. Let's take a look at this component now:

```
import React from 'react';
import { sort } from '../actions/sort';

// Some inline styles for the React view...
var style = {
  textTransform: 'capitalize'
};
```

```
// Renders a "button" element, with the
// "direction" store state as the label
// and the "sort()" action creator function
// is called when the button is clicked.
export default ({ direction }) => (
  <button
    style={style}
    onClick={sort}>{direction}
  </button>
);
```

This element is a simple `button` HTML element, with a style that will capitalize the `direction` label. You can see too that the `onClick` property is used to specify the event handler. In this case, it's simple — we're calling the `sort()` action creator function directly when the button is clicked.

> In practice, other state-handling actions might be dispatched in concert with the SORT action. For example, a PRE_SORT action might be necessary to handle button state.

Routing and actions

The `react-router` library is the de facto routing solution of ReactJS projects. If we're using React component for in the view layer of our Flux architecture, then there's a good chance that we'll want to use this package for routing in our application. However, there are some subtle nuances to be aware of when using `react-router` in the context of Flux. In this final section of the chapter, we'll address some of the tradeoffs we need to make with `react-router` by implementing it in a Flux architecture.

The basic premise of `react-router` is what makes it so attractive in the first place. The router and the routes within it are themselves React components that we can render into the DOM. We can declare that a given route should render a given React component when the route is activated. The router handles all of the nitty-gritty details for us. The question is, how does this work within the context of a Flux application? As we know, stores are where state lives in our application. So this means that they might want to know about the state of the router as well.

Let's start by looking at the `main.js` module, where the router component is declared and rendered:

```
import React from 'react';
import { render } from 'react-dom';
import { Router, Route, IndexRoute } from 'react-router';
```

```
import App from './views/app';
import First from './views/first';
import Second from './views/second';
import { routeUpdate } from './actions/route-update';

// The containiner element for our application.
var appContainer = document.getElementById('app');

// Called by the "Router" whenever a route changes.
// This is where we call the action creator
// "routeUpdate()", passing it the path of the
// new route.
function onUpdate() {
  routeUpdate(this.state.location.pathname);
}

// Renders the router components. Each route
// has an associated React component that's
// rendered when the route is activated.
render((
  <Router onUpdate={onUpdate}>
    <Route path="/" component={App}>
      <IndexRoute component={First}/>
      <Route path="first" components={First}/>
      <Route path="second" component={Second}/>
    </Route>
  </Router>
), appContainer);
```

You can see here that there are three main routes, the default / route, followed by a /first and a /second route. Each route has a corresponding component that's rendered when the route becomes active. What's interesting about these route declarations is that the First and Second components are children of App. This means that when their routes are activated, they're actually rendered within App. Let's take a look at the App component now:

```
import React from 'react';
import { Link } from 'react-router';

// Renders some links to the routes in the app.
// The "props.children" are any sub-components.
export default (props) => (
```

```
  <div>
    <ul>
      <li><Link to="/first">First</Link></li>
      <li><Link to="/second">Second</Link></li>
    </ul>
    {props.children}
  </div>
);
```

This component renders a list of links that point to our two routes—first and second.
It also renders child components through props.children. This is where the child
component is rendered. Let's turn our attention to the routeUpdate() action creator
function now. This is called by the Router component whenever the route changes:

```
import dispatcher from '../dispatcher';

// The action identifiers...
export const ROUTE_UPDATE = 'ROUTE_UPDATE';
export const PRE_ROUTE_UPDATE = 'PRE_ROUTE_UPDATE';

export function routeUpdate(payload) {

  // Immediately dispatch the "PRE_ROUTE_UPDATE"
  // action, giving stores a chance to adjust
  // their state while asynchronous activities happen.
  dispatcher.dispatch({
    type: PRE_ROUTE_UPDATE,
    payload: payload
  });

  // Dispatches the "ROUTE_UPDATE" action
  // after one second.
  setTimeout(() => {
    dispatcher.dispatch({
      type: ROUTE_UPDATE,
      payload: payload
    });
  }, 1000);
}
```

There's actually two actions that are dispatched by this function. First, there's the
`PRE_ROUTE_UPDATE` action, which is dispatched so that stores have an opportunity to
prepare for the changed route. Then, we perform some asynchronous behavior using
`setTimeout()` and then dispatch the `ROUTE_UPDATE` action. Now let's take a look at
one of the stores used by our components. We'll then look at one of the views that
listens to this store. The stores and views are nearly identical, so there's no need to
look at more than one of each:

```javascript
import { EventEmitter } from 'events';
import dispatcher from '../dispatcher';

// We need a couple action constants from
// the same action module.
import {
  PRE_ROUTE_UPDATE,
  ROUTE_UPDATE
} from '../actions/route-update';

class First extends EventEmitter {
  constructor() {
    super();

    // The "content" state is initially an
    // empty string.
    this.state = {
      content: ''
    };

    this.id = dispatcher.register((e) => {
      let { state } = this;

      switch(e.type) {

        // The "PRE_ROUTE_UPDATE" action means the
        // route is about to change once the
        // asynchronous code in the action creator
        // resolves. We can update the "content"
        // state here.
        case PRE_ROUTE_UPDATE:
          if (e.payload.endsWith('first')) {
            state.content = 'Loading...';
            this.emit('change', state);
          }
```

```
        break;

      // When the "ROUTE_UPDATE" action is dispatched,
      // we can change the content to show that it has
      // loaded.
      case ROUTE_UPDATE:
        if (e.payload.endsWith('first')) {
          state.content = 'First Loaded';
          this.emit('change', state);
        }
        break;
    }
  });
  }
}


export default new First();
```

The store updates its `content` state based on the action type and the current route. This is important because other areas of the application might want to know that this store is waiting for a route update to complete. Now let's look at the view that listens to this store:

```
import { default as React, Component } from 'react';
import first from '../stores/first';

export default class First extends Component {
  constructor() {
    super();

    // The initial state comes from the store.
    this.state = first.state;

    // The store "change" callback function is
    // defined here so that it can be bound to
    // "this" and set the component state.
    this.onChange = (state) => {
      this.setState(state);
    };
  }

  // Renders the HTML using "content".
  render() {
    return (
      <p>{this.state.content}</p>
```

```
    );
  }

  // Sets up the store "change" listener.
  componentWillMount() {
    first.on('change', this.onChange);
  }

  // Removes the store "change" listener.
  componentWillUnmount() {
    first.removeListener('change', this.onChange);
  }
}
```

This component is stateful because it has to be. Since it's the router that renders the component initially, we can't re-render it other than by setting its state. This is how we're able to re-render the component to reflect the state of the store—by setting up a handler for the change event. This component also has life cycle methods for listening to the change event of the store, as well as removing the listener. If we didn't remove it, it would try to set the state on a component that isn't mounted.

Summary

This chapter went into detail on the view layer of Flux architectures. Starting with getting information into views, you learned that the change event is fundamental in reflecting the state of the store in the view, and that views often read directly from stores during their initial render. Then, we went over the idea that views are stateless. The state of a given UI element belongs in a store, because other parts of the application might depend on this state, and we don't want to have to query the DOM.

Next, we went over some of the high-level responsibilities of view components. These include rendering store information, composing larger view structures out of smaller view components, and handling user interactivity. We wrapped the chapter up with a walkthrough of using ReactJS components as the view technology in a Flux architecture. In the following chapter, we'll dig into the life cycle of Flux components and how they differ from other architectures.

8

Information Lifecycle

Any information system has a lifecycle. Individual components in these systems have their own lifecycles as well. Cumulatively, these can be easy to deal with or overwhelmingly difficult. In frontend JavaScript architectures, the tendency is toward the latter. The reason is simple, the lifecycles that our components go through, fundamentally alter the flow of information over time in ways that are close to impossible to predict.

This chapter is about the information life cycle in Flux architectures. Flux is different from other architectures in that it puts emphasis on scaling information instead of on JavaScript components. We'll begin exploring this theme with a look at the difficulties we've faced for years, using the typical component lifecycles found in modern JavaScript frameworks. Then, we'll contrast this approach with that of Flux, where high-level components are relatively static.

Next, we'll jump into the concept of scaling information and how this leads to more sane architectures that are much easier to maintain than alternative approaches. We'll close the chapter with a discussion on inactive stores—stores that aren't actively serving a view with data. Let's get to it.

Component life cycle difficulties

One aspect of scaling a frontend architecture is cleaning up unused resources. This frees memory for new resources that get created as the user interacts with the application. JavaScript is garbage-collected, meaning that once an object doesn't have any references to it, it's eligible for collection the next time the collector runs. This gets us partway there; in that, there's no need to manually allocate/de-allocate memory. However, we have a whole other category of scaling issues, and they're all related to the lifecycle of components.

In this section, we'll talk about the scenarios where we want to reclaim unused resources and how this generally happens in frontend architectures. Then, we'll look at the challenges that component dependencies present, in the context of lifecycle management. Finally, we'll look at memory leak scenarios. Even with the best tools in place, there's always the possibility that our code has done something to circumvent memory management.

Reclaiming unused resources

Something that happens a lot throughout the course of an application, is that new resources are created while old resources are destroyed. This is in response to user interactivity—as they traverse the features of the application, new components get created in order to present new information. Much of this creation and destruction of JavaScript objects and DOM elements is transparent to us—the tools we employ can take care of this for us. The following diagram captures the idea of a component that frees internal resources as it changes state:

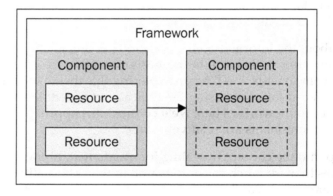

The key lies with the lifecycle of our components. Depending on the framework that's responsible for managing this lifecycle, different things can happen at different times. For instance, your component is instantiated and stored when it's parent component is created. When your component is rendered, it inserts new DOM elements and keeps a reference to them. Finally, when the component's parent is destroyed, our component is instructed to remove its DOM elements and release any references to them. This is an oversimplified work-flow, but the general idea is the same no matter how many moving parts there are. The job of the tools we use is to handle the lifecycle of our components in a way that reclaims unused components.

Why is reclaiming unused components so important? The fundamental limitation we face is that memory is finite, and we're trying to build a robust application that scales well. Removing components from memory when they're no longer needed, makes room for new components to be created when they're needed. So, what's the big deal if we're using a framework that has well-defined lifecycles for our components and handles a lot of the messy details for us?

One limiting factor to this approach is that with a complex application that has lots of moving parts, the framework is constantly creating and destroying objects. This inevitably leads to the garbage collector getting invoked frequently, causing pauses in the main JavaScript execution thread. In the worst case, this can lead to pauses in the user experience due to unresponsive user events. The other potential pitfall of automatically managed component lifecycles is that the framework doesn't always know what we're thinking, and this can lead to hidden dependencies that end up breaking the flow of the component create/destroy lifecycle.

Hidden dependencies

Patterns that define the lifecycle of a particular type of component are a good thing—provided that our components abide by their lifecycle one hundred percent of the time. This rarely works out because we're trying to build something unique that solves a problem for our users, not a piece of software that plays nice with a framework just for the sake of it. The biggest risk here is that we'll accidentally prevent the framework from properly freeing resources by introducing dependencies. These dependencies might make perfect sense in the context of our application, but as far as the framework is concerned, it doesn't know about them, and this breaks in unpredictable ways. Take a look at the following diagram:

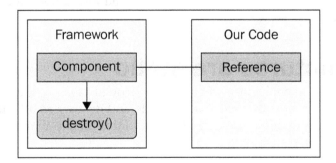

The actual scenarios we face will be a little more nuanced than the scenario depicted here. The general theme is that frameworks that manage lifecycles are unforgiving. All it takes is a dependency in the wrong place to completely invalidate everything that the framework is doing for the application. However, this is the cost/benefit of having lifecycles for architectural components in the first place. The benefit being that we need to reclaim components to make way for new ones, and if a framework can automate this arduous task for us, all the better. The risk is that any time things are created and destroyed, there's a chance that this isn't done properly, leading to memory leaks.

Memory leaks

When our code is constantly creating and destroying objects, the JavaScript garbage collector thrashes, and we experience performance hiccups. However, this is a minor problem compared to leaky JavaScript components that are never fully garbage-collected. This tends to happen when our application code has ideas that don't quite fit with those of the framework that manages the lifecycle of our components. Obviously memory leaks are a huge scalability issue and one that want to avoid at all costs.

So what we have are two related scalability issues with regard to the lifecycle of components in our architecture. First, we don't want to constantly create and destroy objects because this has garbage-collection pausing problems. Second, we don't want to leak memory by introducing hidden dependencies that the framework isn't aware of, breaking the intended lifecycle. As we'll see in the following section, Flux architectures help with both aspects of component lifecycle issues. There isn't a lot of creation/destruction of components in a Flux architecture. This reduces the probability of introducing logic that breaks the lifecycle of a given component. Later in the chapter, we'll see how Flux focuses on information rather than JavaScript components to achieve scale.

Flux structures are static

Given that the need to constantly create and destroy objects presents an opportunity for scaling issues, it seems that we should create and destroy as little as possible. It turns out that Flux architectures are different in this area in that much of the component infrastructure is static.

In this section, we'll look at what sets Flux apart from other architectures in this regard, starting with the singleton pattern that's used by many modules. Then, we'll compare the traditional MVC model approach to Flux stores. Lastly, we'll take a look at static view components and see if this is an idea worth pursuing in order to achieve scale.

Singleton pattern

As you've probably noticed by now, most of the modules we've worked with so far in this book have exported a single instance. The dispatcher exposes a single instance of the `Dispatcher` class from the Facebook Flux package. This is the singleton pattern in action.

The basic idea is that there's only one instance of a class, creating more is never necessary because the first instance is all we'll ever need. This bodes well with the scaling issues we've discussed in this chapter, where constant creation and destruction makes our code vulnerable to errors. These errors ultimately prevent the application from scaling, due to memory leaks or performance problems.

Instead, Flux architectures tend to assemble the plumbing between the components at startup time, and this pluming stays in place permanently. Think about the physical plumbing where you live, it sits idle when it's not being used. However, the cost of tearing out the physical plumbing to reclaim the space, and the cost of replacing it when needed simply doesn't add up. The overhead of having static plumbing structures within our walls isn't a scaling bottleneck in our day-to-day lives.

So while we can avoid some of the creation and destruction of objects by following the singleton pattern, there are tradeoffs. For example, the single pattern isn't necessarily a good pattern. At least not in all our modules where everything is a class, and yet, everything is only instantiated once. Let's look at a store module and see if we can implement something that doesn't actually require a store. First, let's implement a typical store module which exports a singleton class instance for comparison:

```
import { EventEmitter } from 'events';
import dispatcher from '../dispatcher';
import { MY_ACTION } from '../actions/my-action';

// A typical Flux store class. This module
// exports a singleton instance of it.
class SingletonStore extends EventEmitter {
  constructor() {
    super();

    this.state = {
      pending: true
    };

    this.id = dispatcher.register((e) => {
      switch(e.type) {
```

```
        case MY_ACTION:
          this.state.pending = false;
          this.emit('change', this.state);
          break;
      }
    });
  }
}

export default new SingletonStore();
```

There's only a handful of properties that the outside world requires from this module. It needs the state, so other components can read it. It needs the identifier of dispatcher registration, so other components can depend on it using `waitFor()`. And, it needs the `EventEmitter`, so other components can listen for store state changes. Let's now implement a store that doesn't actually require instantiating a new class:

```
import { EventEmitter } from 'events';
import dispatcher from '../dispatcher';
import { MY_ACTION } from '../actions/my-action';

// Exports the state of this store...
export var state = {
  pending: true
};

// Exports the "id" of the dispatcher registration
// so that other stores can depend on this module.
export var id = dispatcher.register((e) => {
  switch(e.type) {
    case MY_ACTION:
      state.pending = false;
      emitter.emit('change', state);
      break;
  }
});

// We need to create a new "EventEmitter" here
// since there's no class to extend it.
const emitter = new EventEmitter();

// Exports the minimal interface that views
// require to listen/unlisten to stores.
export const on = emitter.on.bind(emitter);
export const off = emitter.removeListener.bind(emitter);
```

As you can see, we're exporting the bare necessities that allow other components to treat this module as a store. And it is indeed a store, it's simply structured differently. Instead of exporting a singleton class instance, which has the essential store interface, we're directly exporting the pieces of the interface. Is there any fundamental advantage to either approach? No, there's not. If you prefer classes and the ability to extend a base class, then stick with the singleton pattern. If you feel that classes are ugly and unnecessary, stick with the module approach.

At the end of the day, the architectural result is the same. The store simply exists. There's no need to create and destroy the store as the user interacts with the application. There's nothing preventing us from doing this—setting up and tearing down stores as the state of the application changes. But as we'll see later in the chapter, there's really no advantage to doing this, just as there's no advantage to tearing your walls apart when the sink isn't running.

Let's see these two stores in action. Aside from how they're imported, they're indistinguishable:

```
import { myAction } from './actions/my-action';
import singletonStore from './stores/singleton-store';

// Note that "moduleStore" is a module, with everything
// that it exports, not a class instance.
import * as moduleStore from './stores/module-store';

// Registers a "change" callback with the singleton
// store...
singletonStore.on('change', (state) => {
  console.log('singleton', state.pending);
});

// Registers a "change" callback with the module
// store. Not that it looks and feels exactly
// like a class instance.
moduleStore.on('change', (state) => {
  console.log('module', state.pending);
});

// Triggers the "MY_ACTION" action.
myAction();
```

Comparison to models

Remember the idea that stores represent features at the top-level of our application? Well, top-level features generally aren't created and destroyed constantly throughout the lifetime of the application. Models on the other hand, our friends from the family of MV* architectures, often represent more fine-grained data domains. And because of this, they need to pop in and out of existence.

For example, suppose we're on the search page of an application, and there's a bunch of results displayed. The individual results are likely models, representative of some structure returned by the API. The view that renders the search results probably knows how to display these modules. When the results change or the user navigates to another part of the application, the models are inevitably destroyed. This is part of the whole lifecycle discussion we had earlier in the chapter. It's not a simple deletion—there's cleanup steps that need to be performed.

With Flux stores, we don't have the same level of complexity. There's views that listen to a given store, but that's it. When the state of a store changes, like when some search result data is deleted from the store state, the views are notified. It's then up to the view to reflect this changed data by re-rendering the UI. With Flux, the cleanup is a simple deletion problem, both from the point of view of the DOM and of the store. The fact that we're not blowing away entire stores while the user interacts with the application means that there's less chance for our architectural components to fall out of sync with one another.

Static views

Since views are the components responsible for rendering information that the user can see, it would make sense that the view is cleaned up when the user isn't looking at it, right? Well, not necessarily. Revisiting the plumbing analogy, when we leave the kitchen, we turn the tap in the sink off. We don't get a toolbox and start ripping out pipes. The notion that views in a Flux architecture can be static is in fact viable. It's the water we need to turn off in order to scale, not the plumbing.

Let's look at some views that are created at startup and never destroyed as the user interacts with the application. First, we'll implement a class-based static view:

```
import myStore from '../stores/my-store';

class ClassView {
  constructor() {

    // The "container" DOM element for this view.
    this.container =
```

```
      document.getElementById('class-view');

    // Render the new state when "myStore" changes.
    myStore.on('change', (state) => {
      this.render(state);
    });
  }

  render({ classContent } = myStore.state) {

    // Sets the content of the container element.
    // This is done by reducing the "classContent"
    // array to a single string. If it's empty,
    // any existing DOM elements are removed from
    // the container.
    this.container.innerHTML = classContent.reduce(
      (x, y) => `<strong>${x + y}</strong>`, '');
  }
}

export default new ClassView();
```

This looks like your typical class that you would find in a Flux architecture. It's instantiated within the module and exported. The content itself is rendered by reducing an array to a `<strong>` tag. We'll see why we're rendering such a tag like this when we look at the store. But first, let's look at another static view that takes the form of a function:

```
import React from 'react';

// Renders the view content using a functional
// React component.
export default ({content}) => (
  <strong>{content}</strong>
);
```

This is the functional style of React components that you were introduced to in the previous chapter. As you can see, there's nothing much to it, as React takes care of a lot of the heavy lifting for us. Now let's take a look at the store that both of these views relies on for information:

```
import { EventEmitter } from 'events';
import dispatcher from '../dispatcher';
import { SHOW_CLASS, SHOW_FUNCTION } from '../actions/show';

class MyStore extends EventEmitter {
  constructor() {
```

```
        super();

        // The two content properties of this store's state
        // empty arrays, meaning empty content.
        this.state = {
          classContent: [],
          functionContent: []
        };

        this.id = dispatcher.register((e) => {
          let {state} = this;

          switch(e.type) {

              // If the "SHOW_CLASS" action was dispatched,
              // the "classContent" state gets a single item
              // array and the "functionContent" state gets
              // and empty array.
              case SHOW_CLASS:
                Object.assign(state, {
                  classContent: [ 'Class View' ],
                  functionContent: []
                });

                this.emit('change', state);
                break;

              // If the "SHOW_FUNCTION" action was dispatched,
              // the "functionContent" state gets a single item
              // array and the "classContent" state gets an
              // empty array.
              case SHOW_FUNCTION:
                Object.assign(state, {
                  classContent: [],
                  functionContent: [ 'Function View' ]
                });

                this.emit('change', state);
                break;
          }
        });
    }
}

export default new MyStore();
```

You can see that both actions—SHOW_CLASS and SHOW_FUNCTION—are processed the same way. One action sets a piece of state while deleting another. Let's discuss this approach here for a moment. The classContent and functionContent state properties both use single-item arrays for a string value. Both of our views iterate over these arrays—using map() and reduce(). The reason we're doing it this way is to keep logic out of the views. The business logic that operates on stores should stay in the store. However, views need to know what to display and what to remove. By always iterating over a collection, like an array, the content generation is consistent and logic-free. Let's see how both of these views are used in main.js:

```
import React from 'react';
import { render } from 'react-dom';

import { showClass, showFunction } from './actions/show';
import myStore from './stores/my-store';
import classView from './views/class';
import FunctionView from './views/function';

// The DOM element used by our "FunctionView"
// component.
var functionContainer = document
  .getElementById('function-view');

// Utility to render the "FunctionView" React
// component. Called by the store "change"
// handler and to perform the initial rendering.
function renderFunction(state) {
  render(
    <FunctionView
      content={state.functionContent}/>,
    functionContainer
  );
}

// Sets up the "change" handler for "FunctionView"...
myStore.on('change', renderFunction);

// Perform the initial rendering of both views...
classView.render();
renderFunction(myStore.state);

// Dispatch the "SHOW_CLASS" action.
showClass();
```

```
// Wait one second, then dispatch the "SHOW_FUNCTION"
// action.
setTimeout(() => {
  showFunction();
}, 1000);
```

The `classView` is straightforward to use. It's imported and rendered. The store state handling is encapsulated within the `view` module. The `FunctionView` React component on the other hand, needs to be set up with a handler function that's called when `myStore` changes state. Technically, this isn't a static view, because it's a function that's called whenever `React.render()` is called. However, in the context of Flux, it does behave a lot like a static view, because it's the React rendering system that handles the creation and destruction of view components—our code isn't creating or destroying anything—only passing components to `render()`.

Scaling information

As you've seen so far in this chapter, Flux doesn't try to scale things that don't need to be scaled. For example, stores and views are often created just once during startup. Trying to clean these components repeatedly as the application changes state over time is simply error-prone. It's scaling the information that Flows through our Flux components that will knock our system over if we're not careful.

We'll start this section off with a look at how our Flux architectures can scale well on their own, without massive amounts of data entering the system. This also serves to illustrate the idea that these are in fact two separate problems—scaling the infrastructure of our Flux components versus scaling the volume of data that our architecture is able to process. Then, we'll discuss the topic of designing our user interfaces for less information, to make the design process of scalable components straightforward. We'll explore the role of Flux actions when it comes time to scale our system up to the next level.

What scales well?

As our application grows, it needs to scale in response to things like new feature requests, and growing datasets. The question is, which of these scaling issues is most deserving of our attention? It should be the issue with the highest potential to topple our system. Generally speaking, this has more to do with the input data than it does with the configuration of our Flux components. For instance, there's a potential scaling issue if we're processing input data in polynomial time instead of logarithmic time.

This is why our Flux architecture doesn't need to concern itself with lifecycles and maintaining the plumbing between components the same way other architectures do. Will having a lot of components occupy more memory than they need to and is this expensive in terms of performance? Sure, this is always a consideration—we don't want to have more components then we need. In practice, this type of overhead is hardly noticeable by users. Let's take look at the impact a large component infrastructure has on performance. First, the view:

```
// A really simple view...
export default class MyView {
  constructor(store) {

    // Do nothing except verify that there's
    // a "result" state property.
    store.on('change', ({ result }) => {
      console.assert(
        Number.isInteger(result),
        'MyView'
      );
    });
  }
}
```

There's nothing much to this view because there doesn't need to be. We're not testing the rendering performance of the view itself—we're testing the scalability of the architecture. So all that's required is that the view exists and can listen to a store. We're passing the store instance in through the constructor because we're creating several instances of this view that listen to different stores, as we'll see here in a moment. Let's look at the store code next:

```
import { EventEmitter } from 'events';
import dispatcher from '../dispatcher';
import { MY_ACTION } from '../actions/my-action';

// We're exporting the store class instead of
// an instance from this module because the
// main module will create a bunch of them.
export default class MyStore extends EventEmitter {
  constructor() {
    super();

    // The EventEmitter thinks we're leaking memory
    // there's too many listeners. This circumvents
    // the limitation.
```

```
      this.setMaxListeners(5000);

      this.state = {};

      this.id = dispatcher.register((e) => {
        let {state} = this;

        // Perform some basic arithmetic before emitting
        // the "change" event with the "result" state
        // property.
        switch(e.type) {
          case MY_ACTION:
            state.result = 100000 * e.payload;
            this.emit('change', state);
            break;
        }
      });
    }
  }
```

This is a pretty basic store that does a pretty basic calculation when MY_ACTION is dispatched. Again, this is intentional. Now let's see how these components can scale in a Flux architecture without much data:

```
import MyStore from './stores/my-store';
import MyView from './views/my-view';
import { myAction } from './actions/my-action';

// Holds onto our store and view references...
var stores = [];
var views = [];

// How many items to create and actions to
// dispatch...
var storeCount = 100;
var viewCount = 1000;
var actionCount = 10;

// Setup our Flux infrastructure. This establishes
// all the relevant store listeners and view
// listeners. They all stay active throughout the
// lifetime of the application.
console.time('startup');
for (let i = 0; i < storeCount; i++) {
  let store = new MyStore();
  stores.push(store);
```

```
    for (let i = 0; i < viewCount; i++) {
      views.push(new MyView(store));
    }
  }
console.timeEnd('startup')
// → startup: 26.286ms

console.log('stores', stores.length);
console.log('views', views.length);
console.log('actions', actionCount);
// →
// stores 100
// views 100000
// actions 10

// Dispatches the actions. This is where we either
// succeed or fail at scaling the architecture.
console.time('dispatch');
for (let i = 0; i < actionCount; i++) {
  myAction();
}
console.timeEnd('dispatch');
// → dispatch: 443.929ms
```

We're measuring the startup cost of creating these components and setting up their listeners, because this will typically add to the startup cost of a Flux application. But as we can see here, getting all these components ready is inconsequential in terms of user experience. The big test comes when the actions are dispatched.

This setup causes one million view render calls to happen, and it takes about half a second. This is the plumbing in the wall of our application, and it really doesn't benefit us to tear it down and set it all back up again later. This aspect of the architecture scales well. It's the data that enters the system, and the logic that operates on it that's the real scaling challenge. If we have to run this same test again with an action payload of a 1000 item array that was sorted by the store, we might have a problem.

 We'll address more fine-grained performance testing scenarios in Chapter 13, *Testing and Benchmarking*.

Minimal information required

As you just saw, the notion that Flux components and their connections can be statically-defined is valid. At least, in terms of scaling challenges, having static plumbing in place isn't going to be the thing that knocks our system down when we try to scale it. It's the data that flows into the system, and the means by which we transform it into information for the user. This is the thing that's very difficult to scale, and so, it's best that we do as little of it as possible.

It may sound trivially obvious at first, but having less information to display scales well. This can easily be overlooked because we're out to build features, not to measure the volume of information output from our views. Sometimes, this is the most effective way, or possibly the only way, to fix scaling problems.

When we're designing a Flux architecture for our application, we have to keep information scalability in mind. Often, the best angle to look at the problem is from the UI itself. If there's a way that we can axe certain things, in an effort to reduce clutter, we also reduce the amount of information that views need to generate. Potentially, we can remove an entire data flow from our application simply by changing what the user sees. Lean user interfaces scale well.

Something else to be on the lookout for is information that leaks out of store components. By this, I mean information that a store generates for no real purpose. This could have been something that used to be relevant to how the view worked, but when the feature changed, we forgot to take out the relevant information. Or, it could simply be an oversight in the design—we're generating information that the view doesn't actually need, and its been this way from day one. These problems are difficult to spot, but easy to fix. The only foolproof approach is to periodically audit our views to ensure that they're consuming the information that they need and nothing more.

Actions that scale

Actions are the gatekeepers of any data that wants to enter our Flux system—if it's not an action payload, then it's not data that we care about. Action creator functions aren't problematic to scale, as they don't do much. The most complex aspect of an action creator function is managing asynchronous behavior, if necessary. But this isn't a fundamental scaling problem, every JavaScript application has asynchronous components. There's two fundamental ways that actions can thwart our scaling efforts.

The first is having too many actions. This means that there's more opportunity for programmer error due to all the possibilities. It becomes less obvious which action creator should be used in which context. The same problem can happen when there are few actions and too many action creator parameters. This directly inhibits our ability to get the right data into the stores of our application.

The second way that actions can stumble when we try to scale our system is that the action creator functions are doing too much. For example, an action creator function might try to filter out some of the API response data in an effort to slim down the data that's handed off to the stores through the dispatcher. This is hugely problematic, because it violates the Flux rule that all state and all logic that changes state belongs in stores.

It's understandable how something like this can happen though, when under pressure to scale an application, the most obvious place to fix data problems is at the source. In this case, the source is the handler of the AJAX response. The better way to handle this is to tweak the API itself and have the action creator function supply the appropriate parameters to get the smaller set of data. When state transformations move outside of stores in the frontend, we reduce the likelihood of scaling successfully because we increase the likelihood of other issues taking place.

Inactive stores

In the previous section, we explored the idea that we can have a relatively static component infrastructure in our Flux architecture. This isn't something that causes concerns about scalability. Rather, it's the large amounts of data that's held in our stores. In this final section, we'll cover some scenarios in which we have a store with lots of data as its state, and we don't want our application to become memory-bloated.

The first approach involves deleting the data from the store, freeing resources. We can take this approach a step further by adding heuristics to our store logic that determines that nothing has changed and there's no need to touch the DOM by emitting a change event. Finally, we'll talk about some of the side-effects caused by deleting store data and how to deal with them.

Deleting store data

Something we have to think long and hard about with our Flux components is how data that enters the system will eventually exit the system. If we only put data in without taking any of it out, we've got a problem. In fact, this activity is fundamental to Flux architectures, because removing data from store states is also how we remove other data structures, such as DOM nodes and event handler functions.

Earlier in the chapter, we saw that by emptying an array, we could tell the view to remove UI elements. This is essentially how we scale Flux applications—by removing the data that has potential to cause scaling headaches. Imagine a store that had a collection with thousands of items in it. This collection would not only be expensive to process as is, but it also has the potential to grow much larger.

The simple solution is to empty this collection out when it's no longer needed. Let's revisit this approach. First, here's what the view looks like:

```
import React from 'react';
import { hideAll, hideOdd } from '../actions/hide';

// The view function, renders a button
// that deletes store data by dispatching
// the "HIDE_ALL" action, and renders a list
// of items. The hide odds button only deletes
// some store data by dispatching the "HIDE_ODD"
// action.
export default ({ items }) => (
  <div>
    <button onClick={hideAll}>Hide All</button>
    <button onClick={hideOdd}>Hide Odd</button>
    <ul>
      {items.map(item =>
        <li key={item}>{item}</li>
      )}
    </ul>
  </div>
);
```

A couple of buttons and a list of items—pretty simple. When a button is clicked, it calls an action creator function. Let's turn our attention to the store now:

```
import { EventEmitter } from 'events';
import dispatcher from '../dispatcher';
import { HIDE_ALL, HIDE_ODD } from '../actions/hide';

class MyStore extends EventEmitter {
  constructor() {
    super();

    // The initial state is an "items" array
    // of 100 numbers.
    this.state = {
      items: new Array(100)
        .fill(null)
        .map((x, y) => y)
    };

    this.id = dispatcher.register((e) => {
      let { state } = this;
```

```
        switch(e.type) {

            // When the "HIDE_ALL" action is dispatched,
            // the "items" state is reset back to
            // an empty array.
            case HIDE:
                state.items = []
                this.emit('change', state);
                break;

            // When the "HIDE_ODD" action is dispatched,
            // the "items" state is filtered to include
            // only even numbers.
            case HIDE_ODD:
                state.items = state.items.filter(
                    x => !(x % 2));
                this.emit('change', state);
                break;
        }
    });
    }
}

export default new MyStore();
```

The HIDE_ALL action simply deletes all the items by assigning an empty array. This is exactly what we're after—deleting data when it's no longer needed. This is the real scaling challenge, cleaning up data that has the potential to be big and expensive to process. The HIDE_ODD action is a variation that filters out even numbers. Lastly, let's see how this all comes together in main.js:

```
import React from 'react';
import { render } from 'react-dom';

import myStore from './stores/my-store';
import MyView from './views/my-view';

// The DOM container for the React view...
var container = document.getElementById('my-view');

// Renders the functional "MyView" React
// component.
function renderView(state) {
    render(
        <MyView
            items={state.items}/>,
```

```
        container
    );
}

// Re-render the React component when the store
// state changes.
myStore.on('change', renderView);

// Perform the initial render.
renderView(myStore.state);
```

Optimizing inactive stores

One potential scaling issue with the setup we've used in the preceding example is that the view itself performs some expensive computation. For example, we can't rule out the possibility that even with an empty array as the supplied information to render, the view has some implementation issues. This is problematic in a Flux architecture, because actions are always being dispatched to stores, which in turn notify views that are listening to them. So it's important that views are fast.

This is where React fits really well into Flux. React components are meant to be re-rendered in a top–down fashion, from the root component all the way down to the leaves. It's able to do this efficiently because of the virtual DOM it uses under the hood to compute patches that are then applied to the real DOM. This eliminates many performance issues because issuing a lot of DOM API calls is a performance bottleneck. On the other hand, it would be slightly naive to assume that the store will be publishing changes to an efficient React component.

Stores are responsible for emitting change events when the time is right. Therefore, we could determine within the store that when a given action is dispatched, there's no need to emit a change event. This would involve some sort of heuristic that would determine that the view is already displaying the appropriate information given the state of the store, and that emitting a change event now would be of no value. By doing this, we could avoid any performance challenges in the view. The problem with this approach is that we're building up complexity in our store. It's probably better that we emit change events consistently and deal with views that are doing things inefficiently. Or if we're not using React as the view layer yet, perhaps this is an argument in favor of doing so.

 In the next chapter, we'll look at implementing advanced change detection heuristics in our view components.

Keeping store data

In this chapter, you've seen how to remove data from stores in a way that scales well. If the user has moved from one part of the user interface to another, then we likely want to delete any store data that's no longer needed in this new section. The idea is that rather than take out all of our JavaScript components, we focus on the data in our stores, the aspect of our application that's the most difficult to scale. However, there's a potential problem with this approach that we need to consider.

What happens if another store depends on the data that we've just removed? For example, the user is on a page that's driven by state from store A. They then move on to another page, which is driven by store B, which depends on store A. But we've just deleted the state inside of store A—isn't this going to be a problem for store B?

This isn't a common case—the majority of our stores won't have any dependencies, and we should be safe to delete unused data. However, we need to come up with a game plan for stores that do have dependencies. Let's walk through an example and start with the views. First, we have the radio button view, which is a simple control that allows the user to toggle from a list of users to a list of groups:

```
import React from 'react';
import { id } from '../util';
import { showUsers, showGroups } from '../actions/show';


// This react view displays the two radio
// buttons that determine which list to display.
// Note that they're both using "map()" even
// though it's a single item array. This is to
// keep the logic in the store and out of the view.
export default ({ users, groups }) => (
  <div>
    {users.map(user =>
      <label key={id.next()}>
        {user.label}
        <input
          type="radio"
          name="display"
          checked={user.checked}
          onChange={showUsers}
        />
      </label>
    )}
    {groups.map(group =>
      <label key={id.next()}>
        {group.label}
```

```
          <input
            type="radio"
            name="display"
            checked={group.checked}
            onChange={showGroups}
          />
        </label>
      )}
    </div>
  );
```

The change event for both radio buttons is hooked up to an action creator function, which affects the display of our two other views—we'll look at these next, starting with the user list view:

```
import React from 'react';

// A simple React view that displays a list of
// users.
export default ({ users }) => (
  <ul>
    {users.map(({ name, groupName }) =>
      <li key={name}>{name} ({groupName})</li>
    )}
  </ul>
);
```

Pretty straightforward, and you can see that there's a group dependency here, as we're displaying the group that the user belongs to. We'll dig into that dependency momentarily, but for now, let's look at the group list view:

```
import React from 'react';

// A simple React view that displays a list
// of groups...
export default ({ groups }) => (
  <ul>
    {groups.map(group =>
      <li key={group}>{group}</li>
    )}
  </ul>
);
```

Now, let's take a look at the stores that drive these views, starting with the radio button store:

```
import { EventEmitter } from 'events';
import dispatcher from '../dispatcher';

import { SHOW_USERS, SHOW_GROUPS } from '../actions/show';

class Radio extends EventEmitter {
  constructor() {
    super();

    // This store represents radio buttons for
    // the "users" and "groups" display. Each
    // is represented as an array so that we can
    // easily take the take the button out of
    // the view by emptying the array.
    this.state = {
      users: [{
        label: 'Users',
        checked: true
      }],
      groups: [{
        label: 'Groups',
        checked: false
      }]
    };

    this.id = dispatcher.register((e) => {

      // Easy access to the state properties
      // we need in this handler. See the two
      // getter methods below.
      let { users, groups } = this;

      switch(e.type) {

        // Mark the "users" display as "checked".
        case SHOW_USERS:
          users.checked = true;
          groups.checked = false;

          this.emit('change', this.state);
```

```
            break;

        // Mark the "groups" display as "checked".
        case SHOW_GROUPS:
          users.checked = false;
          groups.checked = true;

          this.emit('change', this.state);
          break;
      }
    });
  }

  // A shortcut for easy access to the "users" state.
  get users() {
    return this.state.users[0]
  }

  // A shortcut for easy access to the "groups" state.
  get groups() {
    return this.state.groups[0]
  }
}

export default new Radio();
```

You can see here that we're using the single-item array technique once again. This is why we have the map() call in the view that uses this store's data. The idea is that to hide one of these buttons, we can do it right here in the store by setting it to an empty collection—keeping logic out of the view. Notice that we've set up some basic getter functions to make dealing with these single-item arrays easier as well. Now let's check out the groups store:

```
import { EventEmitter } from 'events';
import dispatcher from '../dispatcher';
import { SHOW_GROUPS } from '../actions/show';

class Groups extends EventEmitter {
  constructor() {
    super();

    // The default "_group" state is an array of group
    // names.
    this.state = {
      _groups: [
        'Group 1',
        'Group 2'
```

```
    ]
  };

  // The "groups" state is what's actually used
  // by views and is an empty array by default
  // because nothing is displayed by default.
  this.state.groups = [];

  this.id = dispatcher.register((e) => {
    let { state } = this;

    switch(e.type) {

      // The "SHOW_GROUPS" action will map the
      // "_groups" state to the "groups" state
      // so that the view has something to display.
      case SHOW_GROUPS:
        state.groups = state._groups.map(x => x);
        this.emit('change', state);
        break;

      // By default, the "groups" state is emptied,
      // which clears out the view's elements. The
      // "_groups" state, however, remains intact.
      default:
        state.groups = [];
        this.emit('change', state);
        break;
    }
  });
  }
}

export default new Groups();
```

This store has two pieces of state—_groups and groups. Yes, they're basically the same thing. The difference is that the view depends on groups, not on _groups. The Groups store is able to compute the groups state based on _groups. This means that we can safely delete the groups state to update the view rendering while the _groups state isn't touched. Other stores can depend on this store now, without risk of any data disappearing. Let's take a look at the users store now:

```
import { EventEmitter } from 'events';
import dispatcher from '../dispatcher';
import groups from './groups';
import { SHOW_USERS } from '../actions/show';
```

```
class Users extends EventEmitter {
  constructor() {
    super();

    // The default state of the "_users" state is
    // an array of user objects with references to
    // groups from another store.
    this.state = {
      _users: [
        { name: 'User 1', group: 1 },
        { name: 'User 2', group: 0 },
        { name: 'User 3', group: 1 }
      ]
    };

    // Sets the "users" state array, the state
    // that's actually used by views. See
    // "mapUsers()" below.
    this.mapUsers();

    this.id = dispatcher.register((e) => {
      let { state } = this;

      switch(e.type) {

        // If we're showing users, we need to "waitFor()"
        // the "groups" store because we depend on it.
        // Then we can use "mapUsers()" again.
        case SHOW_USERS:
          dispatcher.waitFor([ groups.id ]);

          this.mapUsers();

          this.emit('change', state);
          break;

        // The default action is to empty out
        // the "users" state so that the view
        // will delete the UI elements. However, the
        // "_users" state remains, so that other stores
        // that depend on this one can still access
        // the data.
        default:
          state.users = [];
```

```
                this.emit('change', state);
                break;
        }
    });
  }

  // Maps the "_users" state to the "users" state.
  // The idea being that the "users" array can be
  // emptied to update view displays while the "_users"
  // array remains intact for other stores to use.
  mapUsers() {
    this.state.users = this.state._users.map(user =>
      Object.assign({
        groupName: groups.state._groups[user.group]
      }, user)
    );
  }
}

export default new Users();
```

You can see that the Users store is able to depend on the _groups state from the Groups store in order to build the state that's needed by the user list view. This store follows the same pattern as the Groups store in that it has a _users state and a users state. This allows for other views to depend on _users if necessary, and we can still wipe the users state to clear the UI. However, if it turns out that nothing is dependent on this store, we can revert the pattern so that there's only one piece of state that's deleted when no longer required by the current view. Lastly, let's take a look at the main.js module and see how this all fits together:

```
import React from 'react';
import { render } from 'react-dom';

import radio from './stores/radio';
import users from './stores/users';
import groups from './stores/groups';

import Radio from './views/radio';
import Users from './views/users';
import Groups from './views/groups';

// The container DOM element...
var container = document.getElementById('app');

// Renders the React components. The state for the
```

```
// Flux stores are passed in as props.
function renderApp(
  radioState=radio.state,
  usersState=users.state,
  groupsState=groups.state
) {
  render(
    <div>
      <Radio
        users={radioState.users}
        groups={radioState.groups}/>
      <Users
        users={usersState.users}/>
      <Groups
        groups={groupsState.groups}/>
    </div>,
    container
  );
}

// Renders the app with the new "radio" state.
radio.on('change', (state) => {
  renderApp(state, users.state, groups.state);
});

// Renders the app with the new "users" state.
users.on('change', (state) => {
  renderApp(radio.state, state, groups.state);
});

// Renders the app with the new "groups" state.
groups.on('change', (state) => {
  renderApp(radio.state, users.state, state);
});

// Initial app rendering...
renderApp();
```

Summary

The focus of scaling a Flux architecture is on the information that stores produce, rather than the various components. This chapter started with a discussion on the common practices of other architectures that involve the constant creation and destruction of JavaScript components. This is done to free resources, but it comes at a cost—the potential for error. Next, we looked at the relatively static nature of Flux architectures, where components have a long life. They don't have to constantly create and destroy components, which means that there's less potential for issues.

Next, we covered the concept of scaling information. We did so by demonstrating that our JavaScript components and the connections between them were the least of our worries when it comes to scaling the architecture. The real challenge comes when there's a lot of data to process, and the data that enters the system is likely to grow much faster than the number of JavaScript components we have.

We closed the chapter with some examples of how to deal with unused store data. This is ultimately the most important aspect of scaling a Flux architecture since it gives the browser back unused resources. In the next chapter, we'll tackle the topic of immutable stores. This is something we've alluded to throughout the book, and we'll give it some focused attention now.

9

Immutable Stores

In this chapter, we're going to look at immutable data in Flux stores. Immutability is a term that often coincides with functional programming. Immutable data is data that doesn't change (mutate) once it's been created. The key benefit is that you can predict the root cause of data changes in an application because data can't inadvertently be changed by side-effects. Immutability and Flux get along nicely because they're both about explicitness and predictability.

We'll kick things off by talking about hidden updates or side-effects. Flux by itself discourages such things and immutable data helps enforce the idea. Then, we'll go over what these side-effects entail for the integrity of our Flux architecture. The most severe consequence of side-effects caused by mutating store data are disruptions to the unidirectional data flow of Flux. Next, we'll look at the hidden costs of immutability—these are mostly related to the additional resources required, which can lead to noticeable performance degradation. Finally, we'll look at the Immutable.js library for help with performing transformations on immutable data.

Renouncing hidden updates

The unidirectional nature of Flux is what sets it apart from other modern frontend architectures. The reason that the unidirectional data-flow works is because action creators are the only way that new data can enter the system. However, this isn't strictly enforced by Flux, and this means that some errant piece of code has the potential to completely break our architecture.

In this section, we'll look at how something like this is even possible in Flux. Then we'll look at how views typically get their data from stores and whether or not there's a better way. Finally, we'll think about other components in our Flux architecture and see if anything in addition to store data can be made immutable.

How to break Flux

The easiest way to break Flux is by mutating the state of a store without going through the proper channels. The action dispatcher is the gateway for new data entering the system, and it also coordinates the action handlers of our stores. For example, one action might trigger the handler of a couple stores, using the action payload in different ways. This simply won't happen if the state of stores are being mutated directly. We could get lucky and the changes we make don't have any side-effects. But isn't the whole premise of being explicit with actions that we can't predict complex side-effects?

If we lower the bar and start directly manipulating state here and there, what's to stop us from doing this more frequently? The most likely scenario is a view event handler that mutates store data. This is because views typically have direct references to stores, whereas other Flux components typically do not. So when the user clicks a button and our handler simply changes the state of a store instead of dispatching an action, we could find ourselves in trouble.

Let's walk through an example that highlights just how dangerous operating outside of the Flux playing field can be. We'll check out the button store first:

```
import { EventEmitter } from 'events';
import dispatcher from '../dispatcher';
import { TOGGLE } from '../actions/toggle';

class Button extends EventEmitter {
  constructor() {
    super();

    // The default state is to show the button
    // as enabled and to process click events.
    this.state = {
      text: 'Enabled',
      disabled: false
    };

    this.id = dispatcher.register((e) => {
      let { state } = this;

      switch(e.type) {

        // When the "TOGGLE" action is dispatched,
        // the next state of the button depends on
        // the current state of the "disabled"
        // property.
```

```
        case TOGGLE:
          state.text = state.disabled ?
            'Enabled' : 'Disabled';
          state.disabled = !state.disabled;

          this.emit('change', state);
          break;
      }
    });
  }
}

export default new Button();
```

Seems pretty simple—control the text and the `disabled` status of the buttons. This is pretty simple, but only if we're abiding by the Flux rules and dispatching actions to change the state of a store. Now, let's take a look at a view component that uses this store to render itself:

```
import React from 'react';
import button from '../stores/button';
import { toggle } from '../actions/toggle';

function onClick() {

  // Oh snap! This just totally broke Flux...
  button.state.disabled = !button.state.disabled;

  // Call the action creator as we should...
  toggle();
}

// Renders your typical HTML button, complete
// with properties and a callback handler for
// click events.
export default ({ text, disabled }) => (
  <button
    onClick={onClick}
    disabled={disabled}>{text}</button>
);
```

What's supposed to happen here is that the button should become disabled when it's clicked, because the button store will change the state accordingly when the TOGGLE action is dispatched. This much works as expected. However, the result is that this will never work as expected, due to that one line above the call to toggle(). Here, we're directly manipulating the state of a store. This prevents the expected behavior from taking place when the TOGGLE action is dispatched, because the state has already been changed, so now it will change back.

It's these little hacks that can cause big trouble down the road if we're not careful. When you look at this view module, the problematic code jumps off the screen. Imagine a real project with many more views that are each much bigger than this one—would you be able to spot this issue before it's too late?

Getting store data

Given that referencing store state is a dangerous thing, perhaps we could avoid it altogether? This would drastically reduce the potential for errors, as we saw in the previous section. For example, when two stores depend on one another, they use the dispatcher's waitFor() method to ensure that the store we're dependent on is updated first. Then we can just directly access the store, knowing that its state has already been updated. The approach is visualized as follows:

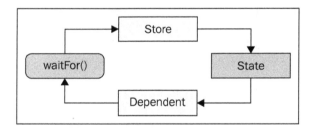

The dependent store is directly referencing the state of the store that it depends on, which is something that can lead to big problems if we're not careful. An alternative approach would be to have the dependent store listen to the change event on the store that it depends on. The callback can then use the new state that's passed to it as an argument. Of course, we would still need to use waitFor() or something along those lines to ensure that the stores update in the correct order. This approach is shown here:

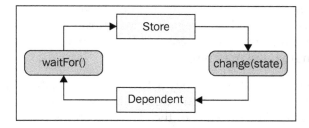

This is starting to look like a view component—views listen to the change event of stores so that they can render UI updates to reflect the changes in state. Views also need to perform an initial rendering of the store data, and this is why they typically reference store state. The problem with any of these ideas is that none of them actually insulate us from directly accessing store state—who knows what kind of reference will be passed in as one of these callback arguments. The other problem is that by introducing callback functions where directly reading a value is possible is an over-complication in design terms. There has to be a better way. Making our store state data immutable is a step in the right direction.

> In the next chapter, we're going to implement our own dispatcher component. While doing so, we'll think about implementing some safeguards against accessing state data from a store while an update round is happening, but the store hasn't been updated. This will make for easier troubleshooting with dependencies.

Everything is immutable

As the last topic before discussing how we might go about enforcing immutability, let's talk about the idea of everything in a Flux architecture being immutable. Theoretically, this shouldn't be that difficult to do since Flux cordons off state from living anywhere other than inside a store. So, let's start with stores.

Should all our stores be immutable, or perhaps just some of them? Having only some immutable stores isn't a good idea because it promotes inconsistency. What about having immutability in place at all, is it even necessary? Now this is a very important question one has to ask about their architecture because there's no cut-and-dried answer here. The immutability argument works when we need that extra assurance that there will be no surprises with store states later on. The counterargument is that we're disciplined enough as programmers that the immutability mechanisms just add overhead.

We'll spend the remainder of this chapter arguing in favor of immutable data, simply because the positives outweigh the negatives in almost every case. Regardless of how you feel about immutability, it's good to know what its strengths are in a Flux architecture—even if you're not going to use it.

What about view components—can they actually be immutable? Well, it turns out that they cannot, because the DOM API doesn't allow this. Our view components have to actually manipulate the state of the elements on the page. However, if we're using a view technology like React, then we get a veil of immutability because the idea is to always re-render components. So it seems as though we're taking old elements and replacing them with new ones when, all the while React figures out the DOM manipulations for us. This promotes the idea that state has no place within a Flux view.

Enforcing unidirectional data flow

If new data only enters the system via action payloads delivered by the dispatcher and our store data is immutable, we have a unidirectional data-flow. This is the goal, so the questions is, how do we enforce this? Can we simply say that our store data is immutable and be done with it? Well, that's something to shoot for, absolutely, but there's more to it than that.

In this section, we'll address the concept of data flowing in unintended directions, and what causes this to happen. We'll then consider the notion of having too many stores and not enough actions as contributors to dysfunctional data-flows. Finally, we'll examine some techniques that we can utilize to make our store data immutable.

Backwards, sideways, and leaky data flow

Flux architectures have a unidirectional data-flow—data enters from the left and exits on the right. This is easy to visualize as a flow that moves forward. What are some of the ways this can go wrong then? Take backwards flow, for instance. If a view instance holds a reference to a store instance and proceeds to mutate its state, then the flow is moving from the view to the store. This is the complete opposite of the expected flow direction, so it is moving backwards. Here's an illustration of what this looks like:

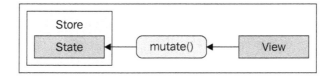

This is obviously not what we'd expect when working with a Flux system. But it's also a likely scenario unless we rule out the possibility by having the store's state return immutable data structures to any other components that want to interact with it. What about stores - can they mutate the state of another store? They shouldn't, and if they do, that would look like a sideways data-flow.

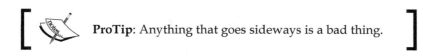

ProTip: Anything that goes sideways is a bad thing.

Here's what a sideways data-flow between two Flux stores might look like:

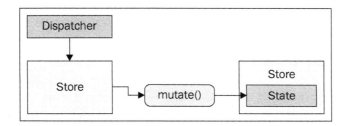

This is just as bad as the view component that directly mutates the state of a store, because the state we just changed could impact the next state that's computed. This is the same situation we saw in the first code example we looked at in the chapter.

What about actions—are they capable of directly manipulating the state of a store? This is probably the least likely scenario, because action creator functions are supposed to just dispatch actions after they coordinate any asynchronous behavior. However, an action creator function could incorrectly mutate a store state in an AJAX callback handler, for example. This is what we refer to as *leaky flows* because they're going around the dispatcher. So, we're leaking mutations without any traceable actions to show where they originated. Here's an illustration of the idea:

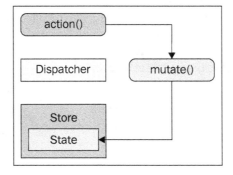

Too many stores?

There's always a possibility that there are too many Flux stores in our architecture. Perhaps the application has grown beyond what we had originally designed for in terms of features. Now, simply mapping a store to a feature won't suffice because there are dozens of stores.

If we're unable to rein in the store count, a possible outcome is more direct state mutations by other components. It's just a matter of convenience, if there's a ton of stores to think about, it means that we're going to have to take care of several other dispatcher-related development activities any time we want to do something. When there's lots of stores, there's the urge to manipulate their state directly. Removing stores reduces this urge.

Not enough actions

Is it possible that our Flux architecture doesn't have enough actions? For example, a view that we're working on needs to change the state of a store. There's no action to handle this for us, so rather than build a new action creator and update the store to handle the logic, we just directly mutate the store. It sounds like an easy enough task—building an action creator function and adding the necessary store update logic. But if we have to keep implementing these one-off action creator functions, eventually we'll just stop caring. There are two ways to fix this issue. The first is to implement more generic actions that apply to more than just one specific situation and can accept parameters. The second is to build a handful of action creator functions that are relevant to the feature that you're working on, even before you need them. When you know that the functions are there, in the back of your mind, you're more likely to use them.

Enforcing immutability

Let's explore some different approaches to keeping store state immutable. The goal is that when some external entity references a store's state, any changes that entity makes to the state doesn't actually affect the store because the data is immutable. We'll start by implementing a store that doesn't actually return a reference to its state—it returns a copy of it using `Object.assign()`:

```
import { EventEmitter } from 'events';
import dispatcher from '../dispatcher';
import { MY_ACTION } from '../actions/my-action';

// The state of this store is encapsulated
// within the module.
var state = {
```

```
    first: 1,
    second: 2,
};

class Copy extends EventEmitter {
  constructor() {
    super();

    this.id = dispatcher.register((e) => {
      switch(e.type) {

        case MY_ACTION:

          // Mutates "state" with new properties...
          Object.assign(state, e.payload);
          this.emit('change', state);
          break;
      }
    });
  }

  // Returns a new copy of "state", not a reference
  // to the original.
  get state() {
    return Object.assign({}, state);
  }
}

export default new Copy();
```

Here, you can see that the actual store state is in a module-level state variable. This means that it isn't accessible directly by the outside world because it isn't exported. We want the state to be encapsulated like this so that it's harder for other components to mutate it. If other components need read access to the store's state properties, they can read the state property of the store. Since this is a getter method, it can compute the value that will be returned. In this case, we'll create a new object on the fly. Now let's look at a store that stores its state in a constant:

```
import { EventEmitter } from 'events';
import dispatcher from '../dispatcher';
import { MY_ACTION } from '../actions/my-action';

// The state of this store is encapsulated
// within this module. It's also stored as
// a constant.
```

```
const state = {
  first: 1,
  second: 2,
};

class Constant extends EventEmitter {
  constructor() {
    super();

    this.id = dispatcher.register((e) => {
      switch(e.type) {

        case MY_ACTION:
          // Mutates "state" with new properties...
          Object.assign(state, e.payload);
          this.emit('change', state);
          break;
      }
    });
  }

  // Returns a reference to the "state" constant...
  get state() {
    return state;
  }
}

export default new Constant();
```

This store has the same structure and patterns as the `Copy` store. The difference is that `state` isn't a variable—it's a constant. This means that we shouldn't be able to mutate it, right? Well, not quite—we just can't assign new values to it. So this approach has limited value because the `state()` getter returns a direct reference to the constant. We'll see how this works momentarily, when other components use the store. Let's look at one more approach, which uses `Object.frozen()` to make objects immutable:

```
import { EventEmitter } from 'events';
import dispatcher from '../dispatcher';
import { MY_ACTION } from '../actions/my-action';

// The store state is encapsulated within
// this module...
var state;
```

```
// Merges new values with current values, freezes
// the new state, and assigns it to "state".
function change(newState) {
  let changedState = Object.assign({}, state, newState);
  state = Object.freeze(changedState);
}

// Sets the initial state and freezes it...
change({
  first: 1,
  second: 2,
});

class Frozen extends EventEmitter {
  constructor() {
    super();

    this.id = dispatcher.register((e) => {
      switch(e.type) {

        case MY_ACTION:

          // Calls "change()" to update the "state"
          // value and re-freeze it.
          change(e.payload);
          this.emit('change', state);
          break;
      }
    });
  }

  // Returns a reference to the frozen "state"...
  get state() {
    return state;
  }
}

export default new Frozen();
```

The state() getter is actually returning a reference to the frozen state variable. What's interesting about this approach is that we don't necessarily need to make a new copy of the data because our change() function has made it immutable. And when the store itself needs to update its state, that's when the state is refrozen.

Let's see how these approaches compare now. First, we'll import the stores and get references to their states:

```
import copy from './stores/copy';
import constant from './stores/constant';
import frozen from './stores/frozen';

var copyState = copy.state;
var constantState = constant.state;
var frozenState = frozen.state;

copyState.second++;
constantState.second++;

try {
  frozenState.second++;
} catch (err) {
  console.error(err);
  // →
  // TypeError: Cannot assign to read only property
  // 'second' of object
}

console.assert(
  copy.state.second !== copyState.second,
  'copy.second mutated'
);

console.assert(
  constant.state.second !== constantState.second,
  'constant.second mutated'
);
// → Assertion failed: constant.second mutated
```

It seems like we were able to successfully change the state of `copyState`. This is sort of true—we changed the state of a copy that doesn't actually reflect the state of the store. The `constantState` change, on the other hand, does have side-effects because any other components that read state from the constant store will see this change.

When we try to change `frozenState`, a `TypeError` is thrown. This might actually be the desired outcome, since it's made explicit that what we're trying to do with `fronzenState` is not allowed. Similar things happen when we add new properties to the store states—copy fails silently, constant fails, and frozen fails explicitly:

```
copyState.third = 3;
constantState.third = 3;

try {
```

```
    frozenState.third = 3;
} catch (err) {
    console.error(err);
    // →
    // TypeError: Can't add property third, object is
    // not extensible
}
```

Finally, let's look at the state data that's sent when the change event is emitted:

```
copy.on('change', (state) => {
    console.assert(state !== copyState, 'copy same');
    console.assert(state.fourth, 'copy missing fourth');
});

constant.on('change', (state) => {
    console.assert(state !== constantState, 'constant same');
    // → Assertion failed: constant same

    console.assert(state.fourth, 'constant missing fourth');
});

frozen.on('change', (state) => {
    console.assert(state !== frozenState, 'frozen same');
    console.assert(state.fourth, 'frozen missing fourth');
});

myAction({ fourth: 4 });
```

The `myAction()` function will extend the store state with new data. As we can see once again, the constant approach has failed us because it returns the same reference that was mutated. Generally speaking, none of these approaches are particularly easy to implement in practice. This is another reason why we'll want to seriously consider using a library like `Immutable.js`, where immutability is the default mode and mostly hidden from our code.

The cost of immutable data

By now you are well aware of the advantage immutable data brings to a Flux architecture—a level of assurance about our unidirectional data-flow. This safety net comes at a cost. In this section, we'll discuss how expensive immutability can be and what can be done about it.

We'll start by covering the biggest immutability issue—transient memory allocations and garbage collection. These things are big threats to the performance of our Flux architecture. Next, we'll think about lessening the amount of memory allocations by batching together transformations on immutable data. Finally, we'll think about the ways in which immutable data eliminates code that's only needed to handle scenarios where data is mutable.

Garbage collection is expensive

One good thing about mutable data structures is that once they're allocated, they tend to stick around for a while. That is, we don't need to copy the properties of an existing structure into a new one, then destroy the old one any time we need to make an update. This is software, so we're going to be making a lot of updates.

With immutable data, we face a memory consumption challenge. Every time we mutate an object, we have to allocate a new copy of that object. Imagine we're in a loop, making changes to immutable objects in a collection—this adds up to a lot of memory allocations in a short period of time—a spike if you will. Furthermore, the old objects that have been superseded by the new ones aren't instantaneously deleted from memory. They have to wait for the garbage collector to clean them up.

When our application uses more memory than it needs to, performance suffers. When the garbage collector has to run frequently because of all our memory allocations, performance suffers. It's the garbage collector more than anything else that triggers laggy user experiences, because our JavaScript code can't respond to any pending events while it's running.

Maybe there's an approach to immutable data that's less memory-intensive than replacing large objects when all we want is a simple update.

Batched mutations

Luckily for us, stores mutate their own state. This means that store dispatcher callbacks encapsulate everything that happens during state transformations. So if our stores have immutable state data, then the outside world doesn't need to know about any shortcuts the store takes internally in order to cut down on the number of memory allocations.

Let's say that a store receives an action and it has to perform three separate transformations on its state: make a transformation that results in a new object, make another transformation on that new object, and so on. That's a lot of transient memory allocations for intermediary data that no other component will ever touch. Here's an illustration of what's going on:

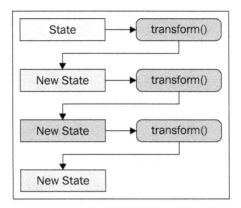

We want the final result to be a new state reference, but the intermediary new state that's created in between is wasteful. Let's see if there's a way that we can batch together these state transformations before the final immutable value is returned:

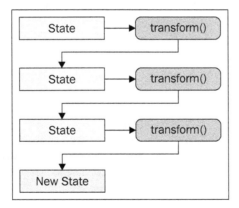

Now, we're only allocating one new object, despite making three state transformations. The mutations we're making within a Flux store are absolutely inconsequential to any other component in the system, yet we're maintaining immutability for anything else that wants to access and read this state.

Offsetting the cost

The painful part of mutable data is that components using this data have to account for side-effects. They don't necessarily know when or how this data will mutate. So they need side-effect handling code. While code that handles unexpected side-effects often doesn't utilize more memory, it isn't free to run either. When there's code to handle edge cases all over our source, the performance degradation can add up. With immutable data, we can remove most, if not all, of this extraneous code that checks the state of something, because we can better predict what it's going to be. This helps to offset the cost of extra memory allocations and garbage collection runs. Even if we're not using immutable data in our stores, Flux architectures make the need for side-effect handling code virtually obsolete. A unidirectional data-flow makes Flux very predictable.

Using Immutable.js

The `Immutable.js` library from Facebook provides immutable JavaScript data structures. This might sound trivial but there's a lot that goes on behind the scenes to make this work, namely creating new instances from transformations as efficiently as possible.

In this section, we'll look at immutable lists and maps. These are viable substitutes for arrays and plain objects, respectively, in our Flux store data. Then, we'll look at how `Immutable.js` can compose complex transformations without the need for intermediary representations. Finally, we'll see how `Immutable.js` returns the same instance when there's no mutations after running through a transformation, allowing for efficient change detection.

Immutable lists and maps

We'll start by looking at lists and maps, since these are fairly common structures that we'll need to implement in our stores. Lists are kind of like arrays and maps are kind of like plain JavaScript objects. Let's implement a store that uses a list:

```
import { EventEmitter } from 'events';
import Immutable from 'Immutable';

import dispatcher from '../dispatcher';
import { LIST_PUSH, LIST_CAPS } from '../actions/list';

// The state of this store is an "Immutable.List"
// instance...
var state = Immutable.List();
```

```
class List extends EventEmitter {
  constructor() {
    super();

    this.id = dispatcher.register((e) => {
      switch(e.type) {

        // When the "LIST_PUSH" action is dispatched,
        // we create a new List instance by calling
        // "push()". The new list is assigned to "state".
        case LIST_PUSH:
          this.emit('change',
            (state = state.push(...e.payload)));
          break;

        // When the "LIST_CAPS" action is dispatched,
        // we created a new List instance by calling
        // "map()". The new list is assigned to "state".
        case LIST_CAPS:
          this.emit('change',
            (state = state.map(x => x.toUpperCase())));
          break;
      }
    });
  }

  get state() {
    return state;
  }
}

export default new List();
```

You can see that the state variable is initialized to an empty Immutable.List() instance (the new keyword isn't necessary because these are functions that return new instances). Whenever we call a method on this list instance, a new instance is returned. This is why we have to assign the result of calling push() and map() to state.

Now let's implement a map store:

```
import { EventEmitter } from 'events';
import Immutable from 'Immutable';

import dispatcher from '../dispatcher';
import { MAP_MERGE, MAP_INCR } from '../actions/map';

// The state of this store is an "Immutable.Map"
// instance...
```

```
var state = Immutable.Map();

class MapStore extends EventEmitter {
  constructor() {
    super();

    this.id = dispatcher.register((e) => {
      switch(e.type) {

        // When the "MAP_MERGE" action is dispatched,
        // we create a new Map instance by calling
        // "merge()". The new map is assigned to "state".
        case MAP_MERGE:
          this.emit('change',
            (state = state.merge(e.payload)));
          break;

        // When the "MAP_INCR" action is dispatched,
        // we create a new Map instance by calling
        // "map()". The new map is assigned to "state".
        case MAP_INCR:
          this.emit('change',
            (state = state.map(x => x + 1)));
      }
    });
  }

  get state() {
    return state;
  }
}

export default new MapStore();
```

As you can see, maps follow the same immutability patterns as lists. The main difference is that they're keyed instead of indexed. Now let's see how both of these stores are used:

```
import list from './stores/list';
import map from './stores/map';
import { listPush, listCaps } from './actions/list';
import { mapMerge, mapIncr } from './actions/map';
```

```
// Logs the items in the "list" store when
// it's state changes.
list.on('change', (state) => {
  for (let item of state) {
    console.log('  list item', item);
  }
});

// Logs the items in the "map" store when
// it's state changes.
map.on('change', (state) => {
  for (let [key, item] of state) {
    console.log(`  ${key}`, item);
  }
});

console.log('List push...');
listPush('First', 'Second', 'Third');
// → List push...
//      list item First
//      list item Second
//      list item Third

console.log('List caps...');
listCaps();
// → List caps...
//      list item FIRST
//      list item SECOND
//      list item THIRD

console.log('Map merge...');
mapMerge({ first: 1, second: 2 });
// → Map merge...
//      first 1
//      second 2

console.log('Map increment...');
mapIncr();
// → Map increment...
//      first 2
//      second 3
```

Immutable transformations

Now, it's time to implement a more involved transformation inside a Flux store. This means chaining together operations on `Immutable.js` structures to create a new structure. But what about intermediary memory allocations—we'll want to keep an eye on these, right? Here's a store that attempts to use less memory while making transformations to a store's state:

```javascript
import { EventEmitter } from 'events';
import Immutable from 'Immutable';

import dispatcher from '../dispatcher';
import { SORT_NAMES } from '../actions/sort-names';

// The state is an object with two immutable
// list instances. The first is a list of user
// maps. The second is a list of user names and
// is empty by default.
const state = {
  users: Immutable.List([
    Immutable.Map({ id: 33, name: 'tHiRd' }),
    Immutable.Map({ id: 22, name: 'sEcoNd' }),
    Immutable.Map({ id: 11, name: 'firsT' })
  ]),
  names: Immutable.List()
};

class Users extends EventEmitter {
  constructor() {
    super();

    this.id = dispatcher.register((e) => {
      switch(e.type) {

        // The "SORT_NAMES" action was dispatched...
        case SORT_NAMES:

          // Determines the "sort" multiplier that's passed
          // to "sortBy()" to sort in ascending or
          // descending direction.
          let sort = e.payload === 'desc' ? -1 : 1;

          // Assigns the sorted list to "users" after
          // performing a series of transforms. The
          // "toSeq()" and "toList()" calls aren't strictly
```

```
      // necessary. Any calls in between them, however,
      // don't result in new structures being created.
      state.names = state.users
        .sortBy(x => x.get('id') * sort)
        .toSeq()
        .map(x => x.get('name'))
        .map(x => `${x[0].toUpperCase()}${x.slice(1)}`)
        .map(x => `${x[0]}${x.slice(1).toLowerCase()}`)
        .toList();

      this.emit('change', state);
      break;
    }
  });
}

get state() {
  return state;
}
}


export default new Users();
```

The SORT_NAMES action results in some interesting transformations happening to our immutable list. The idea is to map it to a list of capitalized user names, sorted by user id. The technique that's employed here involves converting the list into a sequence once it's sorted, using toSeq(). This is done to prevent the map() calls from allocating new structures, because we don't actually need a concrete structure till we're done mapping. To do this, we just have to call toList(), which will call all the mappings we've set up on the sequence and create the list. This means that the only structures we're creating here, are the new list from sortBy(), the new sequence from toSeq(), and the new list from toList().

In this particular example, this might be overkill, simply due to the fact that there are three operations done on a three-element list. So, we would just remove toSeq() and toList() from our code to simplify things. However, as we scale up to larger collections and more complex transformations on them, it doesn't hurt to know about this technique to reduce the memory footprint of our architecture. Let's see this store in action now:

```
import users from './stores/users';
import { sortNames } from './actions/sort-names';

// Logs the user names...
users.on('change', ({names}) => {
```

```
    for (let item of names) {
      console.log('  name', item);
    }
  });

  console.log('Ascending...');
  sortNames();
  // → Ascending...
  //      name First
  //      name Second
  //      name Third

  console.log('Descending...');
  sortNames(true);
  // → Descending...
  //      name Third
  //      name Second
  //      name First
```

Change detection

In this final example of the chapter, we'll see whether we can use Immutable.js structures to implement efficient change detection in our Flux stores. Actually, the detection itself will take place in the React view, but this relies on the store state using an Immutable.js object. Why would we want to do this—isn't React already efficient enough at computing diffs using its virtual DOM? React definitely excels here, but it still has to do a fair amount of work to figure out that no re-rendering is needed. We can lend a hand to our React components by providing hints that the store's state hasn't actually changed. So without further ado, here's the store we'll use:

```
import { EventEmitter } from 'events';
import Immutable from 'Immutable';

import dispatcher from '../dispatcher';
import { MY_ACTION } from '../actions/my-action';

// The store state is an Immutable.js Map instance.
var state = Immutable.Map({
  text: 'off'
});

class MyStore extends EventEmitter {
  constructor() {
```

```
      super();

      this.id = dispatcher.register((e) => {
        switch(e.type) {

          // When "MY_ACTION" is dispatched, we set
          // the "text" property of "state" as the
          // "payload". If the value has change, "state"
          // "set()" returns a new instance. If there's
          // no change, it returns the same instance.
          case MY_ACTION:
            this.emit('change',
              (state = state.set('text', e.payload)));
            break;
        }
      });
    }

    get state() {
      return state;
    }
  }

  export default new MyStore();
```

Nothing fancy is done on our part here; we're simply using an `Immutable.js` Map as our store state. We're then assigning the new `Map` instance to state when `set()` is called, since it returns a new instance. Here's the heuristic we're interested in— if nothing changes, the same instance is returned. Let's see how we can use this property of `Immutable.js` data in our a view:

```
  import { default as React, Component } from 'react';

  export default class MyView extendsComponent {

    render() {

      // Logs the fact that we're rendering because
      // "shouldComponentUpdate()" will prevent it
      // if the store state hasn't changed.
      console.log('Rendering...');

      let { state } = this.props;

      return (
```

```
      <p>{state.get('text')}</p>
    );
  }

  // Since we're using an Immutable.js Map as
  // the store state, we know that if the
  // instances are equal, nothing has changed
  // and there's no need to render.
  shouldComponentUpdate(nextProps) {
    return nextProps.state !== this.props.state;
  }
}
```

The key piece of this component is the `shouldComponentUpdate()` method, which makes the determination that the store has changed by doing a strict inequality comparison. In cases where this component is being rendered a lot but there's no need to change anything, this will avoid a lot of virtual DOM tree checking. Now, let's see how we would go about using this view:

```
import React from 'react';
import { render } from 'react-dom';

import myStore from './stores/my-store';
import MyView from './views/my-view';
import { myAction } from './actions/my-action';

// The container DOM element for our React component.
const container = document.getElementById('app');

// The payload that's sent to "myAction()"...
var payload = 'off';

// Renders the React components using the
// "myStore" state...
function renderApp(state=myStore.state) {
  render(
    <MyView state={myStore.state} />,
    container
  );
```

```
}

// Re-render the app when the store changes...
myStore.on('change', renderApp);

// Performs the initial rendering...
renderApp();

// Dispatches "MY_ACTION" every 0.5 seconds. This
// causes the store to change state and the app
// to re-render.
setInterval(() => {
  myAction(payload);
}, 500);

// After 5 seconds, change the payload that's
// dispatched with "MY_ACTION" so that the store
// state is actually different.
setTimeout(() => {
  payload = 'on';
}, 5000);
```

As you can see, actions that cause our view to re-render are constantly dispatched. However, since the set() call in our store is returning the same instance when nothing changes, the view itself is doing very little work. Then, once we do change the payload value after 5 seconds, the Immutable.js map instance changes, and the view updates. This view is rendered a grand total of two times—the initial rendering and the rendering that takes place when the store data actually changes.

You may have noticed that this implementation could have gone in another direction, one where the store isn't so naive as to emit changes when nothing has changed. It's all a matter of taste and tradeoffs. The approach we've chosen does require that the views take an active role in optimizing the rendering work-flow. This is easy to do with React components, and it simplifies our store logic. On the other hand, we might prefer to keep our views completely logic-less, including the shouldComponentUpdate() checks. If this is the case, we'd simply move this logic back into the store, and not have the change event emitted if the two Immutable.js instances are the same.

Summary

This chapter introduced you to immutability—both in the general sense of the term and from a Flux architecture viewpoint. We began the chapter with a discussion on the various ways that mutable data can break Flux. In particular, this breaks the crown jewel of any Flux architecture—unidirectional data-flow. Next, we looked at the different types of data-flow that emerge when we start mutating data outside of stores, as these are good things to look for when troubleshooting Flux architectures.

There are several ways that our code can enforce immutable data in our Flux stores, and we explored many of them. Immutable data comes at a cost—because the garbage collector constantly needs to run, blocking other JavaScript code from running, to collect all these extra copies of objects. We looked at how to minimize these extra memory allocations and how to offset the overall cost of using immutable data.

We closed the chapter by implementing several stores that used `Immutable.js` data structures. This library buys us immutability, added functionality, and efficient use of intermediary memory allocations by default. In the next chapter, we'll implement our own dispatcher component.

10
Implementing a Dispatcher

Up until this point in the book, we've relied on the reference implementation of the Flux dispatcher. There's nothing wrong with doing this—it's a functional piece of software, and the dispatcher doesn't have many moving parts. On the other hand, it is just a reference implementation of a larger idea—that actions need to be dispatched to stores, and store dependencies need to be managed.

We'll kick things off by talking about the abstract dispatcher interface that's required by Flux architectures. Next, we'll discuss some of the motivations behind implementing our own dispatcher. Finally, we'll devote the remainder of the chapter to implementing our own dispatcher module, and then improving our store components so that they're able to seamlessly interact with the new dispatcher.

Abstract dispatcher interface

The idea with any reference implementation is to directly illustrate, using code, how something is supposed to work. The Facebook reference implementation of the Flux dispatcher does just that—we can use it in a real Flux architecture and get results. We also gain an understating of the abstract dispatcher interface. Put another way, the reference implementation is kind of like software requirements, expressed in code form.

In this section, we'll try to better understand what these minimum requirements are before we dive into our own dispatcher implementation. The first essential piece of functionality that the dispatcher must implement is store registration so that the dispatcher can dispatch payloads to it. Then, we need the actual dispatching mechanism, which iterates over the registered stores and delivers payloads. Finally, we have the dependency semantics to think about while we're dispatching payloads.

Store registration

When we instantiate a store, we have to tell the dispatcher about it. Otherwise, the dispatcher doesn't know about the store's existence. The pattern generally looks something like this:

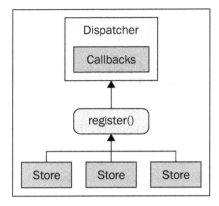

The dispatcher maintains an internal collection of callbacks to run whenever an action is dispatched. It simply needs to iterate over this collection of callback functions, calling each of them in turn. This really is as easy as it sounds, when everything during a Flux update round is synchronous. The question is, what would we want to change about the way the store registration process works?

Maybe instead of registering a callback function within the store constructor, we were to pass the dispatcher a reference to the store instance itself? Then, when it comes time to notify the store about an action that's been dispatched, the dispatcher would iterate over a collection of store instances and call some predefined method. The advantage to this approach would be that since the dispatcher has a reference to the store, it could access other metadata about the store, such as its dependencies.

We'll explore this idea further once we start writing code, a bit later on in the chapter. The bottom line is this—we need a means to tell the dispatcher that a given store instance would like to receive action notifications.

Dispatching payloads

The actual dispatching of payloads is quite simple. The only complicated part is handling dependencies between stores — we'll talk about that next. For now, just imagine an architecture where there are no inter-store dependencies. It's just a simple collection to iterate over, calling each function with the action payload as the argument. Here's an illustration of the process:

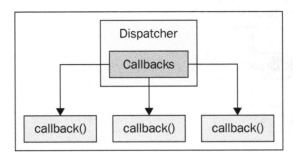

Apart from dependency management, is there anything else that's missing from this picture? Well, there is one situation we could find ourselves in — nested dispatches. These are strictly forbidden in Flux architectures as they would disrupt the synchronous unidirectional update rounds. In fact, the reference implementation of the dispatcher by Facebook tracks the state of any given update round and will catch this if it happens.

This doesn't mean that a dispatcher component that we implement has to check for such conditions. However, it's never a bad idea to fail fast when something so disruptive to the nature of the architecture is taking place.

Something else worth thinking about is the necessity of calling every registered store in a given update round. Sure, it makes sense as far as consistency goes — treat every store the same and notify them about *all the things*. On the other hand, we could have a large application with hundreds of actions being dispatched. Would it make sense to always dispatch actions to stores that never respond to them? When we implement our own dispatcher component, we're free to think about how we can implement such heuristics that benefit our application while staying true to the principles of Flux.

Handling dependencies

Perhaps the most challenging aspect of dispatching actions is making sure that store dependencies are handled correctly. On the other hand, the dispatcher just has to make sure that the store action handlers are called in the correct order. Dispatching actions with dependencies in mind is illustrated here:

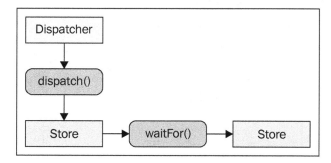

As long as stores that fall on the right-hand side of waitFor() calls get the dispatch notifications first, then all is well. So in essence, store dependencies are an ordering problem as far as the dispatcher is concerned. Order the callbacks in such a way that satisfies the dependency graph, then iterate and call each handler.

Here's the thing—do we really want to rely on the waitFor() dispatcher method as a means to manage store dependencies? Possibly a better way to handle this would be to declare an array of stores that we depend on. This would then be passed to the dispatcher at registration time, and we would no longer require the waitFor() calls.

We have the basic blueprint of what's required to implement our own dispatcher. But before we go ahead with the implementation, let's spend a little more time discussing the challenges faced with the Facebook dispatcher.

Challenges with the dispatcher

In the preceding section, we caught a glimpse of some of the potential challenges with the Facebook reference implementation of a Flux dispatcher. In this section, we'll elaborate on some some of this reasoning, in an attempt to provide motivation to implement our own custom dispatcher.

In this section, we'll reiterate the fact that the Flux NPM package mainly exists as an educational tool. Depending on a package like this is fine, especially since it does the job, but we'll go over some of the risks that something like this carries in a production context. Then, we'll talk about the fact that dispatcher components are singleton instances and they probably don't need to be.

We'll then think about the store registration process and the fact that it's a more manual process than it needs to be. Finally, we'll touch on the store dependency management problem again with a discussion on `waitFor()` and possible declarative alternatives.

Educational purposes

The Facebook Flux NPM package, as we know, provides a reference implementation of a dispatcher. The best way to learn how such a component is supposed to work is to write code that uses it. It's for educational purposes, in other words. This gets us off the ground quickly, as we figure out the best way to write Flux code. Facebook could have just as easily left out the dispatcher implementation and left it up to programmers reading the Flux documentation to figure this out. Code is highly educational though, and serves as a form of documentation. Even if we decide that we're not crazy about how the dispatcher is implemented, we can at least read the code to figure out what the dispatcher is supposed to do.

So is there any risk involved if we were to use this package in a production setting? If we use the default Flux dispatcher in our project, and everything we've developed against it works, there's no reason we couldn't use it in a production application. If it works, it works. However, the fact that this is a reference implementation meant for educational purposes probably means that there's no serious development happening with it. Take React as a counter example, where millions of people use this software in a production environment. There's motivation that this technology moves forward and improves upon itself. This simply isn't the case with a reference dispatcher implementation. Rolling our own is definitely worth thinking about, especially if there's room for improvement.

Singleton dispatchers

If we use the Flux dispatcher from Facebook, we have to instantiate it, as it's just a class. However, since there's only one update round happening at any given time, there's no need for more than one dispatcher instance across the entire application. This is the singleton pattern, and it isn't always the best pattern to use. For one thing, it's needless indirection.

For example, any time we want to dispatch an action, we need to access the `dispatch()` method of the dispatcher. This means that we have to import the dispatcher instance and invoke the method using the instance as the context, like this: `dispatcher.dispatch()`. The same is true with the `register()` method; when a store wants to register itself with the dispatcher, it first needs to access the instance before it calls the method.

So, it would seem that this singleton dispatcher instance serves no real purpose other than to get in the way and make for more verbose code. What if instead of a singleton class instance, the dispatcher were just a simple module that exported the relevant functions? This would greatly simplify the code in places where the dispatcher is required, which is probably quite a few if our application has a lot of stores and actions.

Manual store registration

One invariant of Flux architectures is that stores are connected to dispatchers. There's no other way to change the state of a store, other than by dispatching an action. So unless we want a static store that never changes state, we need to register it with the dispatcher. All the example stores we've looked at in this book so far set up their dispatcher handlers in the constructor. This is where we handle actions that could potentially change the state of a store.

Since dispatcher registration is a given, do we really need to explicitly register a callback function when every store is created? An alternative approach might involve a base store class that takes care of this registration for us; this isn't necessarily a dispatcher-specific problem.

The other aspect of store registration that feels unnecessary for the most part is managing dispatcher IDs. For example, if we implement a store that depends on another store, we have to reference that other store's dispatch ID. The reason IDs are used is simple—a callback function doesn't identify the store. So we have to use the dispatcher to map the callback ID to the store. The whole approach just feels messy, so when we implement our own dispatcher, we can do away with these dispatch IDs entirely.

Error-prone dependency management

The final gripe that we'll want to address with the default Facebook Flux dispatcher is the way that dependencies between stores are handled. The waitFor() mechanism does its job in that it blocks further execution of the handler until all its dependencies have handled the action. This way, we know that the store that we depend on is always up to date. The trouble is that waitFor() feels kind of error-prone.

For one thing, it always has to be in the same place—right at the top of the store action handler. We have to remember to use the dispatch IDs from the stores that we depend on so that `waitFor()` knows which stores to process next. A more declarative approach would mean that we could set the store's dependencies as an array of store references or something along these lines. This way, the dependencies are declared outside of the actual callback function and are a little more obvious. We'll figure out a way to implement this in our dispatcher, which we'll now get started on.

Building a dispatcher module

In this section, we're going to implement our own dispatcher module. This will serve as a replacement for the Facebook reference implementation that we've relied upon so far in this book. First, we'll think about how the dispatcher will track references to store modules. Then, we'll discuss the functions that this module needs to expose, followed by a walk-through of the `dispatch()` implementation. Lastly, we'll figure out how we want to handle dependency management with this dispatcher module.

Encapsulating store references

The first aspect of our dispatcher module to consider are the stores themselves. With Facebook's reference implementation, there are no references to stores—only references to callback functions. That is, when we register with Facebook's dispatcher, we're passing the `register()` method a function instead of the store instance itself. Our dispatcher module will hold onto store references instead of just callback functions. Here's a diagram that illustrates the approach taken by the reference implementation:

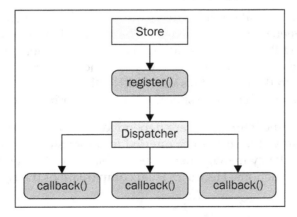

Each time `register()` is called, it adds a callback function to the list of callbacks to be processed by the dispatcher any time an action is dispatched. However, the downside is that the dispatcher might need access to the store for more advanced capabilities that we want to implement, as we'll see shortly. So we'll want to register the store instance itself, rather than just a callback function. This approach is illustrated here:

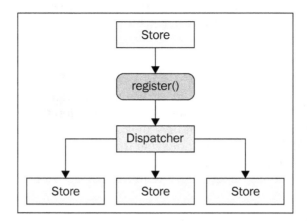

The list of callback functions is now a list of store instances, and when an action is dispatched, the dispatcher now has access to store data, which is useful for things, such as methods and dependency lists. The trade-off here is that callback functions are more generic, and they're simply called by the dispatcher. As we'll see momentarily, there are advantages to this approach that make for simplified store code.

Handling dependencies

The first thing we'll think about in terms of our dispatcher implementation is how dependencies between stores are managed. The standard approach is to implement a `waitFor()` method that blocks execution in the store handler function until the stores it depends on have been handled. As you're now aware, this approach can be problematic due to the fact that it's used within the handler function. A more declarative approach is what we're shooting for with our implementation.

The idea is that the list of stores that are depended upon are declared as a property of the store. This allows the store to be queried for other stores that it depends on. It also takes the dependency management aspect of stores out of the handler code that's supposed to focus on actions. Here's a visual comparison of the two approaches:

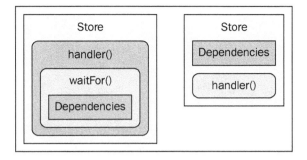

Trying to access dependencies that are specified in `waitFor()` is like peeling back an onion—they're hidden. Our goal is to separate the handler code from the dependency specification. So how do we do that exactly?

Rather than trying to handle dependencies during the dispatching process, we could sort out our dependencies as stores are registered. If a store has its dependencies listed in a property, then the dispatcher can organize the store list in such a way that satisfies those dependencies. Here's an implementation of a `register()` function for our dispatcher module:

```
// This is used by stores so that they can register
// themselves with the dispatcher.
export function register(store) {

  // Don't let a store register itself twice...
  if (stores.includes(store)) {
    throw `Store ${store} already registered`;
  }

  // Adds the "store" reference to "stores".
  stores.push(store);

  // Sorts our stores based on dependencies. If a store
  // depends on another store, the other store is
  // considered "less than" the store. This means that
  // dependencies will be satisfied if the stores are
  // processed in this sort order.
  stores.sort((a, b) => {
    if (a.deps.includes(b)) {
      return 1;
    }
```

```
      if (b.deps.includes(a)) {
        return -1;
      }

      return 0;
    });
  }
```

This is the function that stores can use to register themselves. The first thing this function does is it checks if the store has already been registered with the dispatcher. This is an easy check to perform, because the references are stored in an array; we can use the `includes()` method. If the store hasn't already been registered, then we can push the store onto the array.

Next, we handle store dependencies. Every time a store is registered, we re-sort the `stores` array. This sort is based on the `deps` property of the store. This is where the dependencies of the store are declared. The sort comparator is straightforward. It's based on whether **Store A** depends on **Store B** or vice-versa. For example, let's say these stores were registered in the following order:

Now, let's assume that the follow store dependencies have been declared:

This means that **Store A** depends on both **Store B** and **Store D**. After each of these stores have been registered, the order of the store list in our dispatcher modules would be as follows:

Now the store list is in an order that satisfies the dependencies of the stores. When the dispatcher iterates over the store list and calls each store handler, it will be done in the correct order. Since **Store A** depends on **Store C** and **Store D**, all that matters is that these two stores are handled first. The order of **Store A** and **Store C** are inconsequential since there's no dependency declared between them. Now, let's see how to implement the dispatching logic of our module.

Dispatching actions

In the Facebook reference implementation of a Flux dispatcher, the dispatching mechanism is a method of a dispatcher instance. Since there's really no need for a singleton dispatcher instance, our dispatcher is a simple module with a couple of functions exposed, including a `dispatch()` function. Thanks to the dependency sorting logic, we've implemented in the `register()` function; the work-flow of `dispatch()` will be nice and straightforward. Let's take a look at this code now:

```
// Used by action creator functions to dispatch an
// action payload.
export function dispatch(payload) {

  // The dispatcher is busy, meaning that we've
  // called "dispatch()" while an update round
  // was already taking place.
  if (busy) {
    throw 'Nested dispatch() call detected';
  }

  // Marks the dispatcher as "busy" before we
  // start calling any store handlers.
  busy = true;

  // The action "type" determines the method
  // that we'll call on a the store.
  let { type } = payload;

  // Iterates over each registered store, looking
  // for a method name that matches "type". If found,
  // then we call it, passing it the "payload" that
  // was dispatched.
  for (let store of stores) {
    if (typeof store[type] === 'function') {
      store[type](payload);
    }
  }

  // The dispatcher isn't busy any more, so unmark it.
  busy = false;
}
```

You can see that there's a `busy` variable that's checked at the top of the function. This is set just before we start calling store handlers. Essentially, this checks for anything that calls `dispatch()` as a result of a store handling an action. For example, we could accidentally call `dispatch()` from a store or from a view that's listening to a store. This is not allowed as it breaks the unidirectional data-flow of our Flux architecture. When this happens, it's better to detect it and fail fast than it is to let nested update rounds run their course.

Aside from the busy state handling logic, this function iterates over the stores collection and checks if there's an appropriate method to call. The method name is based on the action type. For example, if the action is `MY_ACTION` and store has a method of the same name, then that method is invoked with the payload as an argument. The process is visualized here:

This is quite the departure from the standard `switch` statement approach we've been using in this book so far. Instead, it's up to the dispatcher to locate the appropriate code to run within the store. This means that if the store doesn't implement a method that corresponds to the action that has been dispatched, it's ignored by the store. This is something that happens often within our store dispatch handlers, only now it happens more efficiently because it sidesteps the `switch` case checking. In the next section, we'll see how our stores can work with this new dispatcher implementation. But first, here's the dispatcher module in its entirety, so you can see how everything fits together:

```
// References to registered stores...
const stores = [];

// This is true when the dispatcher is performing
// an update round. By default, it's not busy.
var busy = false;

// This is used by stores so that they can register
```

```
// themselves with the dispatcher.
export function register(store) {

  // Don't let a store register itself twice...
  if (stores.includes(store)) {
    throw `Store ${store} already registered`;
  }

  // Adds the "store" reference to "stores".
  stores.push(store);

  // Sorts our stores based on dependencies. If a store
  // depends on another store, the other store is
  // considered "less than" the store. This means that
  // dependencies will be satisfied if the stores are
  // processed in this sort order.
  stores.sort((a, b) => {
    if (a.deps.includes(b)) {
      return 1;
    }

    if (b.deps.includes(a)) {
      return -1;
    }

    return 0;
  });
}

// Used by action creator functions to dispatch an
// action payload.
export function dispatch(payload) {

  // The dispatcher is busy, meaning that we've
  // called "dispatch()" while an update round
  // was already taking place.
  if (busy) {
    throw 'Nested dispatch() call detected';
  }

  // Marks the dispatcher as "busy" before we
  // start calling any store handlers.
  busy = true;
```

```
    // The action "type" determines the method
    // that we'll call on a the store.
    let { type } = payload;

    // Iterates over each registered store, looking
    // for a method name that matches "type". If found,
    // then we call it, passing it the "payload" that
    // was dispatched.
    for (let store of stores) {
      if (typeof store[type] === 'function') {
        store[type](payload);
      }
    }

    // The dispatcher isn't busy any more, so unmark it.
    busy = false;
}
```

Improving store registration

We can't improve the work-flow of the dispatcher without improving the work-flow of our stores. Thankfully, the hard work has already been implemented by the dispatcher. We just need to implement our stores in a way that best utilizes the improvements we've made to the dispatcher. In this section, we'll discuss implementing a base store class, followed by some example implementations of stores that extend it and implement their own action methods.

Base store class

The new dispatcher we've just implemented has some important differences from Facebook's reference implementation. The two key differences are that the store registers an instance of itself instead of a callback function, and that the store needs to implement action methods. The base store class should be able to automatically register itself with the dispatcher when it's created. This would mean that stores extending this base class wouldn't need to worry about the dispatcher at all—just implementing action methods that change the state of the store accordingly.

The layout of the dispatcher, the base store, and stores that extend it is illustrated here:

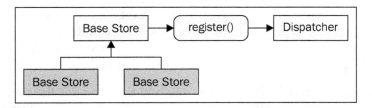

Let's go ahead and look at the implementation of our base store class now. Then, we'll implement some stores that extend it so that we can see our new dispatcher module in action:

```javascript
import { EventEmitter } from 'events';
import { register } from './dispatcher';

// Exports the base store for others to extend.
export default class Store extends EventEmitter {

  // The constructor sets the initial "state" of the
  // store, as well as any dependencies "deps" with
  // other stores.
  constructor(state = {}, deps = []) {
    super();

    // Stores the state and dependencies. The "deps"
    // property is actually required by the
    // dispatcher.
    this.state = state;
    this.deps = deps;

    // Registers the store with the dispatcher.
    register(this);
  }

  // This is a simple helper method that changes the
  // state of the store, by setting the "state"
  // property and then emitting the "change" event.
  change(state) {
    this.state = state;
    this.emit('change', state);
  }

}
```

That's it, pretty simple right? The constructor accepts the initial state of the store and an array of store dependencies. Both of these arguments are optional — they have default argument values. This is especially important for the deps property because our dispatcher module expects it to be there. Then, we call the register() function so that the dispatcher is automatically aware of any stores. Remember, a Flux store is of no use if it's unable to handle actions as they're dispatched.

We've also added a handy little change() method that updates the state and emits the change event for us. Now that we have a base store class, we're free to implement little helper methods like this in order to reduce duplicate store code.

An action method

Let's complete our example that's been running through a few sections now. To do so, we'll implement a few stores that extend the base store we've just created. Here's the first store:

```
import Store from '../store';
import second from './second';
import third from './third';

// The initial state of the store, we'll
// pass this to "super()" in the constructor.
const initialState = {
  foo: false
};

// The dependencies this store has on other
// stores. In this case, it's "second" and
// "third". These too, are passed through
// "super()".
const deps = [ second, third ];

class First extends Store {

  // The call to "super()" takes care for setting up
  // the initial store state, and the dependencies
  // for us.
  constructor() {
    super(initialState, deps);
  }

  // Called in response to the "FOO" action
  // being dispatched...
```

```
  FOO(payload) {
    this.change({ foo: true });
  }

  // Called in response to the "BAR" action
  // being dispatched...
  BAR(payload) {
    this.change(Object.assign({
      bar: true
    }, this.state));
  }
}


export default new First();
```

This store has all of the relevant moving parts to work with our new base store class and our new dispatcher module. You can see in the constructor that we're passing the `initialState` and the `deps` values to the `Store` constructor. You can also see that we have two action methods implemented in this store: `FOO()` and `BAR()`. This means that if any actions with a type of `FOO` or `BAR` are dispatched, this store will respond to them. Now let's implement the two stores that this store depends on:

 If you absolutely can't stand the look of all-caps method names, feel free to change the case of the action types that get dispatched. Another alternative is to implement case-insensitive matching in the dispatcher. The trade-off working against this latter option is that we'd lose the direct mapping from action type to method name. Be careful what you wish for.

```
import Store from '../store';
import third from './third';

class Second extends Store {

  // The call to "super()" sets the initial
  // state for us.
  constructor() {
    super({
      foo: false
    });
  }
```

```
    // Called in response to the "FOO" action
    // being dispatched...
    FOO(payload) {
      this.change({ foo: true });
    }

    // Called in response to the "BAR" action
    // being dispatched. Note that we're
    // dependent on the "third" store, yet
    // we don't make this dependency explicit.
    // This could lead to trouble.
    BAR(payload) {
      this.change({
        foo: third.state.foo
      });
    }
  }
}

export default new Second();
```

The Second store is similar to the First store. It extends the base Store class and sets a default state. It also responds to two actions, as we can see by the two method names. However, this store doesn't declare any dependencies, yet it clearly depends on the third store in the BAR() action handler. This may or may not work, depending on where the third store lands in the collection of stores held by the dispatcher. If we declare third as a dependency, then we know for certain that it'll always be updated before this store. Let's look at our last store now:

```
import Store from '../store';

class Third extends Store {

  // The call to "super()" sets the initial
  // state for us...
  constructor() {
    super({
      foo: false
    });
  }

  // Called in response to the "FOO" action
  // being dispatched.
  FOO(payload) {
```

```
        this.change({ foo: 'updated' });
    }
}


export default new Third();
```

Once again, this store follows the same patterns as its two successors. The key difference being that it has no BAR() action handler. This means that nothing in this store will be called when BAR actions are dispatched. This is in contrast to our earlier handlers where every action would have *funnelled* through a switch statement only to be ignored. Finally, let's look at main.js to tie this all together:

```
import first from './stores/first';
import second from './stores/second';
import third from './stores/third';

import { foo } from './actions/foo';
import { bar } from './actions/bar';

// Logs the state of each store as it changes...
first.on('change', (state) => {
  console.log('first', state);
});

second.on('change', (state) => {
  console.log('second', state);
});

third.on('change', (state) => {
  console.log('third', state);
});

foo();
// →
// third {foo: "updated"}
// second {foo: true}
// first {foo: true}

bar();
// →
// second {foo: "updated"}
// first {bar: true, foo: true}
```

Note that the output of foo() reflects the correct dependency order and that the output of bar() reflects the missing action handler in Third.

Summary

In this chapter, you learned about some of the limitations that are inherent with the Facebook Flux component. For starters, it's not targeted for production environments, because it's a reference implementation for the Flux patterns. We're free to implement these dispatcher patterns however we like.

The essential aspects of a dispatcher are the ability to register store code that handles actions as they're dispatched and the ability to perform the dispatches. Given the simplicity of the requirements, it doesn't make sense to implement another singleton class. Instead, the dispatcher only needs to expose a `register()` and `dispatch()` function.

The big change with our implementation was with regard to dependency management. Instead of figuring out dependencies every time an action is dispatched, the `register()` function sorts the `stores` collection in such a way that satisfies the store dependencies. We then implemented a base store class that's used to simplify our store code by automatically registering the store with the dispatcher for us.

In the next chapter, we'll look at view components that rely on technologies other than ReactJS to render themselves.

11
Alternative View Components

The Flux documentation doesn't have a whole lot to say about view components. And yet, views are an essential part of any Flux architecture. Perhaps what the Flux authors really mean is that Flux doesn't really care about the mechanisms used to render our views—just as long as they're rendered somehow.

It's no secret that Flux was designed with React in mind. Facebook had already built React for their view components—Flux was the missing piece that allows them to formulate a full-fledged, frontend architecture. We'll start this chapter off with a discussion on what makes React such a good fit for Flux architectures. Then we'll weigh these benefits against the downsides of React.

Next, we'll spend some time building views using jQuery and the Handlebars template engine. These are two popular technologies that have likely crossed the path of any given developer at some point. We'll then close the chapter by thinking about views that don't require specific rendering technology, allowing us to be nimble about our views and adopt the new hotness when it arrives.

ReactJS is a good fit for Flux

It's no surprise that React is a good fit for Flux architectures. Both technologies were created by the same company, and they both solve complimentary problems. In this section, we'll dive into some of the details of what it is about React that makes it work so well with Flux. We'll start by looking at the unidirectional flows found in both Flux and React. Next, we'll discuss the idea that re-rendering DOM structures is easier than manipulating specific DOM nodes, and why this is a good fit for store change event handlers. Finally, we'll talk about the relatively small code footprint of React components.

ReactJS is unidirectional

The data-flow in a Flux architecture is unidirectional. It starts with an action and ends with view updates—there's no other way for data to get into a view component. React itself shares this same unidirectional philosophy with Flux. Data flows into a root React component and trickles down into any components used to compose the root. This process is recursive down the component hierarchy.

Data flows into Flux stores through actions, and flows out as change events. React components keep this unidirectional flow going. Once the React component has re-rendered itself based on the store state, the flow is done. The only option is to start all over again by dispatching a new action. The flow between Flux and React components is illustrated here:

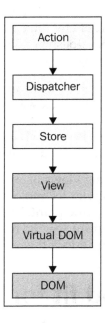

The first three items in our data flow are Flux entities. Any given data flow is kicked off when an action is dispatched. The action itself then enters the dispatcher and is sent to every store. Then the store makes any state changes as appropriate. From here, the data-flow is handed off to the React component. This is where we've specified the structure of the markup we want to render, using JSX. The component then consults with the virtual DOM to figure out what changes, if any, should be made in the actual DOM. Once these changes are made, the end of the data-flow has been reached.

The flow that we've outlined here for React components wouldn't look any different even if they weren't part of a Flux architecture. The Flux components just add predictable state changes in a synchronous way, before handing the data off to components for rendering. Without Flux, React would still need to start from the top and pass data down so that the re-rendering process can start. This fits nicely with the change events that are emitted by the Flux stores.

What doesn't fit so well with React is the idea of two-way data binding. Some people love the idea and have found ways to make it work with React, but I digress. For two-way binding to be effective, our view components need to be in close proximity to mutable data. Then, the view can listen directly to this data in order to re-render itself. We're not setup to handle this with Flux architectures, let alone React. The idea that we can directly mutate the state of something without first entering a work-flow that manages the synchronous update of application-wide state, goes against every idea of Flux. Put simply, Flux architectures favor unidirectional data-flows with predictable outcomes and React helps with this mission.

Re-rendering new data is easy

One thing about ReactJS that really stands out is it's ability to re-render entire DOM trees. Well, any JavaScript code can replace an existing DOM tree by building it again. React uses what's called a virtual DOM to compare the existing elements that the user is currently looking at, against the new elements that we've just rendered. Instead of replacing the entire tree, React will only touch the DOM in places where the two trees differ. Aside from the heuristics React has built into it, the fundamental performance edge comes from the fact that the virtual DOM is in JavaScript memory — we don't have to query the real DOM for elements. It's querying the DOM that can have negative performance implications.

To get around these performance issues, our view code can issue specific queries that are efficient to run, and only fetch the exact elements we need. Our view code can also cache the specific elements that it needs. The problem with this approach is that it feels fragmented once we have more than a few view components. It's difficult for components to share code when they're all tailored for their own specific performance requirements, and this is highly dependent on the DOM structure of the component.

It's more natural for programmers to be able to say *here's a snapshot of what these view elements should look like at this point in time*. We shouldn't have to pick apart the DOM structure and say that this `div` should look like this while this `span` should be hidden and so on. This is why JSX works; we can more easily visualize what the output of our component is going to look like, because it's structured like the elements are structured.

Small code footprint

React components generally have less code than view components that have lots of imperative DOM manipulation code. React doesn't have this type of code because it just needs to express the structure of the DOM through JSX. However, without Flux as the architecture, an application that uses React will probably find that the React components contain much more data transformation code.

For example, when React components are mounted into the DOM, we might need to perform some kind of transformation on data that comes from some source, perhaps an AJAX response. With Flux, the source is always the state of the store, so we know that the data transforms have already happened by the time they're handed off to the React views. Remember, it's the views that drive the structure of our store state, not the stores that drive how our views must be structured.

Event-handling code is another area where React components can have a small code footprint. Well, there's really two dimensions to this. First, event handlers in React are declared right in the JSX, so they're as much a part of the DOM tree structure as any other element properties—there's no need to insert the elements into the DOM and then look them up again later so we can attach an event handler function to them. The second dimension isn't actually specific to React, but more of a Flux phenomenon. The event handlers themselves are usually just action creator functions. All the logic that would have been in our views is now part of our stores.

The downsides of ReactJS

Now that you have a good handle on the benefits of using ReactJS as the view layer in a Flux architecture, it's time to look at some of the downsides. Everything has negative tradeoffs—there's no such thing as a perfect technology. So these things are worth considering in the context of a Flux architecture for your application.

First, we'll consider memory consumption. React is a fairly big library and has a noticeable impact on application load time. However, this is of minor concern compared to the amount of memory consumed by the virtual DOM. Next, we'll look at introducing JSX syntax into our JavaScript modules and the problems that might introduce for those not accustomed to blending other languages into their JavaScript modules.

Virtual DOM and memory

JavaScript applications should strive to be as memory-efficient as possible. Those that don't feel bloated and unresponsive to the user. Applications that use a lot of memory are inherently slower than those that use less memory because they need to perform more work. For example, if we need to look something up in a collection, it's obviously going to take more compute resources if the collection has a ton of objects in it, as opposed to a collection that's much smaller. Another place this can hurt application performance is during garbage collection. This is less of an issue if we have huge collections that are allocated and never freed (possibly due to other problems like leaks). But the more common behavior is to allocate large amounts of memory in response to a user action, then to deallocate that memory when the user moves on. This behavior will trigger frequent garbage collection runs, which translates to pauses in responsiveness.

The architecture of React requires more memory than alternative approaches to memory. This is due to the virtual DOM that React maintains. This in-memory structure is meant to reflect the structure of the real DOM. It doesn't track every single piece of data about every element that the real DOM has. It only tracks the data that's necessary to compute diffs. Here's an illustration of the mapping between our component, the virtual DOM, and the real DOM:

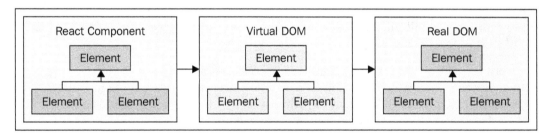

The elements in our React component aren't necessarily occupying much memory, because they're just the declarative part of the component that specify which elements to use and which property values they should have. The virtual DOM reflects the structure and properties as specified in our JSX; these elements actually do occupy memory. Finally, we have the real DOM elements that the user sees and interacts with. These occupy a significant amount of memory too.

The main challenge with this approach is that we're doubling-up on anything that's rendered in the DOM. Put another way, the virtual DOM adds to the total memory consumed by our DOM elements out of necessity. Without the virtual DOM, React and JSX is just another template engine. The virtual DOM solves performance issues in other places. The main area where React excels performance-wise is efficient DOM API interactions, because the virtual DOM eliminates the need for many of these calls.

Is the memory consumed by your typical React application a showstopper? Absolutely not. Memory is quickly becoming a commodity, even in the mobile space. So if we can allocate more memory to solve real performance issues, we should by all means do so. However, there are cases where excessive memory allocation can become a problem with React applications. For instance, what if we simply need to render lots of elements? When and if this becomes a performance issue, your best bet is to probably design for fewer elements.

JSX and markup

JSX is essentially HTML (well, XML technically) mixed in with JavaScript code. If your initial response to this approach wasn't favorable, you're not alone. Over a long period of time, decades actually, we've been conditioned to separate our concerns. Something like HTML should never be in the same module as the JavaScript logic that controls when and how that markup is displayed. If we've been living through the separation-of-concerns principle for so many years, it's only natural to balk at the notion of combining to concerns into a single module.

It's quite possible that the last project you worked on involved specifying markup in template files. These templates are then fed into the view layer for rendering. Coming to Flux from this setting might be a little too much to take in all at once. On one hand, we have a whole new unidirectional data-flow to think about. On the other hand, we're talking about throwing out everything we've worked so hard to build into separate layers.

Let's not forget the fact that the separation of concerns principle does serve a purpose. If two concerns are implemented in two different places, there's less chance that a change in one concern will impact the other. Think of having templates as a way to compartmentalize the visual aspect of any given component. We can, in theory at least, give the design team free reign over the templates and not have to worry about them breaking the JavaScript implementation of the component.

If you've learned anything so far in this book, it's probably that there's a lot more to the complexities of UI components than the sum of their parts. Flux tries to acknowledge these complexities by explicitly modeling them in stores. There's a strict ordering and synchronicity to updating the UI in Flux for a reason: predictability despite all the complexity involved. What does this have to do with JSX, you might ask? Well, before discounting it as something that violates the separation of concerns principle, think about how well it fits with Flux stores. Also consider the idea that markup and the logic that renders it might be the same concern after all.

Vendor lock-in

Have you ever heard someone say something along the lines of *I'm using library x because I don't want to be locked into library y?* Vendor lock-in is a tricky area to navigate. Although these days, where most projects rely on open source projects, it's more like *technology approach lock-in*. I would be remiss if I didn't at least mention the subject here with regard to Flux and React.

Once we start using React and JSX, we've pretty much rolled the dice. It's a safe bet for more reasons than it's an unsafe one. Nonetheless, we've started down a path that's very difficult to get off, which is essentially the point of these past three sections. Even if your mind is 95% made up on choosing React, you'll sleep better at night knowing that you've weighed the tradeoffs.

Using jQuery and Handlebars

Both jQuery and Handlebars are pervasive technologies in modern web applications. There's a high probability that someone new to Flux has used one or both of these technologies, so we'll spend this section implementing some views that use both jQuery and Handlebars.

We'll start with a discussion on what makes jQuery and Handlebars a good fit for implementing view components. Then, we'll implement a basic view that uses these technologies to render the state of Flux stores. After this, we'll think about the various ways that we can compose larger views out of smaller parts and how to best handle user events.

Why jQuery and Handlebars?

Before there were JavaScript frameworks, there was jQuery. This small library set out to solve cross-browser issues prevalent in frontend development, and in general to make development more pleasant. Today, jQuery is still a dominant player in the JavaScript library game. Many larger frameworks depend on jQuery, because it's so effective and the barrier to learn how it works is so low.

One thing that jQuery isn't so great at is specifying the layout of UI components using HTML. For example, we can use jQuery to construct new elements and insert them into the DOM on the fly. However, something about this approach feels cumbersome and unnatural. It's often clearer to be able to write the HTML using the same structure as it would appear on the page. This removes a layer of indirection and makes it easier for us to map the markup to the rendered output.

Enter Handlebars. This library adds a sophisticated template engine to our frontend. Writing Handlebars templates means that we can write HTML, along with some specific Handlebars syntax for the dynamic bits, and avoid the mess of trying to assemble elements using jQuery. Both libraries are complimentary to one another. We have Handlebars templates that declare the structure of our application, and we use the Handlebars rendering engine to render this structure. Then, jQuery can handle every other aspect of the view components, such as selecting DOM elements and handling events. Let's see how this looks in the context of a Flux architecture by implementing a view that renders a Handlebars template.

Rendering templates

Let's start by covering the most basic usage scenario—rendering a Handlebars template into a DOM element using jQuery. Let's first start by looking at the Handlebars template file itself:

```
<p><strong>First: </strong>{{first}}</p>
<p><strong>Last: </strong>{{last}}</p>
```

As you can see, this is essentially basic HTML with a bit of specialized Handlebars syntax mixed in for the dynamic parts. This template is stored inside of a .hbs file (short for *handlebars*—some people use the full .handlebars extension). We can update our Webpack configuration to add the Handlebars loader. This parses and compiles the .hbs templates for us, meaning that our code that uses these templates can import them just like regular JavaScript modules. Let's take a look at what this looks like in our view component:

```
// Imports the compiled Handlebars "template"
// function just like a regular JavaScript module.
import template from './my-view.hbs';
import myStore from '../stores/my-store';

export default class MyView {
  constructor(element) {

    // Sets the container element that
    // we'll use to place the rendered template
    // content. Expected to be a jQuery object.
    this.element = element;

    // When the store state changes, we can
    // re-render the view.
    myStore.on('change', (state) => {
      this.render(state);
```

```
  });
}

// Renders the view. The default state is
// the initial "myStore.state". We use the
// "element" property of the view to set the
// HTML to the rendered output of the Handlebars
// "template()".
render(state = myStore.state) {
  this.element.html(template(state));
  return this;
}
}
```

The `template()` function that this view module imports is created as the result of the Webpack plugin compiling the template into a function for us. The runtime for Handlebars is included as part of the bundle that Webpack creates. The `render()` method of our view component calls the `template()` function, passing it a context and using the return value as the new content for the view's element. The context is just the state of the store, and each time the store state changes, the `html()` jQuery function is used to replace the existing element content.

The fundamental difference between ReactJS and an approach such as this one that uses the Handlebars templating engine, is that React attempts to make small updates. With Handlebars, we could end up replacing a lot of DOM content, and the performance issues could become noticeable by users. To combat these sorts of problems, we have to change the way our application is composed. This in and of itself could put us at a disadvantage compared to using something like React where we can re-render large DOM structures and still be efficient.

Now, let's take a look at the store that drives the content of this view:

```
import { EventEmitter } from 'events';

import dispatcher from '../dispatcher';
import { MY_ACTION } from '../actions/my-action';

// The initial state of the store. Instead of
// empty strings, this state uses labels that
// indicate that there's still data to come.
var state = {
  first: 'loading...',
```

```
      last: 'loading...'
};

class MyStore extends EventEmitter {
  constructor() {
    super();

    this.id = dispatcher.register((e) => {
      switch(e.type) {

        // When the "MY_ACTION" action is
        // dispatched, we extend the state
        // with the value of "payload",
        // overriding any existing property values.
        case MY_ACTION:
          this.emit('change',
            (state = Object.assign(
              {},
              state,
              e.payload
            ))
          );
          break;
      }
    });
  }

  get state() {
    return state;
  }
}

export default new MyStore();
```

This is a fairly typical store—not unlike most stores that we've seen so far in this
book. The payload that's dispatched as part of the MY_ACTION action is used to
extend the state of the store and will override existing property names, if any.
Let's take a look at the main program now:

```
import $ from 'jquery';

import { myAction } from './actions/my-action';
import MyView from './views/my-view';
```

```
// Constructs the new view and performs the
// initial render by calling "render()". Note
// that there's now stored reference to this view,
// because we don't actually need to. If we
// did, "render()" returns the view instance.
new MyView($('#app')).render();

// After 1 second, dispatch "MY_ACTION", which
// will replace the "loading..." labels.
setTimeout(() => {
  myAction({
    first: 'Face',
    last: 'Book'
  });
}, 1000);
```

This is where we initialize the instance of our view component, passing it a jQuery instance. This jQuery object represents the #app element, and is used by the view to hold the rendered Handlebars template content. After a one second delay, we call myAction(), which causes the myStore state to change and the handlebars template to re-render.

Generally, what happens when our Handlebars templates start getting bigger, we'll start adding specialized handlers that only respond to specific store properties. The reason is that the properties change too frequently and they only impact a tiny section of the visible UI. These micro-handlers then proliferate, and we start to lose predictability because we're introducing more paths into the rendering code. With ReactJS, this is less likely to happen, because we seldom have to decompose our view updates like this.

Composing views

If we're using Handlebars templates as the main ingredient of our view components, we probably need the ability to decompose our templates into smaller chunks. Think about the way we decompose our React components—we end up with smaller components that can usually be shared across features. Using Handlebars templates, we can achieve something similar using partial templates. The partial is a smaller part that fits into a larger whole to form the template that gets rendered by the view component.

Let's start by looking at a Handlebars template that serves as the list view for a store that has an array of user data:

```
<ul>
  {{#each users}}
  <li>{{> item-view}}</li>
  {{/each}}
</ul>
```

This template is iterating over the users property of our store, which is an array. However, instead of directly rendering each item, it's simply referring to a partial template using special syntax. Let's look at this partial template now, so we can get a sense of what's being passed to it:

```
<span style="text-transform: capitalize">{{first}}</span>
<span style="text-transform: capitalize">{{last}}</span>
```

In this template, we don't have to qualify the properties that are used in this case: first and last. The context in the parent template is passed to the partial template, in this case the user object. So it's kind of like passing in props to a child React component from a parent component. Once again, however, the difference is that every Handlebars component we use to compose the structure of the DOM elements is re-rendered as there's no virtual DOM to speak of. Let's look at the store that was used to populate this view with data:

```
import { EventEmitter } from 'events';

import dispatcher from '../dispatcher';
import { REVERSE } from '../actions/reverse';

// The initial state is a list of
// user objects.
var state = {
  users: [
    { first: 'first 1', last: 'last 1' },
    { first: 'first 2', last: 'last 2' },
    { first: 'first 3', last: 'last 3' }
  ]
};

class MyStore extends EventEmitter {
  constructor() {
    super();
```

```
    this.id = dispatcher.register((e) => {
      switch(e.type) {

        // When the "REVERSE" action is dispatched,
        // the "state.users" array is reversed by
        // calling "reverse()".
        case REVERSE:
          this.emit('change',
            (state = Object.assign(
              {},
              state,
              { users: state.users.reverse() }
            ))
          );
          break;
      }
    });
  }

  get state() {
    return state;
  }
}

export default new MyStore();
```

And finally, the main program. Here, we'll setup an interval timer that keeps dispatching the REVERSE action. This causes the whole UI to re-render with every dispatch:

```
import $ from 'jquery';

import { reverse } from './actions/reverse';
import ListView from './views/list-view';

// Performs the initial rendering of
// the list view, after initializing
// the view using the "#app" element.
new ListView($('#app')).render();

// Every second, toggle the sort
// order of the list by re-rendering
// the main template and it's partial
// templates.
setInterval(reverse, 1000);
```

Generally speaking, Flux architectures should have as few stores as possible. However, if we're using Handlebars in the view layer, we might be influenced to design our stores differently. For example, we might want to split the collective application state in such a way that results in less DOM structure being re-inserted into the document.

Handling events

Long before any modern web frameworks came into existence, jQuery was addressing cross-browser event-handling issues. Though the API has changed over the years, the powerful capabilities of jQuery's event handling remain intact. This is something that's obviously relevant if we're building views that are powered by jQuery and Handlebars.

The most pressing challenge with event handling in this context is the fact that we're re-rendering elements every time a Handlebars template needs updating. What we don't want is to have to re-attach event handlers to DOM elements every time they're inserted into the DOM. ReactJS utilizes a strategy that doesn't actually bind event handlers directly to the element we want to listen to. Instead, the handler is bound to the body element and as events bubble up, the appropriate handler is invoked. It turns out that this approach has a performance advantage, because it avoids having to bind the same handler function to the same element, over and over. Here's an illustration of the idea:

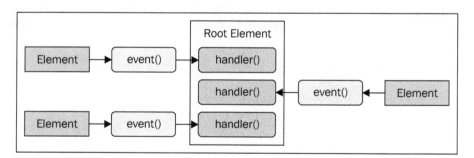

We can achieve something similar to this using jQuery. Let's first look at the Handlebars template files so that we can get a feel for the type of UI we're dealing with here. We'll extend the preceding example by adding a reverse button and selection capabilities. Here's the new item view template:

```
<a href="#{{@index}}" style="font-weight: {{fontWeight}}"
  <span style="text-transform: capitalize">{{first}}</span>
```

```
<span style="text-transform: capitalize">{{last}}</span>
</a>
```

The item is now a link. Note that we're able to use the `@index` Handlebars syntax, which allows access to the index of the current item in the collection we're iterating over. Even though the iteration happens in another template, this special value is still accessible. Now let's see what we have in the main list view Handlebars template:

```
<button>Reverse</button>
<ul>
  {{#each users}}
  <li>{{> item-view}}</li>
  {{/each}}
</ul>
```

The `ul` that builds the list is the same as it was previously. Now we have a new button to reverse the sort order of the list, instead of an interval timer. Let's now take a look at the event handling capabilities of the view component:

```
import template from './list-view.hbs';
import { reverse } from '../actions/reverse';
import { select } from '../actions/select';
import myStore from '../stores/my-store';

export default class ListView {
  constructor(element) {

    this.element = element;

    // When the store state changes, re-render
    // the view.
    myStore.on('change', (state) => {
      this.render(state);
    });

    this.element

      // Binds the click event to "#app", but
      // is only handled if a "button" element
      // generated the event. The "reverse()"
      // action creator is used as the handler.
      .on('click', 'button', reverse)

      // Binds the click event to "#app", but
      // is only handled if an "a" element
```

```
    // generated the event. The index is parsed
    // from the "href" attribute, and this is
    // passed as the payload to the "select()"
    // action creator.
    .on('click', 'a', (e) => {
      e.preventDefault();

      let index = +(/(\d+)$/)
        .exec(e.currentTarget.href)[1];

      select(index);
    });
  }

  // Sets the HTML of "element" to the rendered
  // Handlebars "template()". The context of
  // the template is always the Flux store state.
  render(state = myStore.state) {
    this.element.html(template(state));
    return this;
  }
}
```

We're following the pattern of React where the handler is never directly attached to something that's going to be re-rendered frequently. In fact, you can see that the event handlers are setup in the constructor of the view component, long before anything has ever been rendered by this view. This works because the #app element is already in place, and this is the element we're interested in.

The first handler is for the reverse button, and it uses the reverse() action creator function. It's the second parameter to on() that provides the element context, so that we know this handler is for button elements. The same principle is applied with our second handler, which is called when the user clicks a link. Here, we're simply preventing the default browser behavior and dispatching the select event. Now, let's take a look at some of the changes we had to make to our store to support this new event behavior:

```
import { EventEmitter } from 'events';

import dispatcher from '../dispatcher';
import { REVERSE } from '../actions/reverse';
import { SELECT } from '../actions/select';

// The initial state is a list of
```

```javascript
// user objects. They each have a
// "fontWeight" property which is
// translated to a CSS value when
// rendered.
var state = {
  users: [
    {
      first: 'first 1',
      last: 'last 1',
      fontWeight: 'normal'
    },
    {
      first: 'first 2',
      last: 'last 2',
      fontWeight: 'normal'
    },
    {
      first: 'first 3',
      last: 'last 3',
      fontWeight: 'normal'
    }
  ]
};

class MyStore extends EventEmitter {
  constructor() {
    super();

    this.id = dispatcher.register((e) => {
      switch(e.type) {

        // When the "REVERSE" action is dispatched,
        // the "state.users" array is reversed by
        // calling "reverse()".
        case REVERSE:
          this.emit('change',
            (state = Object.assign(
              {},
              state,
              { users: state.users.reverse() }
            ))
          );
          break;
```

```
            // When the "SELECT" action is dispatched, we
            // need to find the appropriate item based on
            // the "payload" index and mark it as selected.
            case SELECT:
              this.emit('change',
                (state = Object.assign(
                  {},
                  state,
                  { users: state.users.map((v, i) => {

                    // If the current index is the selected
                    // item, change the "fontWeight" property.
                    if (i === e.payload) {
                      return Object.assign({}, v,
                        { fontWeight: 'bold' });

                    // Otherwise, set the "fontWeight" back
                    // to "normal" so that any previously
                    // selected items are reset.
                    } else {
                      return Object.assign({}, v,
                        { fontWeight: 'normal' });
                    }
                  })}
                ))
              );
              break;
          }
        });
      }

      get state() {
        return state;
      }
    }


    export default new MyStore();
```

There are two important changes here that are worth pointing out. The first change is that our users array now has a new fontWeight property for each item within it. This is necessary because it controls the display of our links to indicate that something has been selected. Everything defaults to normal since nothing has been selected yet.

We could put some code in our view component that looks for a `fontWeight` property, and when it can't find one, it defaults to normal. The problem with this tactic is that it introduces unnecessary logic into the view component. We're trying to keep everything in the store, even seemingly trivial things like this. Even if that means adding default values in a store that are also default in the browser.

The second change to the store is the addition of the `SELECT` handling logic. When this action is dispatched, we match up the item index with the payload index and change the font weight. Everything else that doesn't match gets reverted back to a normal `font-weight`.

Using VanillaJS

Not having enough diversity in the ecosystem of frontend JavaScript rendering libraries isn't a problem. In fact, the problem for us is the exact opposite—there's too many libraries and frameworks to choose from. While some people in the JavaScript community view this disjointed plethora of choice as a problem, it doesn't have to be. It's better to have too many technologies to choose from than not enough.

In this section, we'll discuss using VanillaJS as our view technology—no libraries or frameworks. The idea isn't to completely avoid using frameworks, it's to keep our options open as the architecture of our application unfolds. Eventually, we might move our view components to use React, or perhaps there's some other new hotness we've been keeping our eye on.

Keeping my options open

At some point, we have to choose a technology to use with our view components. That depends on which stage of the project we're on. If it's early in the game and we've already decided on a view library, we could end up limiting ourselves to this technology for a long time. Given how fast JavaScript and it's surrounding ecosystem is moving, being stuck with any technology for a length of time usually isn't a good thing. We have to embrace the fact that change is constantly deprecating the thing that was once new hotness.

On the other hand, we don't want to wait too long to make a technology decision for our views, because the more things we build using plain JS, the more difficult it's going to be to migrate these views to a more opinionated approach. Where's the sweet-spot?

The best strategy is to avoid lock-in where possible. This involves keeping things loosely-coupled so that they're substitutable. Thankfully, Flux architectures make this easy because the responsibilities of the view layer are fairly limited. They need to listen to store change events and render the store state. Maybe we should try building two sets of view components. The first set uses a technology such as React, and the other uses something else, such as jQuery and Handlebars. This not only allows us to pick the view technology that works best for our product, but also lets us test our readiness to adopt new technologies, which we'll inevitably want to do.

Moving to React

As you saw in this chapter, we can use technologies like jQuery and Handlebars in the view components of our Flux architecture. What's more, they don't interfere with the unidirectional data-flow found in Flux architectures. That being said, React is probably the best suited view technology to use as part of a Flux architecture. From the perspective of unidirectional data-flow, React picks this up naturally. Even without Flux in place, stateless functional React components behave exactly how we would expect a view to behave in a Flux architecture. When new properties come in, new HTML is rendered.

In addition to React's natural tendency toward unidirectional data-flow, the idea of re-rendering large DOM structures feels less daunting. Thanks to the virtual DOM that React uses to patch the rendered output—instead of replacing the entire thing— we can efficiently pass store state to top-level views for re-rendering. React also handles other edge cases for us too, such as maintaining the focus of a form control during a re-render.

The real question is twofold: how inevitable is a move to React, and how salvageable is our existing code? Well, the first question is generally pretty easy to answer— there's a high probability that you're going to use React in your Flux architecture. It's simply a good fit for a Flux architecture. However, it's naive to assume that there are no negative tradeoffs, like higher memory consumption for example. So if we do decide to move to React after already having developed some view components, do we need to throw everything out? Unlikely. Views play a relatively small role in Flux architectures, as I've stressed throughout the book. So, if moving to React solves problems in your Flux view components, by all means do so—it's a good direction to move in. For now.

New hotness

A couple of years ago, React was brand new hotness. As with any new hotness, developers can and should approach the technology with some degree of skepticism. As it turned out, React was a good bet for many of it's early adopters. On the other hand, not all new and shiny technologies work out. This is how progress is made, and is why so much progress has been made in the JavaScript ecosystem. What's the point of this anecdote? There's always going to be new hotness that's superior to what you've already bet on. Be ready to adopt and re-adopt again.

For example, Google is currently implementing view technology called Incremental DOM (`http://google.github.io/incremental-dom/`), which takes a different approach to rendering that uses a lot less memory. There's `Veu.js` (`http://vuejs.org/`). There are endless other possibilities for the future. Just make sure that you are views can pivot and embrace the latest and greatest view technology—it'll be here soon.

Summary

The focus of this chapter was on the view components of our Flux architecture and how they're loosely-coupled to the point that we can substitute rendering technologies. We started with a discussion on React itself and what makes it a good fit for Flux architectures. Then, we switched gears and covered the potential downsides of using ReactJS.

We spent some time implementing views that leveraged both jQuery and Handlebars. These are two mature technologies that many developers are familiar with and serve as a good jumping off point for implementing a Flux architecture. However, there are strong motivations for anyone implementing Flux to look at React as the view technology of choice.

We wrapped the chapter up with a discussion on using VanillaJS to render our view components. There's no sense in rushing into using a particular technology until we understand the ramifications of that choice. There's always going to be newer and better view libraries, and Flux architectures make it easy to pivot and embrace new hotness.

12
Leveraging Flux Libraries

Flux, first and foremost, is a set of architectural guidelines, specified as patterns for us to follow. While this affords the ultimate flexibility, it can be paralyzing sometimes, when it comes to deciding how to implement a given Flux component. Thankfully, there are some really good Flux libraries out there that provide opinionated implementations of Flux components, which remove the need for a lot of the boilerplate code we would have to write. The idea of this chapter is to look at two of these libraries, to show just how different Flux implementations can be. The goal isn't compliance, but rather a solid architecture that helps our application get the job done.

Implementing core Flux components

In this section, we're going to reiterate the idea that we can change the implementation specifics of the various Flux components in our architecture. We'll start by talking about the dispatcher itself, and think about the various changes that we might make. Then, we'll think about stores and the enhancements we might want to make there. Finally, we'll discuss actions and action creator functions.

Customizing the dispatcher

In Chapter 10, *Implementing a Dispatcher*, we implemented our own dispatcher component. The reference implementation by Facebook is perfectly fine to use, but it's not meant to be the de-facto component found in every production Flux architecture. Instead, it's meant to be a jumping off point, so we can see how the Flux dispatcher specification is supposed to work.

Our solution was to expose the `dispatch()` and `register()` functions from the dispatcher module. By doing so, we made using the dispatcher a little more direct in other areas of our code. There was no longer a dispatcher instance to think about—everything was encapsulated within the dispatcher module.

A generic Flux library might want to take this a step further and completely dissolve the dispatcher, which might sound nuts—it's an essential Flux component. However, we can still achieve the same architectural principle of the dispatcher without explicitly implementing this abstraction. This is the whole point of releasing Flux as a set of specs instead of a concrete implementation. We know conceptually what a Flux architecture should and should not do—we get to pick how to enforce these rules with our implementation.

Implementing a base store

Another improvement we made in *Chapter 10, Implementing a Dispatcher*, was to the store hierarchy. We had each of our stores inherit from a base class. The main reason we implemented this functionality was to automate the registration of the store with the dispatcher, which is good, because there's not much sense in a Flux store that isn't listening to events emitted from the dispatcher. Perhaps a Flux library should handle this type of base functionality for us.

We also implemented method action handlers. This was actually a function of the dispatcher itself in our implementation, and it was quite limiting. Perhaps the base store is the appropriate place for this type of functionality. Libraries should contain this type of generic complexity, not our application.

What's nice about inheriting base functionality with Flux stores is that this is where the brains of our application live. If we were to discover some generic state transformation behavior that applied to more than one store, having a base store in place makes it easy for us to factor out the common code. Maybe a Flux library could ship with some basic transformations in their base store that we would inherit from.

Creating actions

Constants are a great way to be explicit about actions in Flux architectures. The action module defines the constant, and the action creator function passes the constant to the dispatcher. Stores also use these constants when determining how to handle actions as they're dispatched. This creates an explicit tie between the action creator and the code in stores that respond to this action.

In *Chapter 10, Implementing a Dispatcher*, we adopted a different approach. The action creator functions still defined constants and used them when dispatching the action. However, we made changes that allowed for our stores to define method handlers. So instead of one function that listened to the dispatcher, the stores defined methods that matched the constant defined for the action. This is convenient from the store's perspective, but it diminishes the value of having constants if they're only used by the action creator functions.

A Flux library could help make dispatching and handling actions a little more straightforward. Using constants and `switch` statements is good insofar as it makes what's happening explicit. We like explicitness in our Flux architecture. The challenge is that this approach requires diligence on the part of the programmers implementing the system. In other words, there's plenty of opportunity for human error. A Flux library could remove the error-prone aspects of dealing with constants in two places.

Another area that a Flux library could help is with asynchronous action creator functions. The asynchronous behavior of our application is likely to follow a similar pattern:

- Dispatch an action that changes the state of a store before the asynchronous code runs
- Dispatch an action when the response arrives
- Dispatch a different action if the asynchronous behavior fails.

It's almost like asynchronous actions have a lifecycle that could be abstracted into a common function by a Flux library.

Implementation pain points

In the preceding section, we covered the areas of Flux that might benefit from a custom implementation. Before we dive into `Alt.js` and Redux, we'll briefly talk about some of pain points with implementing Flux architectures. Asynchronous actions are tough to get right, in any architecture, let alone Flux. The way we partition our application state into stores can be a tricky design problem. If we get this wrong, it can be hard to recover from. Finally, we have data dependency challenges to think about.

Dispatching asynchronous actions

As we discussed in the preceding section, asynchronous action creators are difficult to implement. It's challenging because we usually have to let the stores know that this asynchronous action is about to take place so that the UI can be updated to reflect this. For example, when a button is clicked that sends one or more AJAX requests, we probably want to disable that button before actually sending the request, to prevent duplicate requests. The only way to do this in Flux is to dispatch an action, because everything is unidirectional.

Libraries can help with this, to an extent. For example, the pre-request actions and success/error response actions can be somewhat abstracted into something that's easier to use, because that's a common pattern. However, even doing this leaves the issue of assembling requests to go fetch all the data that's needed for a given action, synchronize the responses and pass them each to the store so that it can transform them into something that the view needs.

Maybe it's best if we were to leave this asynchronous problem outside the scope of Flux. Facebook has introduced GraphQL, for example, a language that simplifies building complex data from backend services and only responding with what the store actually needs. This is all done in one response, so we save on bandwidth and latency as well. This approach isn't for everyone, and so it's up to the Flux implementer to choose how they want to deal with asynchronicity, just as long as the unidirectional data-flow on the client remains intact.

Partitioning stores

Incorrectly partitioning the stores in our Flux architecture is perhaps one of the biggest design risks we face. What generally happens is that the stores are roughly balanced; then, as the system evolves, all the new features end up going into one store while the responsibilities of the other stores aren't clear. The stores become unbalanced, in other words. The store that holds onto the majority of the application state gets too complex to maintain.

Another potential issue with the partitioning of our stores is that they grow to be too fine-grained. We don't want this to happen either. Though the state that's managed by individual stores is simple enough, the complexity resides in the dependencies between all these stores. Even if there aren't too many dependencies, when there's more stores to think about, it's more difficult to hold enough state in our heads as we're trying to reason about something. When related state is all in one place, it's much easier to predict what will happen.

What if a Flux library, like Redux, took a radical approach and eliminated all sources of confusion by only allowing a single store? This indeed prevents design issues like partitioning stores. Instead, as we'll see later on the chapter, Redux uses reducer functions to transform the state of the single store.

Using Alt

`Alt.js` is a Flux library that implements a lot of the boilerplate code for us. It completely adheres to the Flux concepts and patterns, but let's us focus on the architecture from the perspective of our application, rather than worrying about action constants and `switch` statements.

In this section, we'll touch on the core concepts of Alt before diving into a simple todo list example. The example is intentionally simple—you'll be able to map the code back to the Flux concepts you've learned about so far in this book.

The core ideas

The main goal of the Facebook Flux package is to provide a reference implementation of a basic dispatcher component. This serves well as an aide to the concepts of Flux— actions are dispatched to stores in a synchronous, unidirectional fashion. As we've seen through the book, the dispatcher concept doesn't even necessarily need to be exposed to those who are implementing Flux. We can simplify the Flux abstractions and yet still fall within the constraints of a Flux architecture.

Alt is a Flux library that's supposed to be used in production applications—it's not a reference implementation. Let's go over a few of it's goals as a Flux library before we jump into the code.

- **Compliant**: Alt doesn't borrow ideas from Flux—it's truly meant for Flux systems. For example, the concept of stores, actions, and views are all relevant. Likewise, the principles of Flux architecture are followed closely by Alt. Things like synchronous update rounds and unidirectional data-flow are enforced.

- **Automates boilerplate**: Some of the more tedious programming tasks associated with implementing Flux are handled nicely by Alt. These include things like automatically creating action creator functions and action constants. Alt will also take care of store action handler methods for us—reducing the need for long `switch` statements.

- **No dispatcher**: There's no dispatcher for our code to interface with. Dispatching actions to all the stores is taken care of behind the scenes, when we call our action creator functions. Things like dependency management between stores are handled directly within the stores themselves.

Creating stores

The simple application that we're going to create will display two lists for the user. One list is for the todo items, the other list is for the items that have been completed. We'll use two stores—one for each list. Let's take a look at how we create stores using `Alt.js`. First, we have the `Todo` store:

```
import alt from '../alt';
import actions from '../actions';

class Todo {
  constructor() {

    // This is the state of the input element
    // used to create a new Todo item.
    this.inputValue = '';

    // The initial list of todo items...
    this.todos = [
      { title: 'Build this thing' },
      { title: 'Build that thing' },
      { title: 'Build all the things' }
    ];

    // Sets up the handler methods to be called
    // when the corresponding action is dispatched.
    this.bindListeners({
      createTodo: actions.CREATE_TODO,
      removeTodo: actions.REMOVE_TODO,
      updateInputValue: actions.UPDATE_INPUT_VALUE
    });
  }

  // Creates a new Todo using the action "payload"
  // as the title.
  createTodo(payload) {
    this.todos.push({ title: payload });
  }

  // Removes the Todo based on the index, which is
  // passed in as the action payload.
  removeTodo(payload) {
    this.todos.splice(payload, 1);
  }
```

```
    // Updates the Todo value that the user is currently
    // entering in the Todo input box.
    updateInputValue(payload) {
      this.inputValue = payload;
    }
}


  // The "createStore()" function hooks our store class
  // up with all the relevant action dispatching machinery,
  // returning an instance of the store.
  export default alt.createStore(Todo, 'Todo');
```

This probably doesn't look very familiar, relative to what we've seen so far in this book. Not to worry; we'll walk through the moving parts here now. The first question you probably have is — where's the state? It's not clear by looking at the code, but the state is any instance variables of the class. In this case, it's the inputValue string and the todos array.

Next, we have a call to bindListeners() with a configuration object passed to it. This is how Alt stores map actions to methods. You can see that we have methods defined that correspond to what's passed into bindListeners(). Lastly, we have the call to createStore(). This function instantiates the Todo store class for us, but it also hooks up the dispatch mechanism.

That's all there is to the store definition — it's ready to be used by views that need to render it's state. Now let's take a look at the Done store, which follows the same approach, only with fewer moving parts:

```
import alt from '../alt';
import actions from '../actions';
import todo from './todo';


class Done {
  constructor() {

    // The "done" state holds an array of
    // completed items.
    this.done = [];

    // Binds the only listener of this store.
    this.bindListeners({
      createDone: actions.CREATE_DONE
    });
  }
```

```
    // This action payload is the index of an item
    // from the "todo" store. This is called when
    // the item is clicked, and the item is added
    // to the "done" array.
    //
    // Note that this action handler does not mutate
    // the "todo" state as that is not allowed.
    createDone(payload) {
      const { todos } = todo.getState();
      this.done.splice(0, 0, todos[payload]);
    }
  }
}

// Creates the store instance, and hooks it
// up with the Alt dispatching machinery.
export default alt.createStore(Done, 'Done');
```

You can see here that this store actually uses the Todo store to copy over item data
when an item is marked as done. However, this store doesn't mutate the Todo store,
as that would violate the unidirectional data-flow.

> These store classes aren't event emitters, so they don't explicitly
> emit anything when the state changes. For example when a todo
> is added, how do the views know that anything has changed?
> Since the createTodo() method is called automatically for
> us, the notification mechanism also happens automatically once
> our method has finished executing. We'll see more on the state
> change notification semantics momentarily.

Declaring action creators

We've seen how stores respond to actions being dispatched. Now we need a means
to actually dispatch these actions. This is probably the easiest aspect of our Alt
application. Alt can generate the functions we need, as well as the constants that
are used by the bindListeners() call in our stores. Let's take a look at the actions
module and see how this works with Alt:

```
import alt from './alt';

// Exports an object with functions that accept
// a payload argument. These are the action
// creators. Also creates action constants
// based on the names passed to "generateActions()"
export default alt.generateActions(
```

```
    'createTodo',
    'createDone',
    'removeTodo',
    'updateInputValue'
);
```

This will export an object with action creator functions that have the same names as the strings passed to `generateActions()`. And it'll generate the action constants used by the store. Since our action creator functions are all very similar, `generateActions()` has high utility. There's a lot of boilerplate code that we no longer have to maintain. On the other hand, there are more complex cases that involve asynchronous actions that need more code than this. Take a look at the Alt documentation for asynchronous actions if you're interested in using this library for your project.

Listening for state changes

All throughout this book, we've added event handler functions to the change event emitted by our stores. With libraries like Alt, this is somewhat managed for us already. Let's take a look at the main module of our application which uses the `AltContainer` React component to feed store data into our other React components:

```
// The React and Alt components we need...
import React from 'react';
import { render } from 'react-dom';
import AltContainer from 'alt-container';

// The stores and React components from
// this application...
import todo from './stores/todo';
import done from './stores/done';
import TodoList from './views/todo-list';
import DoneList from './views/done-list';

// Renders the "AltContainer" component. This
// is where the stores are tied to the views.
// The "TodoList" and "DoneList" components
// are children of the "AltContainer", so
// they get the "todo" and the "done" stores
// as props.
render(
  <AltContainer stores={{ todo, done }}>
    <TodoList/>
    <DoneList/>
  </AltContainer>,
  document.getElementById('app')
);
```

The `AltContainer` component accepts a `stores` property. The container will listen to each of these stores and re-render it's children when the state of the any store changes. This is the only setup involved for getting our views to listen to stores—no manual `on()` or `listen()` calls all over the place. In the next section, we'll look at the `TodoList` and the `DoneList` components to see how they work with `AltContainer`.

Rendering views and dispatching actions

The job of the `TodoList` component is to render items from the `Todo` store. There are two other things this view needs to handle as well. First, there's the `input` element that the user uses to enter new todo items. Second, we also need to mark items as done when they're clicked, by moving them to the done list. These latter two responsibilities involve event handling and dispatching actions. Let's take a look at the implementation of the todo list view:

```
import React from 'react';
import { Component } from 'react';

import actions from '../actions';

export default class TodoList extends Component {
  render() {

    // The relevant state from the "todo" store
    // that we're rendering here.
    const { todos, inputValue } = this.props.todo;

    // Renders an input for new todos, and the list
    // of current todos. When the user types
    // and then hits enter, the new todo is created.
    // When the user clicks a todo, it's moved to the
    // "done" store.
    return (
      <div>
        <h3>TODO</h3>
        <div>
          <input
            value={inputValue}
            placeholder="TODO..."
            onKeyUp={this.onKeyUp}
            onChange={this.onChange}
            autoFocus
          />
```

```
        </div>
        <ul>
          {todos.map(({ title }, i) =>
            <li key={i}>
              <a
                href="#"
                onClick={this.onClick.bind(null, i)}
              >{title}</a>
            </li>
          )}
        </ul>
      </div>
    );
  }

  // An active Todo was clicked. The "key" is the
  // index of the Todo within the store. This is
  // passed as the payload to the "createDone()"
  // action, and next to the "removeTodo()" action.
  onClick(key) {
    actions.createDone(key);
    actions.removeTodo(key);
  }

  // If the user has entered some text and the
  // "enter" key is pressed, we use the
  // "createTodo()" action to create a new
  // item using the entered text. Then we clear
  // the input using the "updateInputValue()"
  // action, passing it an empty string.
  onKeyUp(e) {
    const { value } = e.target;

    if (e.which === 13 && value) {
      actions.createTodo(value);
      actions.updateInputValue('');
    }
  }

  // The text input value changed - update the store.
  onChange(e) {
    actions.updateInputValue(e.target.value);
  }
}
```

You might be wondering why we can't just clear `e.target.value` when the **Enter** key is pressed. Indeed we could do this, but this would go against the nature of Flux where state is kept in stores. This includes transient values as they're being entered by the user. What if another part of the application wanted to know about the text input value? Well, all it needs is to depend on the `Todo` store. If the state wasn't there, then our code would have to query the DOM, which we don't want to do.

Finally, let's look at the done list component. This component is simpler than the todo list because there's no event handling:

```
import React from 'react';
import { Component } from 'react';

export default class DoneList extends Component {
  render() {

    // The "done" array is the only state we need
    // from the "done" store.
    const { done } = this.props.done;

    // We want to display these items
    // as strikethrough text.
    const itemStyle = {
      textDecoration: 'line-through'
    }

    // Renders the list of done items, with
    // the "itemStyle" applied to each item.
    return (
      <div>
        <h3>DONE</h3>
        <ul>
          {done.map(({ title }) =>
            <li style={itemStyle}>{title}</li>
          )}
        </ul>
      </div>
    );
  }
}
```

Using Redux

In this section, we're going to look at the Redux library for implementing a Flux architecture. Unlike Alt.js, Redux doesn't aim for Flux compliance. The goal of Redux is to borrow the important ideas from Flux, leaving the tedious bits behind. Despite not implementing Flux components as specified in the official documentation, Redux is the go-to solution for React architectures now. Redux is proof that simplicity always wins over advanced features.

The core ideas

Before implementing some Redux code, let's take a moment to look at the core ideas of Redux:

- **No dispatcher**: This is just like Alt.js, which also purges the dispatcher concept from it's API. The fact that these Flux libraries don't expose a dispatcher component serves to illustrate the point that Flux is just a set of ideas and patterns, not an implementation. Both Alt and Redux dispatch actions, they just don't require a dispatcher to do it.

- **One store to rule them all**: Redux eschews the notion that a Flux architecture requires multiple stores. Instead, one store is used to hold the entire application state. At first glance, this might sound like the store would get too large and be too difficult to understand. This is just as likely to happen with multiple stores, the only difference there is that the application state is split into different modules.

- **Dispatch to the store**: When there's only one store to worry about, we can make design concessions, such as treating the store and the dispatcher as the same concept. This is exactly what Redux does—it dispatches actions directly to the store.

- **Pure reducers**: The idea behind multiple Flux stores is to split the application state into a few logically separated domains. We can still do this using Redux, the difference is that we separate our state into domains using reducer functions. These functions are responsible for transforming the state of the store when actions are dispatched. They're pure because they return new data and avoid introducing any side-effects.

Reducers and stores

We're now going to implement the same simple todo application that we made using Alt—this time using Redux. There's a lot of overlap between the two libraries, particularly with the React components themselves; not much needs to change there. Where Redux departs from Alt and Flux in general is with it's single store, and the reducer functions that change it's state. With that said, we'll look at the store and it's reducer functions first.

We'll create a module for the initial state of the the Redux store. This is an important first step because it provides the initial structure for the reducer functions that transform the store state. Let's take a look at the initial state module:

```
import Immutable from 'immutable';

// The initial state of the Redux store. The
// "shape" of the application state includes
// two domains - "Todo" and "Done". Each domain
// is an Immutable.js structure.
const initialState = {
  Todo: Immutable.fromJS({
    inputValue: '',
    todos: [
      { title: 'Build this thing' },
      { title: 'Build that thing' },
      { title: 'Build all the things' }
    ]
  }),
  Done: Immutable.fromJS({
    done: []
  })
};


export default initialState;
```

The state is a simple JavaScript object. You can see that the single store isn't just a tangled mess of properties, it's organized by two main properties—Todo and Done. This is like having multiple stores, except they're in one object. Something else you'll notice is that each store property is an Immutable.js data structure. The reason for this is that we need to treat the state that's passed into our reducer functions as immutable. This library makes enforcing immutability easy.

The state transformations that take place with the store state will be divided into two reducer functions. In fact, the two functions map to the two initial properties of the store: Todo and Done. Let's look at the Todo reducer first:

```
import Immutable from 'immutable';

import initialState from '../initial-state';
import {
  UPDATE_INPUT_VALUE,
  CREATE_TODO,
  REMOVE_TODO
} from '../constants';

export default function Todo(state = initialState, action) {
  switch (action.type) {

    // When the "UPDATE_INPUT_VALUE" action is dispatched,
    // we set the "inputValue" key of the Immutable.Map.
    case UPDATE_INPUT_VALUE:
      return state.set('inputValue', action.payload);

    // When the "CREATE_TODO" action is dispatched,
    // we push the new item to the end of the
    // Immutable.List
    case CREATE_TODO:
      return state.set('todos',
        state.get('todos').push(Immutable.Map({
          title: action.payload
        }))
      );

    // When the "REMOVE_TODO" action is dispatched,
    // we delete the item at the given index from
    // the Immutable.List.
    case REMOVE_TODO:
      return state.set('todos',
        state.get('todos').delete(action.payload));
    default:
      return state;
  }
}
```

The `switch` statement that's used here should look familiar — it's the same pattern we've been implementing the stores throughout this book. In fact, this function is just like a store, with two main differences. The first difference is that it's a function instead of a class. This means that instead of setting state property values, we return the new state. The second difference is that Redux handles the mechanics of listening to stores and calling this reducer function. With classes, we have to write a lot of this code ourselves.

> It's important that these reducer functions do not mutate the state argument. This is why we're using the `Immutable.js` library — to make it easier to transform existing state by creating new data. It's not necessary to use `Immutable.js` for transforming Redux store state, but it does help with code brevity.

Now let's look at the `Done` reducer function:

```
import Immutable from 'immutable';

import initialState from '../initial-state';
import { CREATE_DONE } from '../constants';

export default function Done(state = initialState, action) {
  switch (action.type) {

    // When the "CREATE_DONE" action is dispatched,
    // we insert the new item into the beginning
    // of the Immutable.List.
    case CREATE_DONE:
      return state.set('done',
        state.get('done')
          .insert(0, Immutable.Map(action.payload))
      );

    // Nothing to do, return the state "as-is".
    default:
      return state;
  }
}
```

We're almost done with our Redux store. At this point, we have two reducer functions, each in their own module. We need to tie them together using `combineReducers()` and `createStore()`. Let's take a look at our store module now:

```
import { combineReducers, createStore } from 'redux';

import initialState from './initial-state';
import Todo from './reducers/todo.js';
import Done from './reducers/done.js';

export default createStore(combineReducers({
  Todo,
  Done
}), initialState);
```

As you can see, the `combineReducers()` function creates a new function. This is the main reducer function that maintains the state of the application. So instead of your typical Flux dispatcher that needs to handle getting actions to several stores, Redux actions are dispatched to this single store, and our reducer functions are called in response.

Redux actions

As you know, there's a difference between actions and action creators. Actions are the payloads that get sent to the various Flux stores, whereas action creators are responsible for creating the action payloads, and then sending them to the dispatcher. With Redux, action creator functions are slightly different in that they only create the action payloads, they don't talk directly with the dispatcher.

We'll see how the action creators are called in the following section when we implement the view components. But for now, here's what our actions module looks like:

```
import {
  CREATE_TODO,
  CREATE_DONE,
  REMOVE_TODO,
  UPDATE_INPUT_VALUE
} from './constants';

// Creates a new Todo item. The "payload" should
// be an object with a "title" property.
export function createTodo(payload) {
  return {
```

```
    type: CREATE_TODO,
    payload
  };
}


// Creates a new Done item. The "payload" should
// be an object with a "title" property.
export function createDone(payload) {
  return {
    type: CREATE_DONE,
    payload
  };
}


// Removes the todo and the given "payload" index.
export function removeTodo(payload) {
  return {
    type: REMOVE_TODO,
    payload
  };
}


// Updates the "inputValue" state with the given
// "payload" string value.
export function updateInputValue(payload) {
  return {
    type: UPDATE_INPUT_VALUE,
    payload
  };
}
```

These functions just return the data that's going to be dispatched by the store—they don't actually dispatch the data. The exception to this is when asynchronous actions are involved. In this case, we actually need to dispatch the action once the asynchronous values have resolved. See the official Redux documentation where there are plenty of asynchronous action examples.

Rendering components and dispatching actions

At this point, we have a Redux store and action creator functions. All that's left to do is implement our React components and connect them to the store. We'll start with the `TodoList` view:

```
import React from 'react';
import { Component } from 'react';
import { connect } from 'react-redux';

import {
  updateInputValue,
  createTodo,
  createDone,
  removeTodo
} from '../actions';

class TodoList extends Component {
  constructor(...args) {
    super(...args);
    this.onClick = this.onClick.bind(this);
    this.onKeyUp = this.onKeyUp.bind(this);
    this.onChange = this.onChange.bind(this);
  }

  render() {

    // The relevant state from the "todo" store
    // that we're rendering here.
    const { todos, inputValue } = this.props;

    // Renders an input for new todos, and the list
    // of current todos. When the user types
    // and then hits enter, the new todo is created.
    // When the user clicks a todo, it's moved to the
    // "done" array.
    return (
      <div>
        <h3>TODO</h3>
        <div>
          <input
            value={inputValue}
```

```
              placeholder="TODO..."
              onKeyUp={this.onKeyUp}
              onChange={this.onChange}
              autoFocus
            />
        </div>
        <ul>
          {todos.map(({ title }, i) =>
            <li key={i}>
              <a
                href="#"
                onClick={this.onClick.bind(null, i)}
              >{title}</a>
            </li>
          )}
        </ul>
      </div>
    );
  }

  // An active Todo was clicked. The "key" is the
  // index of the Todo within the store. This is
  // passed as the payload to the "createDone()"
  // action, and next to the "removeTodo()" action.
  onClick(key) {
    const { dispatch, todos } = this.props;

    dispatch(createDone(todos[key]));
    dispatch(removeTodo(key));
  }

  // If the user has entered some text and the
  // "enter" key is pressed, we use the
  // "createTodo()" action to create a new
  // item using the entered text. Then we clear
  // the input using the "updateInputValue()"
  // action, passing it an empty string.
  onKeyUp(e) {
    const { dispatch } = this.props;
    const { value } = e.target;

    if (e.which === 13 && value) {
      dispatch(createTodo(e.target.value));
      dispatch(updateInputValue(''));
```

```
    }
  }

  // The text input value changed - update the store.
  onChange(e) {
    this.props.dispatch(
    updateInputValue(e.target.value));
  }
}


// The props that get passed to this component
// from the store. We just need to convert the
// "Todo" Immutable.js structure to plain JS.
function mapStateToProps(state) {
  return state.Todo.toJS();
}


// Exports the "connected" version of the
// component that's connect to the Redux store.
export default connect(mapStateToProps)(TodoList);
```

The key thing to note about this module is that it's not the component class that's exported. Instead, we use the connect() function from the react-redux package. This function connects the Redux store to this view. The state from the store passes through the mapStateToProps() function, which determines how the React component properties are assigned. In this case, we just need to transform the Immutable.js structure into a plain JavaScript object.

The downside of the event handlers is that we need to bind their context in the constructor, because React doesn't auto-bind the context for ES2015 style components. The handlers need access to this.props because it has the dispatch() function needed to dispatch our action data to the store, as well as the store data used to construct the action payloads. Now let's look at the DoneList component:

```
import React, { Component } from 'react';
import { connect } from 'react-redux';

class DoneList extends Component {
  render() {

    // The "done" array is the only state we need
    // from the "done" store.
    const { done } = this.props;
```

```
      // We want to display these items
      // as strikethrough text.
      constitemStyle = {
        textDecoration: 'line-through'
      }

      // Renders the list of done items, with
      // the "itemStyle" applied to each item.
      return (
        <div>
          <h3>DONE</h3>
          <ul>
            {done.map(({ title }, i) =>
              <li key={i} style={itemStyle}>{title}</li>
            )}
          </ul>
        </div>
      );
  }
}

// The props that get passed to this component
// from the store. We just need to convert the
// "Done" Immutable.js structure to plain JS.
function mapStateToProps(state) {
  return state.Done.toJS();
}

// Exports the "connected" version of the
// component that's connect to the Redux store.
export default connect(mapStateToProps)(DoneList);
```

As you can see, this works in much the same way as the TodoList component.
In fact, these components haven't changed much relative to the Alt implementation
of the same application. The last step is to hook up the two components with the
Redux store, which can be accomplished using the Provider component:

```
import React from 'react';
import { render } from 'react-dom';
import { Provider } from 'react-redux';

import store from './store';
import TodoList from './views/todo-list';
import DoneList from './views/done-list';
```

```
// Renders the "TodoList" and the "DoneList"
// components. The "Provider" component is
// used to connect the store to the components.
// When the store changes state, the children
// of "Provider" are re-rendered.
render(
  <Provider store={store}>
    <div>
      <TodoList/>
      <DoneList/>
    </div>
  </Provider>,
  document.getElementById('app')
);
```

Summary

In this chapter, you learned about leveraging Flux libraries. In particular, we looked at two of the prevailing libraries that can be used to implement Flux architectures.

We started the chapter off with a discussion that was mostly a recap of the fundamental principles of Flux and how we implemented them throughout the previous chapters of this book. We then covered some of the various pain points of implementing Flux—like singleton dispatchers, repetitive action code, and partitioning store modules. These are areas that a library like Alt.js or Redux could address for us.

We then proceeded to implement a simple todo application using the Alt.js Flux library. The idea behind Flux is to implement all the relevant Flux components while automating the typical arduous implementation chores behind the scenes for us. After this, we turned our attention to the Redux library. Redux is less concerned with following the Flux patterns exactly. Instead, Redux aims for simplicity while borrowing some of the more important Flux ideas like unidirectional data-flow.

In the next chapter, we'll cover two very important aspects of any Flux architecture—functional and performance testing.

13
Testing and Performance

We want the architecture of our application to be the best that it can possibly be. It may sound silly to have to state this, but it does bear repeating from time to time, as a reminder that the work we're doing with Flux has the potential to make or break the success of the application. The best tools we have in our arsenal are unit tests and performance tests. These two activities are equally important. Being functionally-correct but slow as hell is a failure. Being fast as hell and riddled with bugs is a failure.

A huge contributing factor to implementing successful tests is to focus on what's relevant. We'll spend time in this chapter thinking about what the important tests are for Flux architectures—from both a functional and a performance perspective. This is especially important to think about given how new Flux is to the community. We'll focus on specific Flux components and design some unit tests for them. We'll then think about the difference between benchmarking low-level code versus performance testing end-to-end scenarios.

Hello Jest

Jasmine is the widely accepted tool of choice when it comes to writing effective unit tests for JavaScript code. There's no shortage of add-on tools for Jasmine that make it possible to test just about anything and to use any tool to run your tests. For example, it's common practice to use a task runner such as Grunt or Gulp to run tests, along with the other various build tasks associated with the project.

Jest is a unit testing tool, developed by Facebook, which leverages the best parts of Jasmine while adding new capabilities. It's also easy to run Jest in our projects. For example, projects that depend on Webpack generally rely on NPM scripts to perform various tasks, as opposed to a task runner. This is easy to do with Jest, as we'll see in a moment.

There are three key aspects to Jest that will help us test our Flux architectures:

- Jest provides a virtualized JavaScript environment, including a DOM interface

- Jest spawns multiple worker processes to run our tests, leading to less time waiting for tests to complete and an overall faster development lifecycle

- Jest can mock JavaScript modules for us, making it easier to isolate units of code to test

Let's take a look at a quick example to get things rolling. Suppose we have the following function that we'd like to test:

```
// Builds and returns a string based
// on the "name" argument.
export default function sayHello(name = 'World') {
  return `Hello ${name}!`;
}
```

This should be easy enough, we just need to write a unit test that checks for expected output. Let's see what this test looks like in Jest:

```
// Tells Jest that we want the real "hello"
// module, not the mocked version.
jest.unmock('../hello');

// Imports the function we want to test.
import sayHello from '../hello';

// Your typical Jasmine test suite, test cases,
// and test assertions.
describe('sayHello()', () => {
  it('says hello world', () => {
    expect(sayHello()).toBe('Hello World!');
  });

  it('says hello flux', () => {
    expect(sayHello('Flux')).toBe('Hello Flux!');
  });
});
```

If this looks a lot like Jasmine, that's because it is. Jasmine is actually used under the hood to perform all the test assertions. However, at the top of the test module, you can see that there's a Jest function call to unmock(). This tells Jest that we don't want a mocked version of the sayHello() function. We want to test the real thing.

There's actually quite a bit of tinkering involved with getting Jest set up to work with ES2015 module imports. But rather than try to explain that here, I'd recommend looking at the source code that ships along with this book. And now, back to the important stuff.

Let's create a `main.js` module that imports the `sayHello()` function and calls it:

```
import sayHello from './hello';
sayHello();
```

The Jest unit test that we created for the `sayHello()` function isolated the `sayHello()` function. That is, we didn't have to test any other code in order to test this function. If we apply this same logic to the main module, we shouldn't have to rely on the code that implements `sayHello()`. This is where the mocking capability of Jest comes in handy. Our last test turned off the mocking feature for the hello module, where `sayHello()` is defined. This time, we actually want to mock the function. Let's see what the main test looks like:

```
jest.unmock('../main');

// The "main" module is the real deal. The
// "sayHello()" function is a mock.
import '../main';
import sayHello from '../hello';

describe('main', () => {

  // We're expecting the "main" module to call
  // "sayHello()" exactly once. Since the "sayHello()"
  // function we've imported here is the same mock
  // called by main, we can verify this is indeed
  // what main is actually doing.
  it('calls sayHello()', () => {
    expect(sayHello.mock.calls.length).toBe(1);
  });
});
```

This time around, we're making sure that the `main.js` module is not mocked by Jest. This means that the `sayHello()` function that we've imported is in fact the mocked version. To verify that the main module is working as expected, as simple as the module is, we just need to verify that the `sayHello()` function was called once.

Testing action creators

Now that we have a rough idea of how Jest works, it's time to start testing the various components of our Flux architecture. We'll start with action creator functions, since these determine the data that enters the system and are the starting point of the unidirectional data-flow. There are two types of action creators we'll want to test. First, we have the basic synchronous functions, followed by the asynchronous ones. Both types of actions lead to very different types of unit tests.

Synchronous functions

The job of an action creator is to create the necessary payload data and to dispatch it to stores. So to test this functionality, we'll want the real action creator function and a mocked dispatcher component. Remember, the idea is to isolate the component as the single unit that's being tested—we don't want any side-effects from the dispatcher code to influence the test outcome. With that said, lets take a look at the action creator:

```
import dispatcher from '../dispatcher';

export const SYNC = 'SYNC';

// Your typical synchronous action creator
// function. Dispatches an action with
// payload data.
export function syncFunc(payload) {
  dispatcher.dispatch({
    type: SYNC,
    payload
  });
}
```

This sort of function is probably looking familiar by now. We want our unit test for this function to verify whether or not the `dispatch()` method is called correctly. Let's take a look at the test now:

```
// We want to test the real "syncFunc()" implementation.
jest.unmock('../actions/sync-func');

import dispatcher from '../dispatcher';
import { syncFunc } from '../actions/sync-func';

// The "dispatch()" method is mocked by
// Jest. We'll use it in the test to validate
// our action.
```

```
const { dispatch } = dispatcher;

describe('syncFunc()', () => {
  it('calls dispatch()', () => {

    // Calling "syncFunc()" should dispatch an
    // action. We can verify this by making sure
    // that the "dispatch()" was called.
    syncFunc('data');
    expect(dispatch.mock.calls.length).toBe(1);
  });

  it('calls dispatch() with correct payload', () => {
    syncFunc('data');

    // After calling "syncFunc()", we can get
    // argument information from the mock.
    const args = dispatch.mock.calls[1];
    const [ action ] = args;

    // Make sure the correct information was
    // passed to the dispater.
    expect(action).toBeDefined();
    expect(action.type).toBe('SYNC');
    expect(action.payload).toBe('data');
  });
});
```

This works exactly as we expect it to. The first step is to tell Jest not to mock what's in the sync-func module, using the unmock() function. Jest will still mock everything else, including the dispatcher. So when this test calls syncFunc(), it's calling the mock dispatcher in-turn. When it does so, the mock records information about the call, which we then use in our test assertions to make sure that everything is working as expected.

Nice and easy, right? Things get a little trickier when we need to mock asynchronous action creator functions, but we'll try to simplify everything in the next section.

Asynchronous functions

Jest makes it easy for us to isolate the code that a given unit test should be testing by mocking all the irrelevant parts. Some things are easily handled by the Jest mock generator. Others need our intervention, as you'll see in this example. So let's start off and take a look at the asynchronous action creator function that we're trying to test:

```
import dispatcher from '../dispatcher';
import request from '../request';

export const ASYNC = 'ASYNC';

// Makes a "request()" call (which is really
// just an alias for "fetch()") and dispatches
// the "ASYNC" action with the JSON response
// as the action payload.
export function asyncFunc() {
  return request('https://httpbin.org/ip')
    .then(resp => resp.json())
    .then(resp => dispatcher.dispatch({
      type: ASYNC,
      payload: resp
    }));
}
```

This action creator makes a request to a public JSON endpoint, and then dispatches the ASYNC action with the response as the action payload. If the request() function that we're using to make the network request looks a lot like the global fetch() function, that's because it is that function. The request module simply exports it, as follows:

```
// We're exporting the global "fetch()" function
// so that Jest has an opportunity to mock it.
export default fetch;
```

It seems pointless, but there's really no overhead involved. This is how we're able to mock all network requests in our code easily. If we mock this request module for our unit tests, it means that our code won't be trying to reach a remote server. To mock this module, we just have to create a module by the same name in the __mocks__ directory, alongside the __tests__ directory. Jest will mock find this mock and substitute it for the real module when it's imported. Let's look at the source of the mock request() function now:

```
// Exports the mocked version of the "request()"
// function our action creators use. In this case,
```

```
// we're emulating the "fetch()" function and the
// "Response" object that it resolves.
export default function request() {
  return new Promise((resolve, reject) => {
    process.nextTick(() => {
      resolve({
        json: () => new Promise((resolve, reject) => {

          // This is where we put all of our mock fetch
          // data. A given function should just test
          // the properties that it's interested in,
          // ignoring the rest.
          resolve({ origin: 'localhost' });
        })
      });
    });
  });
}
```

If this code looks a little gross, don't worry—it's confined to this one place. All it's doing is replicating the interface of the native `fetch()` function that this module replaces (because we don't actually want to fetch anything). The tricky part of this approach is that any `request()` calls in our code are going to get the same resolved values. But this should be fine, assuming that our code can just ignore properties that it doesn't care about and that we can keep the test data in here to a minimum.

At this point, we have a mocked network layer, which means that we're ready to implement the actual unit test now. Let's go ahead and do that:

```
jest.unmock('../actions/async-func');

// The "dispatcher" is mock while "asyncFunc()"
// is not.
import dispatcher from '../dispatcher';
import { asyncFunc } from '../actions/async-func';

describe('asyncFunc()', () => {

  // For testing asynchronous code that returns
  // promises, we use "pit()" in place of "it()".
  pit('dispatch', () => {

    // Once the call to "asyncFunc()" has resolved,
    // we can perform our test assertions.
    return asyncFunc().then(() => {
```

```
        // Collect stats about he mock
        // "dispatch()" method.
        const { calls } = dispatcher.dispatch.mock;
        const { type, payload } = calls[0][0];

        // Make sure that the asynchronous function
        // dispatches an action with the appropriate
        // payload.
        expect(calls.length).toBe(1);
        expect(type).toBe('ASYNC');
        expect(payload.origin).toBe('localhost');
      });
    });
  });
```

There are two important things to note about this test. One, it's using the `pit()` function as a drop-in replacement for `it()`. Two, the `asyncFunc()` function itself returns a promise. These two aspects of Jest are what make writing asynchronous unit tests so straightforward. The difficult part of this example isn't the test, it's the infrastructure we need in place in order to mock things like network requests. Thanks to everything Jest takes care of for us, our unit test code is actually a lot smaller than it would otherwise be.

Testing stores

In the previous section, we used Jest to test action creator functions. This wasn't much different from testing any other JavaScript function, except that Flux action creators need to somehow dispatch the actions they create to stores. Jest helps us achieve this by automatically mocking certain components, and it will certainly help us test our store components.

In this section, we'll look at testing the basic path of an action being dispatched to a store and the store emitting a change event. Then, we'll think about the initial store state and how this can lead to bugs that unit tests should be able to catch. Making all of this work is going to involve thinking about implementing testable store code, which is something we have yet to think about in this book.

Testing store listeners

Store components can be tricky to isolate from other components. This in turn makes designing unit tests for stores difficult. For example, a store will typically register itself with the dispatcher by passing it a callback function. This is the function that will change the state of the store, depending on the action payload that's passed to it. The reason this is a challenge is that it's tightly-coupled with the dispatcher.

Ideally, we want the dispatcher removed from the unit test completely. We're only testing our store code in the unit test, so we don't want anything that's happening in the dispatcher to interfere with the outcome. The odds of this happening are slim, since the dispatcher doesn't really have much to do. However, it's better to be consistent with all our Flux components and somehow isolate them completely. We've seen how Jest can help us out in the previous section. We just need to somehow apply this principle to stores—to decouple them from the dispatcher during unit tests.

This is a case where we might need to reconsider how we write our store code— sometimes for code to be good, it needs to be changed slightly so that it's good and testable. For example, the anonymous function that we would normally register with the dispatcher becomes a store method. This allows the test to call the method directly, skipping the whole dispatching mechanism, which is exactly what we want. Let's take a look at the store code now:

```
import { EventEmitter } from '../events';
import dispatcher from '../dispatcher';
import { DO_STUFF } from '../actions/do-stuff';

var state = {};

class MyStore extends EventEmitter {
  constructor() {
    super();

    // Registers a method of this store as the
    // handler, to better support unit testing.
    this.id = dispatcher.register(this.onAction.bind(this));
  }

  // Instead of performing the state transformation
  // in the function that's registered with the
  // dispatcher, it just determines which store
  // method to call. This approach better supports
  // testability.
  onAction(action) {
```

```
    switch (action.type) {
      case DO_STUFF:
        this.doStuff(action.payload);
        break;
    }
  }

  // Changes the "state" of the store, and emits
  // a "change" event.
  doStuff(payload) {
    this.emit('change', (state = payload));
  }
}

export default new MyStore();
```

As you can see, the onAction() method is registered with the dispatcher, and will be called any time an action is dispatched. The doStuff() method breaks the specific state transformation that takes place in response to the DO_STUFF action out of the onAction() method. This isn't strictly necessary, but it does provide us with another target for our unit tests. For example, we could have just left the anonymous callback function in place and have our tests target the doStuff() method directly. However, if our tests call onAction() with the same type of payload data that comes from the dispatcher, we get better test coverage of the store.

The astute reader might have noticed that this store is importing EventEmitter from a different place than usual—../events. We have our own events module? We do now, and it's the same idea as with the fetch() function in the preceding section. We're providing a module of our own that Jest can mock. This is an easy way for Jest to mock the EventEmitter class. We were so busy thinking about the dispatcher, that we forgot to decouple our store from the event emitter for our test. Let's take a look at the events module so that you can see we're still exposing the good old EventEmitter we all know and love:

```
// In order to mock the Node "EventEmitter" API,
// we need to expose it through one of our own modules.
import { EventEmitter } from 'events';
export { EventEmitter as EventEmitter };
```

This means that the methods inherited by our store will be mocked by Jest, which is perfect because now our store is completely isolated from other component code and we can use data collected by the mock to perform some test assertions. Let's implement the unit test for this store now:

```
// We want to test the real store...
jest.unmock('../stores/my-store');

import myStore from '../stores/my-store';

describe('MyStore', () => {
  it('does stuff', () => {

    // Directly calls the store method that's
    // registered with the dispatcher, passing it
    // the same type of data that the dispatcher
    // would.
    myStore.onAction({
      type: 'DO_STUFF',
      payload: { foo: 'bar' }
    });

    // Get some of the mocked "emit()" call info...
    const calls = myStore.emit.mock.calls;
    const [ args ] = calls;

    // We can now assert that the store emits a
    // "change" event and that it has the correct info.
    expect(calls.length).toBe(1);
    expect(args[0]).toBe('change');
    expect(args[1].foo).toBe('bar');
  });
});
```

What's nice about this approach is that it closely resembles how the data flows through the store, but without actually depending on other components in order to run the test. The test data enters the store the same way it would with an actual dispatcher component. Likewise, we know that the correct event data is being emitted by the store by measuring the mock implementation. This is where the store's responsibilities end, and so too do the test's responsibilities.

Testing initial conditions

One thing we'll learn soon after our Flux stores grow large and complex is that they become increasingly difficult to test. For example, if the number of actions that a store responds to goes up, then the number of state configurations we'll want to test with will also go up. To help accommodate the unit tests for our stores, it would be helpful to be able to set the initial state of the store. Let's take a look at a store that allows us to set the initial state and responds to a couple of actions:

```javascript
import { EventEmitter } from '../events';
import dispatcher from '../dispatcher';
import { POWER_ON } from '../actions/power-on';
import { POWER_OFF } from '../actions/power-off';

// The initial state of the store...
var state = {
  power: 'off',
  busy: false
};

class MyStore extends EventEmitter {

  // Sets the initial state of the store to the given
  // argument if provided.
  constructor(initialState = state) {
    super();
    state = initialState;
    this.id = dispatcher.register(this.onAction.bind(this));
  }

  // Figure out which action was dispatched and call the
  // appropriate method.
  onAction(action) {
    switch (action.type) {
      case POWER_ON:
        this.powerOn();
        break;
      case POWER_OFF:
        this.powerOff();
        break;
    }
  }

  // Changes the power state to "on", if the power state is
```

```
    // currently "off".
    powerOn() {
      if (state.power === 'off') {
        this.emit('change',
          (state = Object.assign({}, state, {
            power: 'on'
          }))
        );
      }
    }

    // Changes the power state to "off" if "busy" is false and
    // if the current power state is "on".
    powerOff() {
      if (!state.busy && state.power === 'on') {
        this.emit('change',
          (state = Object.assign({}, state, {
            power: 'off'
          }))
        );
      }
    }

    // Gets the state...
    get state() {
      return state;
    }
  }

export default MyStore;
```

This store responds to the POWER_ON and POWER_OFF actions. If you look at the methods that handle the state transformations of these two actions, you can see that the result depends on the current state. For example, powering on a store requires that the store already be off. Powering off a store is even more restrictive — the store has to be off and cannot be busy. These types of state transformations need to be tested using different initial store states, to make sure that the happy path works as expected, as well as the edge cases. Now let's take a look at the test for this store:

```
// We want to test the real store...
jest.unmock('../stores/my-store');

import MyStore from '../stores/my-store';
```

```
describe('MyStore', () => {

  // The default initial state of the store is
  // powered off. This test makes sure that
  // dispatching the "POWER_ON" action changes the
  // power state of the store.
  it('powers on', () => {
    let myStore = new MyStore();

    myStore.onAction({ type: 'POWER_ON' });

    expect(myStore.state.power).toBe('on');
    expect(myStore.state.busy).toBe(false);
    expect(myStore.emit.mock.calls.length).toBe(1);
  });

  // This test changes the initial state of the store
  // when it is first instantiated. The initial state
  // is now powered off, and we've also marked the
  // store as busy. This test makes sure that the
  // logic of the store works as expected - the state
  // shouldn't change, and no events are emitted.
  it('does not powers off if busy', () => {
    let myStore = new MyStore({
      power: 'on',
      busy: true
    });

    myStore.onAction({ type: 'POWER_OFF' });

    expect(myStore.state.power).toBe('on');
    expect(myStore.state.busy).toBe(true);
    expect(myStore.emit.mock.calls.length).toBe(0);
  });

  // This test is just like the one above, only the
  // "busy" property is false, which means that we
  // should be able to power off the store when the
  // "POWER_OFF" action is dispatched.
  it('does not powers off if busy', () => {
    let myStore = new MyStore({
      power: 'on',
      busy: false
    });
```

```
    myStore.onAction({ type: 'POWER_OFF' });

    expect(myStore.state.power).toBe('off');
    expect(myStore.state.busy).toBe(false);
    expect(myStore.emit.mock.calls.length).toBe(1);
  });
});
```

The second test is perhaps the most interesting because it makes sure that no events were emitted as a result of the action, due to the way the state transformation logic of the store works.

Performance goals

It's time to switch gears and think about testing the performance of our Flux architecture. Testing the performance of a particular component can be difficult for the same reason that testing the functionality of a component is difficult—we have to isolate it from other code. On the other hand, our users don't necessarily care about the performance of individual components—just the overall user experience.

In this section, we'll discuss what we're trying to achieve with our Flux architecture in terms of performance. We'll start with the user perceived performance of the application, because this is the most consequential aspect of an under-performing architecture. Next, we'll think about measuring the raw performance of our Flux components. Finally, we'll consider the benefits of putting performance requirements in place for when we develop new components.

User perceived performance

From the point of view of our users, our application either feels responsive or laggy. This *feeling* is called user-perceived performance, because the user isn't actually measuring how long something takes to complete. Generally speaking, user-perceived performance is about frustration thresholds. Whenever we have to wait for something, frustration grows because we don't feel in control of the situation. We can't do anything to make it hurry up, in other words.

One solution is to distract the user. There are times when our code has to process something and there's no way around the length of time it takes. While this is happening, we can keep the user updated on the task progress. We might even be able to show some of the output that's already been processed, depending on the type of task. The other answer is to write performant code, which is something we should always strive for anyway.

User-perceived performance is critically important for the software product that we're building because if it's perceived as being slow, it's also perceived as being of poor quality. At the end of the day, it's the user's opinion that matters—this is how we measure whether or not our Flux architecture scales to an acceptable level. The downside of user perceived performance is that it's impossible to quantify, at least at a granular level. This is where we need tooling in place to help us measure how our components perform.

Measured performance

Performance metrics tell us specifically where the performance bottlenecks in our code are. If we know where the performance issues are, then we're better equipped to address them. From the perspective of a Flux architecture, for example, we would want to know whether the action creators are taking a long time to respond, or whether the stores are taking a long time to transform their state.

There are two types of performance testing that can help us stay on top of any performance issues during the development of our Flux architecture. The first type of testing is profiling, and we'll look at this in more detail in the next section. The second type of performance testing is benchmarking. This latter type of testing is done at a lower level and is good for comparing different implementations.

The only question is—how do we make performance measurement a fact of daily life, and what can we do with the results?

Performance requirements

Given that we have the tools necessary for performance testing at our disposal, it would seem that it's possible to define some requirements around performance. For example, if someone is implementing a store, could we introduce a performance requirement that says a store can take no longer than x milliseconds to emit a change event? The plus side is that we could be reasonably confident about the performance of our architecture, right down to the component level. The down side is the complexity involved.

For one thing, development of new code would noticeably slow down, because not only would we have to test for functional correctness, we would also have a strict performance bar to clear. This takes time, and the payoff is most likely nothing. Let's say that we end up spending a bunch of time improving the performance of some component because it's barely failing the requirement. This would mean that we're spinning our wheels on something that's intangible to the user.

This isn't to say that performance testing cannot be automated or that it shouldn't be done at all. We simply have to be smart about where we invest our time testing the performance of our Flux code. The ultimate decider of performance is the user, so it's difficult to set concrete requirements that mean *good enough* performance, but it's really easy to waste time trying to achieve optimal performance that nobody will notice, least of all your customers.

Profiling tools

The various profiling tools available to us through a web browser are often enough to address any performance issues in our interface. These include the components that make up our Flux architecture. In this section, we'll go over the three main tools found in browser developer tools that we'll want to use to profile our Flux architecture.

First are the action creator functions, specifically asynchronous functions. Then we'll think about the memory consumption of our Flux components. Finally, we'll discuss CPU utilization.

Asynchronous actions

The network is always going to be the slowest layer of the application. Even if the API call we're making is relatively fast, it's still slow compared to other JavaScript code. If our application didn't make any network requests, it would be blazing fast. It also wouldn't be of much use. Generally speaking, JavaScript applications rely on remote API endpoints as their data resources.

To make sure that these network calls aren't causing performance issues, we can leverage the networking profiler of the browser developer tools. This shows us, in great detail, what any given request is doing, and how long it takes to do it. For example, if the server is taking a long time to respond to a request, this will be reflected in the timeline of the request.

Using this tool, we can also see the number of requests that are outstanding at any given point. For instance, maybe there's a page in our application that's hammering the server with requests and overwhelming it. In that case, we have to rethink the design. Each request that we look at in this tool allows us to drill down into the code that initiated the request. In Flux applications, this should always be an action creator function. With this tool, we always know which action creator functions are problematic from a network point of view and we can do something about them.

Store memory

The next developer tool that can help us test the performance of our Flux architecture is the memory profiler. Memory is obviously something that we have to be careful with. On the one hand, we have to be considerate of other applications running on the system and avoid hogging memory. On the other hand, when we try to be careful with memory, we end up with frequent allocations/deallocations, triggering the garbage collector. It's hard to put a number on the maximum amount of memory a component should use. The application needs what it needs.

In terms of Flux, we're most interested in what the memory profiler can tell us about our stores. Remember, stores are where we're likely to face scalability issues as our application grows, because they'll have to handle more input data. Of course, we'll also want to keep an eye on the memory consumed by our view components as well, but ultimately it's the stores that control how much or how little memory views will consume.

There are two ways the memory profiler can help us better understand the memory consumption of our Flux stores. First, there's the memory timeline. This view shows how memory is allocated/deallocated over time. This is useful because it lets us see how memory is used as we interact with the application the same way a user would. Second, the memory profiler lets us take a snapshot of the current memory allocations. This is how we determine the type of data that's being allocated, and the code that's doing it. For example, with a snapshot, we can see which store is taking up the most memory.

CPU utilization

As you saw in the previous section on the memory profiler, the frequent garbage collections can cause issues with responsiveness. This is because the garbage collector will block any other JavaScript code from running. The CPU profiler can actually show us how much CPU time the garbage collector is taking away from other code. If it's a lot, then we can figure out a better memory strategy.

Once again, however, we should turn our attention to the store components of our Flux architecture when profiling the CPU. The simple reason is that this will have the biggest return on investment. The scalability issues that we're likely to face are centered around the data transformation functions used to handle action payloads within stores. Unless these functions are efficient enough to handle the data that enters the system, the architecture won't scale because the CPU is being over-utilized by our code. And with that, we'll turn our attention to benchmarking the functions that are critical to the scalability of our systems.

Benchmarking tools

On one end of the performance testing spectrum, there's user-perceived performance. This is where one of our customers is complaining about laggyness, and sure enough, it's easy for us to replicate the problem. This could be an issue with view components, network requests, or something in our store that's causing the suboptimal user experience. On the other end of the spectrum, we have raw benchmarking of code, where we want accurate timings to ensure that we're using the most efficient implementation.

In this section, we'll briefly introduce the concept of benchmarking, and then we'll show an example that uses `Benchmark.js` to compare two state transformation implementations.

Benchmarking code

When we benchmark our code, we're comparing one implementation to another, or we can compare three or more implementations. The key is to isolate the implementations from any other components and to make sure that they each have the same input and produce the same output. Benchmarks are like unit tests in a sense, because we have a unit of code that we isolate as a unit and use a tool to measure and test its performance.

One challenge with performing these sorts of micro-benchmarks is accurate timing. Another challenge is creating an environment that isn't disrupted by other things. For example, trying to run a JavaScript benchmark in a web page is likely to face interference by other things, such as the DOM. `Benchmark.js` handles the nitty-gritty details of getting the most accurate measurement for our code. With that said, let's jump into an example.

 Unlike unit tests, benchmarks aren't necessarily something we want to keep around and maintain forever. It's simply too much of a burden, and the value of benchmarks tends to diminish when there's hundreds of them. There are probably a few exceptions, where we want to keep benchmarks in the repository for illustrative purposes. But generally speaking, benchmarks can safely be discarded once the code has been implemented or once the performance of existing code has been improved.

State transformations

The state transformations that happen inside of Flux stores have the potential to
bring the system to a halt when we try to scale it up. As you know, the rest of the
Flux components in our architecture scale well. It's the added request volume and
added data volume that cause problems. Low-level functions that transform this data
need to perform well. We can use a tool like Benchmark.js to build benchmarks for
the code that works with store data. Here's an example:

```
import { Suite } from 'benchmark';

// The "setup()" function is used by each benchmark in
// the suite to create data to used within the test.
// This is run before anything is measured.
function setup() {

  // The "coll" array will be available in each
  // benchmark function because this source gets
  // compiled into the benchmark function.
  const coll = new Array(10000)
    .fill({
      first: 'First',
      last: 'Last',
      disabled: false
    });

  // Disable some of the items...
  for (let i = 0; i<coll.length; i += 10) {
    coll[i].disabled = true;
  }
}

new Suite()

  // Adds a benchmark that tests the "filter()"
  // function to remove disabled items and the
  // "map()" function to transform the string
  // properties.
  .add('filter() + map()', () => {
    const results = coll
      .filter(item => !item.disabled)
      .map(item => ({
        first: item.first.toUpperCase(),
        last: item.last.toUpperCase()
```

```
    }));
  }, { setup: setup })

  // Adds a benchmark that tests a "for..of" loop
  // to build the "results" array.
  .add('for..of', () => {
    const results = [];

    for (let item of coll) {
      if (!item.disabled) {
        results.push({
          first: item.first.toUpperCase(),
          last: item.last.toUpperCase()
        });
      }
    }
  }, { setup: setup })

  // Adds a benchmark that tests a "reduce()"
  // call to filter out disabled items
  // and perform the string transforms.
  .add('reduce()', () => {
    const results = coll
      .reduce((res, item) => !item.disabled ?
        res.concat({
          first: item.first.toUpperCase(),
          last: item.last.toUpperCase()
        }) : res);
  }, { setup: setup })

  // Setup event handlers for logging output...
  .on('cycle', function(event) {
    console.log(String(event.target));
  })
  .on('start', () => {
    console.log('Running...');
  })
  .on('complete', function() {
    const name = this.filter('fastest').map('name');
    console.log(`Fastest is "${name}"`);
  })
  .on('error', function(e) {
    console.error(e.target.error);
  })
```

```
// Runs the benchmarks...
.run({ 'async': true });
// →
// Running...
// filter() x 1,470 ops/sec ±1.00% (86 runs sampled)
// for..of x 1,971 ops/sec ±2.39% (81 runs sampled)
// reduce() x 1,479 ops/sec ±0.89% (87 runs sampled)
// Fastest is "for..of"
```

As you can see, we just need to add two or more benchmark functions to the suite, then run it. The output is specific performance data that compares the various implementations. In this case, we're filtering and mapping an array of 10,000 items. The "for..of" approach stands out as the best bet performance-wise.

What's important about benchmarking is that it can rule out false assumptions fairly easily. For example, we might assume that because "for..of" outperforms the alternative implementations, that it's automatically the best choice. Well, the two alternatives aren't that far behind. So if we really would rather implement the functionality using reduce(), there's probably no scaling risk in doing so.

 The code that ships with this book implements a few tricks to make this example work with ES2015 syntax using Babel. This is an especially good idea if you're transpiling your production code using Babel, so your benchmarks reflect reality. It's also handy to add an npm bench script to your package.json for easy access.

Summary

The focus of this chapter has been testing our Flux architectures. There are two types of tests that we employ to do this: functional and performance. With functional units, we verify that the units of code that make up our Flux architecture are behaving as expected. With performance units, we're validating that the code is performing at the expected levels.

We introduced the Jest testing framework to implement unit tests for our action creators and our stores. We then discussed the various tools in the browser that can help us troubleshoot performance issues at a high-level. These are the types of things that impact the user experience in a tangible way.

We closed the chapter with a look at benchmarking our code. This is something that takes place at a low-level and is most likely related to the state transformation functionality of our stores. Now it's time to consider the implications a Flux architecture has on the overall software development lifecycle.

14
Flux and the Software Development Lifecycle

Flux is about information architecture, first and foremost. This is the reason that Flux is a set of patterns instead of a framework implementation. When we design front-end architectures that scale, the specific implementation matters very little, relative to the design of the overall system. It's things like unidirectional data-flows and synchronous update rounds that have a lasting impact on the scalability of the system. In fact, Flux can be influential enough that it changes the way we develop our software.

In this chapter we'll look at the software development lifecycle through the lens of Flux. We'll open the chapter with a discussion on the open-ended possibilities with Flux implementations. Then we'll compare the types of development activities that take place at the beginning of a new Flux project with what happens with a maturing Flux project.

We'll also think about the concepts that make Flux appealing to begin with, and how to extract these ideas and apply them to other software systems. Lastly, we'll end the chapter with a look at creating monolithic Flux systems versus packaging Flux components.

Flux is open to interpretation

One problem with JavaScript frameworks is that they're just one instantiation of a full spectrum of possible solutions. One solution isn't as universal as we might hope. Even a specification such as Flux that contains just a handful of patterns is open for interpretation. The fact that they're just patterns makes it easier for one group to go and implement their software one way, while another group uses the same patterns to implement their software how they see fit.

In this section, we'll reiterate the fact that Flux is just a set of patterns to follow. We'll revisit the possibility of using a Flux library, each of which has a different take on implementing the Flux patterns. Then we'll consider the trade-offs of implementing our own Flux components.

Implementation option 1 – just the patterns

Flux is just patterns for us to follow. We might not even follow them exactly. Pattern efficacy isn't what's important—what's important is that we get the fundamental value of Flux out of our design. For example, actions describe something that has happened, and they carry with them a payload of new data to enter the system. Once the new data has been dispatched, it continues in one direction until it is rendered. Flux just happens to use the concept of a dispatcher and a store. We could call our implementation of Flux a conveyor belt if we wanted to. If the data-flow is unidirectional and predictable, then we've met one Flux goal.

Likewise, we can implement the dispatcher and the store components to our liking. There are probably tweaks that we could make to a store component that would better serve our application. These could be for performance reasons, or they could be simple developer conveniences. Either of these things are fine to introduce, as long as the data-flow stays unidirectional and synchronous.

These ideas of unidirectional data-flow and synchronous update rounds aren't unique to Flux. We could work within the confines of other architectures, such as MVC, and achieve the same principles. What is unique about Flux is that it was born out of frustration. Engineers at Facebook decided that they needed a vehicle to explicitly state just how to get these design principles right.

Implementation option 2 – use a Flux library

We certainly don't have to implement every Flux component ourselves. There's plenty of choice out there when it comes to Flux libraries. What's interesting is that this Flux library ecosystem reinforces the assertion that Flux is open to interpretation. Perhaps the best example of this is Redux. This library is not an implementation of the concepts outlined in the Flux documentation. Instead, Redux takes a different route to implementing Flux principles.

For example, there's no dispatcher in Redux, and we can only create one store, which consists of reducer functions. What's important is that we still get the unidirectional data-flow and that the update rounds are synchronous. Then there's Alt.js, which takes a more traditional approach to implementing Flux in that it has the same abstractions as outlined in the Flux documentation. But Alt.js also builds its own ideas on top of these concepts to make implementing Flux that much easier and more enjoyable.

Is it all-or-nothing when we decide to leverage a Flux library? Not necessarily. This fear of all-or-nothing stems from monolithic frameworks that prescribe a certain way of doing things, and there's no easy way to work around these. With libraries, the idea is to be able to pick and choose the bits that you need in order to compose larger behavior. Take the view layer in a Flux architecture—this is most commonly made up of React components. However, neither Redux or Alt.js require that we use React. Redux is small enough that we can just use its store component for our application state, and Alt.js has several smaller modules that we can pick and choose from—there are probably several that we'll never use.

Roll your own Flux

Given that there are so many approaches to implementing a Flux system, is there any utility in implementing our own? In other words, would we be re-inventing the wheel by rolling our own Flux components instead of depending on one of the many Flux libraries out there? Not at all. There's a strong possibility that none of the Flux libraries meet the needs of what we're trying to accomplish. Or maybe there are several things about the Flux components that we want to customize, so that it makes less sense to depend on an implementation that we're going to change completely.

Most of the code in this book has been based on our own implementations of Flux components. We've relied on the reference implementation of the Flux dispatcher, but then we went and implemented our own, without much difficulty. The positive aspect of implementing our own Flux components is that we have the freedom to tweak the components to meet the needs of our application as it evolves. This is more difficult to do when we depend on someone else's implementation.

One possibility is that we use a library like Alt.js for inspiration for rolling our own implementation. This way, we can implement the cool features from that library while modifying them as we see fit. On the other hand, we could be better off just using a Flux library as-is. The best bet is to think about this sort of thing while you're building a skeleton Flux architecture. Don't depend on any libraries upfront, but decide early on if you're going to use something like Redux, so you don't have to throw out too many components.

Development methodologies

In this section, we'll look at the development methodologies that take place at different stages of a Flux project. Keep in mind that these are just guidelines, as methodologies can vary quite drastically from team to team. If two different teams are implementing a Flux system, there will no doubt be some commonalities.

First we'll think about what happens during the initial phases of a new Flux project. Then we'll think about Flux projects that have had a chance to mature, and what the process might look like for adding a new feature to the system.

Upfront Flux activities

Many software development methodologies frown upon big upfront design. The reason is simple—we spend too much time designing before any software is written and tested. Incrementally delivering pieces of software gives us a chance to validate any assumptions we may have made while writing code. The question is, does Flux require big upfront design, or can we incrementally implement parts of a Flux system?

As you saw earlier in the book, the first step to designing a Flux architecture is writing code. At first, we're only interested in producing a skeleton architecture so that we can get a feel for the types of information our components will need. We don't spend time implementing UI components initially, because doing so will likely be a time sink and a distraction from thinking about the other Flux components that we'll need—such as stores and actions.

The question is, can building a skeleton architecture fit into the regular flow of developing software without being big on upfront design? I think so.

We don't want to spend too much time on a skeleton architecture, because that's just a recipe for bike-shedding. We could, however, set sprint goals for building pieces of the skeleton architecture and reviewing with a larger group. Something like a sprint demo might actually be the ideal forum to decide whether or not we've built enough of the skeleton architecture and whether we're happy with it. Then it's time to start building features in earnest.

Maturing a Flux application

Once we've moved well beyond the skeleton architecture phase, we hopefully have in place a solid product with features that our customers will enjoy using. Ideally, this means that we've hit a sweet spot with our Flux architecture—it scales well, it's easy to maintain, and we're able to keep our customers happy by delivering new features. The application is mature, in other words. So how did we get to this point, and how do we keep it going?

Let's consider a feature that we've been asked to build. We have a team of all-purpose programmers to build it. How should we go about decomposing the feature into implementation tasks? Flux makes this fairly easy to figure out, because there are a limited number of component types. So if we can get a small team assembled to deliver a feature, then one person can focus on implementing the views, another on the stores and actions, and another to build the back-end data services. Here's an illustration of a team and the Flux components they build to realize a feature of the application:

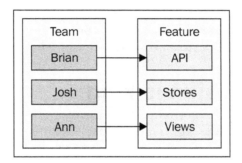

An alternative approach would be to have teams that focus on the same types of components. For example, a store team would be spread across features but each member would work on a store component at any given time. This approach is inferior because a team of Flux programmers working on the same deliverable have collective insight into how the feature is going to provide maximum customer value.

Borrowing ideas from Flux

Flux forces us to think about the information architecture of our application in new and interesting ways. Rarely does adopting a new approach like this happen in a vacuum. The ideas tend to spread to other parts of the technology stack. With Flux, it's the architectural principles of data-flow direction and feature-driven information that stand out as having a positive impact. If these things can have a positive impact on the frontend code, why couldn't they influence the design of the system as a whole?

Unidirectional data flow

The unidirectional flow of data through a Flux architecture is probably the key aspect that enables it to scale. By itself, unidirectional data-flow makes the code we write easy to reason about. In places, this approach can be a little more verbose, but this is a conscious trade-off that we make in order to facilitate predictability. For example, with the two-way data binding capabilities found in some frameworks, we can get away with writing less code. This, however, is a developer convenience that trades off predictability.

This is the type of lesson from Flux that may in fact be applicable to other areas of our technology stack. For example, are there pieces of code that are difficult to reason about because the data that flows through them moves in several directions? Can we change that?

It might be hard to enforce unidirectional data-flows to the extent that Flux does, but we can at least think about the benefits that this brings to the front-end of the application and try to apply the same principles to other code. For instance, maybe we can't get a unidirectional data-flow in place but we can slim down the component by removing flows that are particularly difficult to predict.

Information design is king

Flux architectures start with information that the user interacts with, and work their its way backward, toward the API. This approach is different from other front-end architectures where you have the API entities, and you then create front-end models, and the views (or view models) figure out the transformations necessary to create information that's relevant to the user. The challenge with putting information first is that we might come up with something that's just not feasible from the API perspective.

However, if this is the case then we probably have a dysfunctional team structure to begin with, because it's easy to isolate oneself in one's own technology bubble (back-end, network, front-end, and so on), but this simply does not work in a feature-driven product. All contributing members need to know what's going on in every layer of the stack.

If we can sort out the teams so that each contributor is fully aware of what's happening in the various parts of the code-base, then we can adopt an *information is king* attitude toward feature development. Flux works well for this, and it turns out that this is actually the best way to serve our customers. If we know what information is needed, we can figure out how to get it.

On the other hand, we're biased about what can and cannot be done because we already have an API to work with. This, however, should never be the determining factor of when and how we're able to implement a feature. Like Flux, we should design our abstractions around the information required by the feature, and not the other way around.

Packaging Flux components

In this last section, we'll think about the composition of large Flux applications from the point of view of packages. First, we'll make the case for a monolithic distribution of a Flux application, and the point at which this approach becomes untenable. Then we'll talk about packages, and how they help us scale up the Flux application development effort. Finally, we'll walk through an example of how this might work.

The case for monolithic Flux

Anyone who has been caught in dependency hell knows that it's an unpleasant place to be. Generally speaking, we bring these issues on ourselves by relying too heavily on third-party packages. For example, we might use a couple components from a gigantic library, or we might use an exceedingly simple library for something we could have written ourselves. In any case, we end up with more dependencies than what's justified for the size and scope of our project.

Just because we're implementing a Flux architecture for our application, we don't have to scale it up for scaling's sake. In other words, we can still use Flux for simple applications and acknowledge the fact that there's no need to scale it yet. In this case, we're probably better off avoiding dependencies wherever possible.

The composition of our simple Flux application can be monolithic as well. By this, I don't mean putting everything into a few modules. A monolithic Flux application would be distributed as a single NPM package. We can probably do this for quite some time. For example, we could successfully ship software for years without this ever being a problem. However, when extensibility becomes an issue, we have to rethink the best way to compose and package our Flux application.

Packages enable scale

Applications will eventually become a victim of their own success. If an application manages to stay around long enough and gain enough attention from customers, it will eventually have more features than it can feasibly handle. That's not to say that our Flux architecture can't handle a lot of features—it can. But look at things from the customers' viewpoint. They probably don't want or need everything that other customers use.

This requires that we seriously think about the composition of our Flux architecture, because you can bet that we're going to need more fine-grained management of features. Installable features, in other words. But just how fine-grained do these components, and the packages through which we install them, need to be? Well, I think a top-level feature might be a good unit of measurement.

For example, we typically model the state of a given top-level feature of our application in a single store. Other features have their own stores, we can depend on them, and so on. This means that our application needs to take into consideration that a given feature component might not be installed on the system. For instance, if we were to create a Flux component that implements user management functionality, our application that loads these components would require this feature as though it were any other third-party package.

Installable Flux components

In this section, we'll walk through an example application—albeit a simple one—to illustrate how we can go about installing the major pieces of our application components. It's beneficial to be able to excise the major parts from our core application, because this decouples them from the application, and it makes it easier to use the package elsewhere.

Let's start by looking at the main module of the application, which will help set the context for the other two NPM packages that make up two main features:

```
// The React components we need...
import React from 'react';
import { render } from 'react-dom';

// The stores and views from our "feature packages".
import { Users, ListUsers } from 'my-users';
import { Groups, ListGroups } from 'my-groups';

// The components that are core to the application...
import dispatcher from './dispatcher';
```

```
import AppData from './stores/app';
import App from './views/app';
import { init } from './actions/init';

// Constructs the Flux stores, passing in the
// dispatcher as an argument. This is how we're
// able to get third-party Flux components to
// talk to our application and vice-versa.
const app = new AppData(dispatcher);
const users = new Users(dispatcher);
const groups = new Groups(dispatcher);

// Re-render the application when the store
// changes state.
app.on('change', renderApp);
users.on('change', renderApp);
groups.on('change', renderApp);

// Renders the "App" React component, and it's
// child components. The dispatcher is passed
// to the "ListUsers" and the "ListGroups"
// components since they come from different
// packages.
function renderApp() {
  render(
    <App {...app.state}>
      <ListUsers
        dispatcher={dispatcher}
        {...users.state}
      />
      <ListGroups
        dispatcher={dispatcher}
        {...groups.state}
      />
    </App>,
    document.getElementById('app')
  );
}

// Dispatches the "INIT" action, so that the
// "App" store will populate it's state.
init();
```

We'll start at the top—where we're importing stores and views from the my-users and the my-groups packages. This is the code for our application, but note that we're not using a relative import path. This is because they're installed as NPM packages. This means that another application could easily share these components, and that they can be updated independently of the applications that use them. After these imports, we have the rest of the application components.

 Apple's legal team will be happy to see that I named the store *AppData* instead of *AppStore*.

Next, we create the store instances. You can see that each store has a reference to the dispatcher passed to it. This is how we communicate with Flux components that we're dependent on for composing a larger application. We'll look at the stores shortly.

The renderApp() function then renders the main App React component, and the two components from our NPM packages as children. It's this function that we've registered with each of the store instances, so that when any of these stores change state, the UI is re-rendered. Finally, the init() action creator function is called, which populates the main navigation.

This main module is key to being able to compose larger applications out of smaller, separately installable Flux packages. We import them and configure them all in one place. The dispatcher is the main communication mechanism—it's passed to both the stores and the views. We don't have to touch more than one file in order to important and make use of big application features, which is hugely important for scaling up the development effort.

Now we'll take a look at the app store (not Apple's) to see how the navigation data is driven:

```
import { EventEmitter } from 'events';
import { INIT } from '../actions/init';

// The initial state of the "App" store has
// some header text and a collection of
// navigation links.
const initialState = {
  header: [ 'Home' ],
  links: [
    { title: 'Users', action: 'LOAD_USERS' },
    { title: 'Groups', action: 'LOAD_GROUPS' }
  ]
};
```

```
// The actual state is empty by default, meaning
// that nothing gets rendered.
var state = {
  header: [],
  links:[]
};

export default class App extends EventEmitter{
  constructor(dispatcher) {
    super();

    this.id = dispatcher.register((action) => {
      switch(action.type) {

        // When the "INIT" action is dispatched,
        // we assign the initial state to the empty
        // state, which triggers a re-render.
        case INIT:
          state = Object.assign({}, initialState);
          break;

        // By default, we empty out the store's state.
        default:
          state = Object.assign({}, state, {
            header: [],
            links: []
          });
          break;
      }

      // We always emit the change event.
      this.emit('change', state);
    });
  }

  get state() {
    return Object.assign({}, state);
  }
}
```

Here you can see that this store has two sets of state–one is for the initial state of the store, and one is the actual state that's passed to view components for rendering. The state has empty properties by default so that views using this store don't actually render anything. The INIT action will cause the state to be populated from initialState, and this results in the view being updated.

Let's take a look at this view now:

```javascript
import React from 'react';
import dispatcher from '../dispatcher';

// The "onClick()" click handler will dispatch
// the given action. This argument is bound when
// the link is rendered. Actions that are dispatched
// from this function can be handled by other packages
// that are sharing this same dispatcher.
function onClick(type, e) {
  e.preventDefault();
  dispatcher.dispatch({ type });
}

// Renders the main navigation links, and
// any child elements. Nothing is rendered
// if the store state is empty.
export default ({ header, links, children }) => (
  <div>
    {header.map(title => <h1 key={title}>{title}</h1>)}
    <ul>{
      links.map(({ title, action }) =>
        <li key={action}>
          <a
            href="#"
            onClick={onClick.bind(null, action)}>{title}
          </a>
        </li>
      )
    }</ul>
    {children}
  </div>
);
```

When the store state is empty, as it is by default, all that's rendered is an empty div, and an empty ul. This is enough to completely remove the view from the screen. The click event is interesting. It's using the dispatcher to dispatch actions. The action type comes from the store data, and, by default, this application doesn't actually do anything with the LOAD_USERS or LOAD_GROUPS actions. But the two packages we've imported and set up in the main module do listen to these actions. This is a big part of what makes this approach scale-different NPM Flux packages can dispatch or react to actions-but this doesn't mean either will actually happen.

This is the gist of our application. Now we'll walk through the `my-users` package. The `my-groups` package is nearly identical, so we won't list that code here. First we have the store:

```
import { EventEmitter } from 'events';
import { LOAD_USERS } from '../actions/load-users';
import { LOAD_USER } from '../actions/load-user';

// The initial state of the store has some header
// text and a collection of user objects.
const initialState = {
  header: [ 'Users' ],
  users: [
    { id: 1, name: 'First User' },
    { id: 2, name: 'Second User' },
    { id: 3, name: 'Third User' }
  ]
};

// The state of the store that gets rendered by
// views. Initially this is empty so nothing is
// rendered by the view.
var state = {
  header: [],
  users: []
};

export default class Users extends EventEmitter{
  constructor(dispatcher) {
    super();

    this.id = dispatcher.register((action) => {
      switch(action.type) {

        // When the "LOAD_USERS" action is dispatched,
        // we populate the store state using the initial
        // state object. This causes the view to render.
        case LOAD_USERS:
          state = Object.assign({}, initialState);
          break;

        // When the "LOAD_USER" action is dispatched,
        // we update the header text by finding the user
        // that corresponds to the "payload" id, and using
```

```
      // it's "name" property.
      case LOAD_USER:
        state = Object.assign({}, state, {
          header: [ state.users.find(
            x => x.id === action.payload).name ]
        });
        break;

      // By default, we want to empty the store state.
      default:
        state = Object.assign({}, state, {
          header: [],
          users: []
        });
        break;
    }

    // Always emit the change event.
    this.emit('change', state);
  });
}

get state() {
  return Object.assign({}, state);
}
}
```

There are two key actions that this store handles. The first is LOAD_USERS, which takes the initial state and uses it to populate the store state. The LOAD_USER action changes the content of the header state, and this action is dispatched when a user link is clicked. By default, the store state is cleared out. Now let's take a look at the React component that renders the store data:

```
import React from 'react';
import { LOAD_USER } from '../actions/load-user';

// The "click" event handler for items in the users
// list. The dispatcher is passed in as an argument
// because this Flux package doesn't have a dispatcher,
// it relies on the one from the application.
//
// The "id" of the user that was clicked is also passed
// in as an argument. Then the "LOAD_USER" action
// is dispatched.
```

```
function onClick(dispatcher, id, e) {
  e.preventDefault();

  dispatcher.dispatch({
    type: LOAD_USER,
    payload: id
  });
}


// Renders the component using data from the store
// state that was passed in as props.
export default ({ header, users, dispatcher }) => (
  <div>
    {header.map(h => <h1 key={h}>{h}</h1>)}
    <ul>{users.map(({ id, name }) =>
      <li key={id}>
        <a
          href="#"
          onClick={
            onClick.bind(null, dispatcher, id)
          }>{name}
        </a>
      </li>
    )}</ul>
  </div>
)
```

The key difference between this view and your typical Flux view is that the dispatcher itself is passed in as a prop. Then, as the links are rendered, the dispatcher instance is bound as the first argument to the handler function.

I strongly recommend downloading and experimenting with the code from this example. The two packages that are installed are very simple, just enough to illustrate how we can get the basic mechanisms in place that enable us to break major features out of the application and into their own installable packages.

Summary

This chapter looked at Flux in the larger context of the software development life-cycle. Since Flux is a set of architectural patterns for us to follow, they're largely open to interpretation as far as implementation goes. At the beginning of a Flux project, the emphasis is on iteratively delivering pieces of a skeleton architecture. Once we have a mature application with several features, the focus shifts to managing complexity.

We then discussed the possibility that other areas of our technology stack might want to borrow ideas from Flux. Things like unidirectional data-flows mean that there's less chance of side-effects and that the system as a whole is more predictable. Finally, we closed the chapter with a look at how we could potentially compose larger applications out of separately installable features made out of Flux components.

I hope this book has been an enlightening read on Flux architecture. The goal wasn't necessarily to nail down the *ideal* Flux implementation–I don't think there is such a thing. Instead, I wanted to impart the style of thinking that goes along with the important principles of Flux. If you find yourself implementing something, and start thinking about unidirectional data-flows and predictability, then I might have succeeded.

Index

A

abstract dispatcher interface
about 219
dependencies, handling 222
payloads, dispatching 221
store registration 220
action constants
organizing 71, 72
action creators
asynchronous functions 290-292
synchronous functions 288, 289
testing 288
action names
about 67
conventions 68
static action data 69, 70
actions
about 117
scaling 178, 179
Alt
action creators, declaring 268
actions, dispatching 270-272
core ideas 265
state changes, listening for 269
stores, creating 266-268
using 265
views, rendering 270-272
API calls
action creators, composing 106-108
and user interactivity 99-103
as common case 98, 99
combining 103

complex action creators 103-106
making 97
application data
and UI state 35
feature centric 37
tightly coupled transformations 36, 37
transforming 35, 36

B

bare bone views, skeleton architecture
about 61
actions, identifying 62-64
missing data, finishing 61, 62
benchmarking tools
about 303
code, benchmarking 303
state transformations 304, 306
benefits, explicit actions
architectural layers 34, 35
data changes state 31
data-flow 34, 35
hierarchical structures 32
hierarchy depths 33
multiple actions 31
multiple component hierarchies 32
side-effects 33
updates via hidden side-effects 29, 30
benefits, ReactJS
about 239
new data, re-rendering 241
small code footprint 242
unidirectional 240, 241

www.ingramcontent.com/pod-product-compliance
Lightning Source LLC
Chambersburg PA
CBHW062055050326
40690CB00016B/3097